Also by Francis Steegmuller

COCTEAU: A BIOGRAPHY
"YOUR ISADORA": THE LOVE STORY OF ISADORA DUNCAN
AND GORDON CRAIG
APOLLINAIRE: POET AMONG THE PAINTERS
THE CHRISTENING PARTY
THE GRAND MADEMOISELLE
THE TWO LIVES OF JAMES JACKSON JARVES
MAUPASSANT: A LION IN THE PATH
FLAUBERT AND MADAME BOVARY: A DOUBLE PORTRAIT
SILENCE AT SALERNO: A COMEDY OF INTRIGUE
STATES OF GRACE
FRENCH FOLLIES AND OTHER FOLLIES
THE MUSICALE

Under the name Byron Steel

O RARE BEN JONSON
JAVA-JAVA
SIR FRANCIS BACON

Under the name David Keith

A MATTER OF IODINE
A MATTER OF ACCENT
BLUE HARPSICHORD
(later reprinted in paperback under the name
Francis Steegmuller)

Translations

THE SELECTED LETTERS OF GUSTAVE FLAUBERT
MADAME BOVARY
GUSTAVE FLAUBERT: INTIMATE NOTEBOOK, 1840–1841
PAPILLOT, CLIGNOT ET DODO (with Norbert Guterman)
SAINTE-BEUVE: SELECTED ESSAYS (with Norbert Guterman)
FLAUBERT IN EGYPT
LE HIBOU ET LA POUSSIQUETTE
THE LETTERS OF GUSTAVE FLAUBERT, 1830–1857
THE LETTERS OF GUSTAVE FLAUBERT, 1857–1880

A WOMAN,
A MAN,
AND
TWO KINGDOMS

Francis Steegmuller

A WOMAN,
A MAN,
AND
TWO KINGDOMS

*The Story of Madame d'Épinay
and the Abbé Galiani*

Alfred A. Knopf   New York

1991

For LILIANE *and* OLIVIER ZIÉGEL,
in long friendship

CONTENTS

ILLUSTRATIONS

AUTHOR'S NOTE

DURING the several years that elapsed between the conception of the present book and its completion, I was helped by innumerable friends, acquaintances, and strangers, and am grateful to them all.

My particular thanks go to my wife, Shirley Hazzard; and to the Révérend Père Jean-Pierre Jossua, Liliane Ziégel, Patrizia Antignani, Elisabeth Sifton, Harry Ford, Carlo Knight, and the late Roberto Pane.

I also wish to thank George Andreou, Colin Bailey, Mirella and Maurizio Barracco, Jacques Barzun, Maria Elena Bertoldi, Clara Binswanger, Erse and Leroy Breunig, Victor Brombert, Morton N. Cohen, Giulio Colavolpe, James Coulter, Benedetta Craveri, Olivier Lalive d'Épinay, Everett Fahy, the late Brian Fothergill, Marcello Gigante, Lily Gravino, George Jellinek, Martin Kreeb, Raffaele LaCapria, John A. Marino, William Maxwell, Franca and the late Benedetto Nicolini, Robert Pounder, Richard Swift, William F. Weaver, and Ruth Plaut Weinreb. Other acknowledgments are incorporated in the notes.

Among the numerous libraries to which I am indebted, I wish especially to thank the New York Public Library and the libraries of Columbia University and Harvard University; in Naples, the Biblioteca Nazionale and the libraries of the Università degli Studi and the Società Napoletana di Storia Patria; in New York, the New York Society Library, the Morgan Library, and the library of the French Institute—Alliance Française.

PREFACE

TALLEYRAND'S assertion that anyone who had not lived in pre-Revolutionary France could not fully know life's pleasure—*"Qui n'a pas vécu dans les années voisines de 1787 ne sait pas ce que c'est le plaisir de vivre"*—is the most familiar of many tributes to the quality of a society that still exercises its fascination over the modern mind. That this civilized well-being had been enjoyed by privileged classes within a darker context of suffering, exploitation, and injustice was traumatically illustrated by the Revolution itself, and by the deranged excesses of the ensuing Terror. Yet the pleasures to which Talleyrand alluded were not the merely frivolous and selfish amusements of courtiers or persons of great wealth.

Talleyrand was thinking, above all, of a social and intellectual flowering that, ever extending its boundaries, has caused the age to be called that of Enlightenment, creating, as it did, an increase in human consideration, as distinguished from formal manners. Limitations on friendship—between classes, sexes, and generations—were eased, as was objective discussion. The circles enjoying these changes were intimate but not parochial; their companionable discussions were often subtle, and didactic in no baneful sense. Civilized conduct, which encompassed wit, self-humor, and sociability, necessarily excluded bombast. And the presence of women in an active—at times, a presiding—role contributed a new measure of incisiveness, sensibility, and grace.

This prospering of knowledge in an ambiance not only of unaffected charm but of keen observation and diverse genius could no more have been imagined, at the time, as a prelude to the violence that erupted in 1789 than the Belle Époque, with its parallel currents of privilege, social consciousness, and reform, could have been interpreted by its denizens as an overture to the immense tragedy of the First World War. Writing, in 1779, of ancient Gaul, Edward Gibbon contrasted the aspect of that province with "the present state of the

xiii

same country, as it is now governed by the absolute monarch of an industrious, wealthy and affectionate people." Dean Milman, in one of his notes to Gibbon's history, called attention to that "remarkable passage," and, in particular, to the date of its composition—ten years before the fall of the Bastille and twelve before the beheading of the absolute monarch by the representatives of his "affectionate people." In a later chapter of his history, Gibbon wrote: "In France, the remains of liberty are kept alive by the spirit, the honour, and even the prejudices of fifty thousand nobles." Here Gibbon is referring to the resistance, in 1787, by portions of the French nobility, to that same Bourbon absolutism. This resistance to the royal power caused many French peers, early in the Revolution, to espouse a number of the revolutionary reforms—only, as events accelerated, to find their support rejected and themselves condemned to the guillotine.

A few years after Gibbon had extolled, in this way, the condition of France, Johann Wolfgang von Goethe was visiting Naples, then the capital of a powerful kingdom ruled by another branch of the house of Bourbon. "Naples is a paradise," he wrote to a friend on 16 March 1787. "Everyone lives in a state of intoxicated self-forgetfulness, myself included. I seem to be a different person, whom I hardly recognize. Yesterday I thought to myself, 'Either you were mad before, or you are mad now.' " Once again, as with Gibbon and France, the foreigner's praise came a decade before the convulsion. The story of the Neapolitan revolution of 1799 is not familiar outside Italy—because of its brevity, and also because its disastrous cultural consequences long weakened Naples's intellectual communion with the world. The so-called Parthenopean Republic, proclaimed by the Neapolitan bourgeoisie and intelligentsia in January 1799 and temporarily supported by French republican troops, lasted barely six months; reprisals by the re-established monarchs—who had, for a time, fled to Sicily—were so savage as to inhibit the life of the mind at Naples for decades to come.

The central personalities of the present work—the French

Louise d'Épinay and the Neapolitan Ferdinando Galiani—"escaped" these revolutions. Mme d'Épinay died, in Paris, at the age of fifty-seven, in 1783; and Galiani, in Naples, at fifty-nine, four years later. Theirs were the *"années voisines de 1787"* invoked in Talleyrand's nostalgic pronouncement. Talleyrand had, of course, assumed that his *"vécu"* would be recognized as meaning, in particular, *"vécu à Paris."* Mme d'Épinay lived continuously in Paris or near it, for most of her life. The Neapolitan abbé Galiani was a Parisian for ten years, until his official recall—a trauma that launched a long correspondence between these two; by predilection, he remained "Parisian" for the rest of his life.

Melchior Grimm, a pivotal figure in the friendship of Galiani and Mme d'Épinay, fled the French Revolution and survived it. Another such associate, Denis Diderot, died five years before the fall of the Bastille. Had he lived longer, the great Encyclopaedist would certainly have been a hero to the Girondists. But the Girondists fell. And who—remembering that many a good and eminent man has been destroyed at the order of lesser men—would be bold enough to conjecture Diderot's fate?

PART ONE

THE FRIENDS

Madame d'Épinay, by Jean-Étienne Liotard

I

Madame d'Épinay; *or*, Poor Relations

"I AM NOT at all pretty," Mme Louise d'Épinay wrote of herself in one of her early, privately printed books, "but I am not ugly. I am *petite*, thin, with a good figure. I have a youthful look, but without freshness: noble, gentle, lively, and interesting." Voltaire wrote of her "*grands yeux noirs*"; a young Genevan admirer said, "her eyes are so beautiful, so tender, so eloquent of her soul, that one is scarcely aware of the rest"; and there is Diderot's description of a portrait—its painter and its present whereabouts unknown—for which he had seen her pose in her château de La Chevrette, a few miles north of Paris: "The portrait of Mme d'Épinay is finished. Her bust is *demi-nu*. A few curling locks of hair fall to her neck and shoulders: the rest is caught up by a blue ribbon around her forehead. Her mouth is slightly open: one sees her breathe: and her eyes are filled with languor. It is the very image of tenderness and voluptuousness." The picture, Diderot wrote, was also an excellent likeness.

Today we know her from two portraits in Geneva, where she lived for two years in her early thirties, under the medical supervision of the esteemed Dr. Théodore Tronchin. One of the portraits—both are by Jean-Étienne Liotard—was given to Dr. Tronchin, with Mme d'Épinay's thanks, when she left that city to return to France; and he, in turn, bequeathed it to the Musée d'Art et d'Histoire in Geneva, where one sees it today. The other, perhaps a preparatory sketch, but very "finished," is closer to Diderot's description of the portrait he saw later, at La Chevrette; it is privately owned in Switzerland. Both portraits are spirited, each of them emphasizing a different aspect of the volatile subject. In these eighteenth-century invocations—of soul and wit, of the voluptuous and the tender—one "sees her breathe" indeed.

But it is her written word that most strongly reveals Mme d'Épinay as a woman of character, entirely recognizable in our modern context: penetrating, swift, resilient, and filled with intelligent life.

In January 1783, three months before her death, she was awarded the first Prix Montyon, a prize that had been recently established at the French Academy to honor the author of "the book published in the current year that might be of greatest benefit to society." *Les Conversations d'Émilie*—her memories, in dialogue form, of the education of her granddaughter Émilie de Belsunce—remains an intelligent and charming work. Although Mme d'Épinay has always been best, and most unfairly, known for the role Jean-Jacques Rousseau maliciously gives her in his *Confessions*, it is for *Les Conversations d'Émilie*, displaying her as teacher and "liberated woman," that she is admired in the present day.

Very different from the exemplary *Conversations* are the volumes of Mme d'Épinay's much longer work: her novel, or "pseudo-memoirs," *L'Histoire de Madame de Montbrillant* (referred to in the following pages as "Memoirs"), begun when she was thirty and unpublished in her lifetime. Of this work she writes in the preface:

4

My aim in publishing the story of my misfortunes is to absolve myself in the eyes of the public from suspicions of frivolity, coquetry, and lack of character. . . . These memoirs should also serve as a lesson to mothers. In them they will see the dangers of unconsidered and formless education, and the necessity of studying a child's nature before imposing a rigid program of instruction.

No one, Sainte-Beuve said, better describes the society and customs of eighteenth-century France: "Madame d'Épinay's memoirs are not a book: they are an epoch." Just as she gives herself a pseudonym as author (Montbrillant is the name of a village near Geneva she had reason to visit), so throughout the book Mme d'Épinay rebaptizes her relations, friends, and acquaintances; and at the end of this extraordinary "autobiography" she even recounts, with considerable pathos, the exemplary death of "Madame de Montbrillant" herself. As biography the book must be read with caution—although, in its most modern edition, admirable guidance has been provided by the editors, who have included many identifying notes.[1] The reader comes away both historically informed and with a sense of having read a French equivalent of one of those eighteenth-century English novels which Mme d'Épinay tells us she herself enjoyed—*Pamela* or *Sir Charles Grandison*.

She was christened Louise-Florence-Petronille-Tardieu d'Esclavelles, born on 11 March 1726 in the fortress at Valenciennes, a stronghold on the Franco-Flemish border, where her father, the baron d'Esclavelles, ex-musketeer, ex–lieutenant colonel in the wars of Louis XIV, was commanding officer. He and his wife, both of old aristocratic stock, were not at all rich; and when the baron died suddenly, he left his widow and nine-year-old daughter in modest circumstances. Because Mme d'Esclavelles was occupied in dismantling the quarters at Valenciennes to make way for the new commandant and arranging the sale of superfluous effects,

Louise was sent to Paris to stay with an aunt, her mother's sister. Although this lady's husband, Louis-Denis de Lalive de Bellegarde, an immensely wealthy bourgeois, a *fermier-général*,[2] was a kindly man, his wife was something of a termagant; and Louise found herself a Cinderella, continually reminded of her inferior, impoverished state and her lack of beauty. She was an intelligent, serious-minded child, and immediately began to profit from the meager lessons in "heraldry, French history and geography" given to her younger cousin Sophie by the latter's governess—lessons which her aunt grudgingly and intermittently allowed her to share. She wrote later:

> When I was a child it was not the custom to teach girls anything. They were more or less inoculated with their religious duties, to prepare them for their first communion: they were given a very good dancing-master, a very poor music teacher, and in rare cases a mediocre teacher of drawing. Add to this a bit of history and geography, devoid of any incentive to further learning: it was merely a question of memorizing names and dates, which were forgotten as soon as the teacher was let go. Such was the extent of what was considered a superior education. Above all, we were never taught to think; and any study of science was scrupulously avoided as being inappropriate to our sex.

Back from Valenciennes after several months, Mme d'Esclavelles took a small flat in Paris. Being extremely devout, she was pleased when Louise, benefiting from a scholarship endowed by a distant relation, went to live as a student boarder in a convent. The nuns did their wretched work;[3] and, two years later, her "education" completed, the girl who had shown such early promise—and it seems to have been her father, never her mother, who had encouraged the child to use her mind—emerged at fourteen ignorant and pietistic. An elderly cousin of her father's, the shrewd Mme de Roncherolles, who was fond of Louise and who is often quoted in the Memoirs as a source of worldly wisdom, put it this way to Mme d'Esclavelles, who was encouraging her daughter to frequent a certain religious-minded couple: "Those people are 36-karat bigots. Not good for your daughter. That sort of thing leads straight to *l'amour*. Make no mistake: when a girl is devout at fifteen, it's not God whom she loves—it's her lover, and she only adores God as a substitute while she awaits the lover's appearance."

During her unhappy stay with her aunt Bellegarde, Louise had seen something of her young cousin Sophie's brothers and sisters. Marie-Charlotte, between Louise and Sophie in age, home from her convent school, was erratic, nasty, patronizing; Ange-Laurent, a sweet-natured, timid boy, was a stammerer; and there was the principal heir, Denis-Joseph, two years Louise's senior.[4] The last's formal name at the time, derived from a remote maternal connection, was Monsieur de Preux (a name later to be given by Rousseau, when he became acquainted with the family, to the hero of *La Nouvelle Héloïse*). The boys lived at school, with their tutor, in another part of the city, and during visits to their home they were kind to their fatherless cousin. On Epiphany, 6 January, when the family celebrated Twelfth Night (she calls it "*La Nuit des Rois*") with the traditional cutting of a cake, it was twelve-year-old Monsieur de Preux who found the hidden ring and thus became king. Called to choose his queen, he beckoned to Louise, whose pleasure gave rise to spiteful remarks from her aunt.

Two and a half years later, when Louise emerged from her convent school, she and her mother were asked to a summer house-party at the château de La Chevrette: it was Louise's first visit to the house that would later be her home, and her entry into *le monde* as a young lady. Among those assembled one evening to play games was Denis-Joseph, now almost fifteen, handsome, headstrong, and spoiled. A few days before, when he had said something Louise thought improper, she had not hesitated, following the precepts given by her confessor in the convent, to offer him a few sage words of reproval. His tutor had "applauded" what she said, and he himself had "listened to her very attentively." One of the games they played that evening in the salon of the château was *"le jeu du secrétaire,"* in which each player writes a line on a piece of paper and the slips are passed in turn to every other player, each of whom adds a line which he thinks in some way appropriate: the slips are then read aloud. "I confess," Mme d'Épinay writes, "that my vanity was flattered to find written on my card, in my cousin's hand, the words 'She was born to please, and she will succeed.' "

Thus, while they were both in their mid-teens, Louise had attracted her cousin's particular attention; and one hundred fifty very Richardsonian pages later—which in the Memoirs cover six years—we learn that they were married in the church of Saint-Roch, in the rue Saint-Honoré, a little after midnight on the day before Christmas 1745. Mme d'Escla-velles had provided her daughter with a dowry of thirty thousand livres; on his son, M. de Bellegarde had settled three hundred thousand. Denis-Joseph was twenty-one, Louise twenty. Now of age, he assumed a new surname, Lalive d'Épinay, legally bestowed on him by his father (in 1742 M. de Bellegarde had bought the *seigneurie* of the village of Épinay, on the Seine close to Paris); and the young man was soon appointed, through his father's influence, to a post in the *fermes* of Brittany and Périgord.[5]

During the courtship of the young couple, after the family had discovered that they were passing each other secret notes, Denis-Joseph had been sent for a time to a military school, the "Académie du Roi pour l'éducation des jeunes gentilhommes," in the rue de Tournon, where he was taught fencing, mathematics, dancing, languages, drawing, and music. And later—after his mother died and Mme d'Esclavelles consented to manage her widowed brother-in-law's household, taking Louise to live with her there—the young man, although decorous in his behavior with his cousin, was again sent away, this time to Brittany.

In the earliest pages of the Memoirs, this period is recounted in some charming passages. On one of his last evenings at home, before she had been told of his impending exile, Mme d'Épinay writes:

My uncle had just left the harpsichord: my cousin took his place and asked me to sing an aria from an opera. I agreed. My uncle and my mother were sitting beside the fire with my cousin Sophie. While I was singing a recitative from *Thétis et Pelée*,[6] he said to me in a low voice: "At last I have a moment to talk to you. I suspect you've been unfair to me."

"I? In what way?"

"You have been attributing my silence to indifference."

"What silence?"

"If you knew what I've been suffering because of you! Never, never have you been absent from my heart, but now there's to be no end to my suffering. You must have noticed how depressed I've been during this past week. There's a good reason. In a fortnight I'm to go away for six months, perhaps longer."

I was so astonished, so affected by the news, that as I sang I gave an exclamation of astonishment, and what was to have been a simple "Ah!" came out strangely.

"No, no!" my uncle called out. "What are you doing? Sing the right notes!"

"We turned the wrong page, father," my cousin said.

That little lie made me unhappy, and I wanted to stop, but my mother, who thought I was offended by my uncle's words, told me to stay where I was and begin the scene again. As soon as I had sung one or two bars, my cousin resumed: "What worries me most about my absence is that you'll have some bad times with my other sister, and nobody to comfort you. . . . If you'll write to me when things go wrong . . ."

"No," I said. "Not unless my mother approves. I show her all my letters."

"Will she see mine?" he asked.

"Of course."

"What? All?"

That exchange took place while we were singing alternately; and since the passage ended as he asked me that last question, I made no answer, and walked away.

M. de Bellegarde's farewell to his son, the evening before Denis-Joseph left for Brittany, is a scene suggestive of a depiction by Greuze, whose fine, fashionable, sentimental canvases would later be collected by Ange-Laurent:

I am still upset [Mme d'Épinay writes, in a "letter to a friend"] by the farewell given him by his father. What a parting! It was touching and terrible. We were all assembled in M. de Bellegarde's study to bid good-bye to the "poor exile," as he calls himself. It was after lunch. He embraced us all, finally going to his father. M. de Bellegarde put his hands on his son's shoulders, indicating that he should kneel. He did so, and then his father, with tears in his eyes, gave him his blessing. "May God bless my first-born," he said, "and with His grace keep him good, happy, and well."

Then, collecting himself a little, and speaking affectionately, with his son still kneeling, he said: "My son, never forget the lessons you learned in your father's house, and the advice your mother gave you as she lay dying." His voice broke, he wept, and we all wept with him. He reminded him of his conduct since his mother's death, in a way that could only have pleased him, since he stressed everything he could praise; but then he spoke strongly, too strongly perhaps, of his tendency to dissipation, his lack of application, his spirit of independence, and his stubbornness. I confess that I have not been particularly aware of those last-mentioned failings. Isn't it a bad policy for mothers and fathers to exaggerate the failings of their children? It seems to me that my cousin has not, as yet, given signs of being so entirely willful.

"As yet." That was two years before they were married. During the interval that followed, Louise had reason to conceive many doubts about Denis-Joseph, to note many bad "signs"; and friends, while acknowledging his ability to charm, gave her warnings. When she learned that he had contracted a venereal disease in Brest she was "horrified," and resolved to give him up and accept one of the other, flattering marriage proposals she tells us she had received; but in her infatuation she believed those who told her that he had been cured. As her wedding day approached he showered her with jewels—diamonds, gold, "buckles, a necklace, an aigrette"; and from M. de Bellegarde came a gift of spending money, one hundred louis d'or—a thousand dollars, or, perhaps, pounds, today. Nevertheless, she tells us, she walked to the church on that winter night in 1745 in "fear and trembling." As well she might: she was in thrall to a monster.

In the Memoirs, an anecdote, the account of an episode in Mme d'Épinay's daily life, is rarely without its larger significance.

A few months before her marriage, she tells us, Denis-Joseph had written her that Martin, the fashionable Parisian designer of furniture, sedan chairs, and carriages, had sent him four colored drawings to choose from for two carriages he wanted made, "a fine *berline* for you and a *diligence* for me. Don't mention this to my father. His simple tastes would be shocked: he doesn't realize how young people do things nowadays. I'll wait a few months before showing him my coach."

"A few months" later, M. de Bellegarde had apparently accepted the ordering of the carriages as a *fait accompli*, and Mme d'Épinay tells of writing to a friend about her first outing in hers, a few weeks after her marriage:

I'm still trembling from what just happened to me. My beautiful coach was delivered this morning. It's really charming. I decided to celebrate its arrival by going out in it alone this afternoon—I thought I would attend vespers at the convent and then pay a call on my great-aunt. The grooms were deathly slow in harnessing up, but I finally climbed in: my mother and father-in-law were on the balcony to see me off. We hadn't gone four paces when the horses bolted. The coachman lost control and shouted to the footman to jump off: the horses raced along the Ramparts, and we were headed straight for the ditch. I was too frightened to cry out: seeing that we were in for it I quickly lowered the windows, crouched on the floor and pulled both cushions over my head. The coach overturned. I wasn't hurt, and people came at once to help. I decided to walk on to my great-aunt's. A very nicely dressed young man offered me his arm: I was afraid to accept—didn't quite know whether I should. Finally I did, and we set off as fast as my trembly legs could carry me. My mother, who had seen the horses bolt and had been told by one of the footmen what had happened, sent my maid in my father-in-law's coach to fetch me home.

My coachman claims that I'm to blame, because I was in such a hurry he didn't have time to see that everything was in order. In fact, he had forgotten to secure what they call the curbs. . . .

A simple, straightforward little narrative and at the same time an artful, metaphorical passage: her husband's extravagance; her father-in-law's old-fashioned caution followed by paternal indulgence; her delight in the new luxury provided by her husband—a luxury that quickly brings terror and near disaster; succor from a stranger and from her elders. All these elements, here compressed into one episode, are, in fact, present throughout the first third of the Memoirs.

There were only a few weeks, barely months, of honeymoon before Mme d'Épinay's husband proved to be, and hastened to do, everything that might have been feared. His adulteries, countless and costly, began very soon; her father-in-law's wedding gift of louis d'or disappeared from the drawer into which she had put it; in a shop she discovered her husband's portrait, a copy of one he had had painted for her, being framed for a well-known courtesan; he roistered around the clock with companions—sometimes, in drink, bringing them to her bedside. Her first child, a son—he was christened Louis-Joseph—was born while her husband was in Brittany on official business, combined, she later learned, with more debauchery; in a letter he forbade her to nurse the child, and only long after his return consented to visit with her the home of the wet nurse. Just as she began to realize that she was all but free of the monster's charm, she suddenly, to her horror, found herself infected by a recurrence of his venereal disease—a recurrence of which he had been well aware but said nothing.

Frightened by the anger of his father, who had tolerated his earlier, bachelor infection but now ordered him to make every effort to avoid scandal, he agreed to her demand for an end to sexual relations. His consent, she says, was given in a mocking tone:

> "So be it, then, Madame: have it as you wish. I see your mind is made up, and I don't blame you in the least. Let us each live peacefully in his own way. Anything you do will be satisfactory to me. I expect you to give me the same freedom; and whenever we see each other we'll be happy and content. That way of living is divine: it makes for good marriages."
>
> "What! You're suggesting that I . . ."
>
> "I suggest nothing. I merely approve."
>
> "You imply that it's I who want to . . ."
>
> "Come, now: no scolding. Emulate my moderation. Adieu, Madame," he said, very gaily, making me two deep bows. "I have things to do in town. If I hear any amusing gossip I'll bring it back with me this evening to enliven the family circle. You may rely on me as a husband ready to pay homage to your charms whenever you wish; and if you remain adamant toward that husband he will nonetheless continue to be your friend and"—he ended—"your servant, Madame."

During the year that followed, d'Épinay continued promiscuous and irresponsible, accumulating new debts—creditors indulged him as the heir of a wealthy man—and failing to provide his wife with household money. It would be his way of life until the end. In her desperation Mme d'Épinay appealed to her father-in-law and, with his reluctant consent, went to law. With the supporting testimony of his business adviser and of her doctor, she was awarded, on 14 May 1749, a *séparation des biens*—the return of her dowry. (She had wanted to ask for a *séparation des corps*, a complete legal separation, physical as well as financial, but was dissuaded by her advisers' fear of scandal.) In addition, for the payment of her household expenses, M. de Bellegarde saw to it that a portion of his annual allowance to his son be paid directly to her, to provide an income sufficient for her support and that of her household. And he was able to arrange for an annual sum to be paid to her after his own death. It was then quite exceptional—and may not be usual even now—that a father-in-law should show such solidarity with a victimized young wife.

Legally, however, apart from her dowry, Mme d'Épinay continued to be independent financially only to the extent that her husband respected his father's intent. And sexually, she was her own mistress only for as long as her husband would keep his word.

Now Mme d'Épinay embarked on her first love affair outside marriage.

It was in the house of friends that she met Charles-Louis Dupin de Francueil, a handsome, well-connected young official in the Treasury—married, and known to have a daughter, but in society always seen alone. He was politely attentive to her, and she found him charming.[7] At this time, however, she was depressed and agitated by recent events; and on discovering that Francueil was a friend of her husband, she was on her guard. Épinay began to bring Francueil occasionally to their house, and although this new acquaintance behaved impeccably, Louise d'Épinay continued aloof. Then, from her diary:

Denis-Joseph Lalive d'Épinay, artist unknown

27 February. *[1748, Paris]* M. de Francueil has now called twice while I was out. I shall let him know that I'll be home tomorrow.

28 February. *[Paris]* I have seen M. de Francueil. He seems pleasant, much more so than I first thought. No one else came, so after we had talked for an hour and I was at a loss for further conversation, I suggested that we have some music. We played together well into the evening. I asked him to stay to supper, but he was already engaged.

6 March. *[Paris]* Of all the people I know, M. de Francueil is the most enlivening. He has the best mind and is the most talented. He urged me to take up my long-neglected music, and has even given me a few lessons in composition.

5 April. *[La Chevrette]* We have come here for Easter. My husband invited M. de Francueil, and I have been very happy to have him with us. He is so naturally and unaffectedly polite; everything he does is done gracefully; his conversation is so agreeable and interesting that one can't help greatly liking him. My father-in-law is much taken with him. Who wouldn't be? He paints beautifully, composes, has a very wide knowledge, and a gaiety I find delightful. I confess that it's been a long time since I've spent the days so pleasantly.

My husband is about to leave for a new tour of duty. This time he'll be away for at least six months.

15 April. *[Paris]* The day before M. d'Épinay left, M. de Francueil paid his usual visit. I happened to remark, I don't know in what connection, that one thing I particularly enjoyed in the country was hearing the sound of huntsmen's horns as we sat at table in the early evening. He made no reply, and at eight o'clock he left. My husband, coming in, told me that he had met him on the stairs and invited him to return for supper, so that they could say farewell, and he had accepted. This surprised me, as he had seemed eager to leave. He returned at nine, and when we were at table in my father-in-law's apartment we suddenly heard the sound of hunting horns—the most delightful of all sounds—coming from the next room. I looked at M. de Francueil, who smiled and said he supposed I had arranged it as a farewell serenade to my husband. I denied I had anything to do with it, but said nothing more, and I saw that M. de Francueil appreciated my silence.

After supper, since it was a particularly beautiful night, M. d'Épinay suggested that we walk around Place Vendôme in the moonlight. We agreed. Francueil gave me his arm. He pressed my hand several times, but only when there seemed to be a good reason—to prevent my stumbling in the dark, or making a misstep.

Back in our house, my husband, who was in high spirits and would be setting out at six in the morning, proposed that we entertain ourselves with music until that time. At first there was general acceptance, but Francueil pointed out that I might well be tired. Whereupon he left, asking my permission to come the next day and inquire how I was.

That following day, he and I were both invited to supper at the abbé de V———'s. There I was taken ill: Francueil's kindness and concern were beyond description. I left early, expecting that he would see me to my coach, and I confess I felt offended when he didn't. But on reaching my house I was surprised to see that his coach had followed mine. He stepped down and saw me to my door—no farther. He asked with the utmost kindness how I was feeling, and immediately left. I was greatly touched.

And there follow, in the Memoirs, twenty pages recounting days and nights of low-voiced talk and secret notes, of expert siege and half-hearted resistance. In Paris, self-defense may have seemed essential, but things were different at La Chevrette, where Francueil was again invited, this time by

M. de Bellegarde, and where he was attentive to the old gentleman and even won the regard of the always-suspicious Mme d'Esclavelles. "Nature had never been so calm" nor April evenings in the park so mild; the only sound was the song of the nightingale, "filling the soul with *volupté*." Mme d'Épinay, writing of her "fall" nine years after the event, is *en plein romantisme*:

> *21 April. (La Chevrette, five o'clock in the morning)* Remorse can never banish thee from my heart, I know. Every thought, every reflection, fixes thee there more firmly. Yes, thou wilt ever be the object of all my affection. Oh! What love thou owest me for the sacrifice I have made for thee! Day is breaking: the righteous man, lifting his eyes to heaven, gives thanks to the Creator for the rest he has enjoyed, and asks his blessing for the work of the day. Whereas the guilty will betray, by an uneasy glance, the agitation in which he forfeited that benediction. Come, oh come, oh thee whom I adore! Only in thy arms, in thy bosom, can I hide my shame and stifle my remorse.
>
> *The same day. Later.* What happiness could be compared with mine, if only I could avow it? Never will I accustom myself to the need to conceal the delicious agitation of my heart. My very face must be my accuser. How shall I bear my husband's gaze when he returns, since the merest glance from those around me fills me with terror? Only to myself, in the darkness of the night, am I able to avow the transports of yesterday.
>
> May today be as happy! . . . And may the rapture that fills my heart finally stifle my scruples. . . .

Mme d'Épinay was indeed happy: so different from her former self that she "no longer knew who she was."

She was happy with Francueil for three years. Thanks to him she began to feel, and to display, some of the liveliness of mind and spirit, the intellectual curiosity, that had first been awakened during her childhood, before her father died.

Her daughter by Francueil, born 1 August 1749, was christened Angélique-Louise-Charlotte. All the conventions were
observed: her husband made no legal difficulty; Mme d'Esclavelles, while constantly lecturing Louise about propriety,
was not deceived; M. de Bellegarde was silent; their friends
knew the truth, but there was no scandal. For a time, Épinay,
by now an accomplished sadist, had enjoyed teasing his wife
and her lover in company and berating her in private, but
he was soon silenced by his own indiscretions. Scandals arising from his riotous conduct with various "actresses," particularly a pair of sisters, "les demoiselles de Verrières," had
become so blatant as to displease his governmental employ-
ers, and they abruptly punished him with another six months
in the provinces. According to the Memoirs, his principal
parting words to his wife as he left for Poitiers were a request
that she beg his father not to sell *all* his saddle horses to pay
his debts.

Private theatricals had become the mode in Paris and in
country houses, and M. de Bellegarde, seeing his daughter-
in-law emerge from the suffering inflicted by his son, agreed
to her suggestion, inspired by Francueil, that the orangery
at La Chevrette be transformed into a theatre. "You never
suspected, any more than I, did you, that I had a talent for
acting?" Mme d'Épinay wrote to a friend in the summer of
1748. "People tell me so, at least. M. de Francueil, who has
all the talents and accomplishments one could wish, is among
other things a good actor. It is he who has set our little
company going. He is our director."

Members of the family, reinforced by houseguests and
country neighbors, made up the little theatrical company led
by Francueil. Mme d'Épinay seems indeed to have been a
star, acting "divinely," according to one of her fellow players,
"especially roles of ladies in love." Except on special occa-
sions, Mme d'Épinay tells us, the audience consisted chiefly
of servants and the local peasantry, everyone else being on
stage. "M. de Bellegarde and Mme d'Esclavelles were enchanted, and seemed ten years younger."

One of the performances, given to celebrate the annual fête of the village of Épinay on 14 September 1748, was a three-act comedy in verse called *L'Engagement téméraire*. The author, a friend of Francueil's, was the thirty-three-year-old Jean-Jacques Rousseau, come from Geneva to La Chevrette for the occasion.

Rousseau in 1748 was not yet a public figure. He had written several plays; in Paris he had presented "a new method of musical notation" before the Académie des Sciences; and for a time he had been the secretary of Francueil's stepmother, Mme Dupin, in the château de Chenonceaux, then in her possession. Mme d'Épinay, writing a decade after the event, says that at La Chevrette she found him uncouth but interesting: "He is flattering without being polite. He lacks conventional manners, but it is easy to see that he is immensely intelligent. He is of dark complexion, with bright eyes that give him a lively expression. Indeed, he seems good-looking while conversing, but you recall him as almost ugly. His health is said to be poor, as he is reputed to suffer from certain ailments: it is these that make him glum at times"—a discreet reference to Rousseau's well-known urinary difficulties.

Among the ladies at La Chevrette, Rousseau was the subject of much talk. "Francueil has brought with him a poor devil of an author," Mme d'Épinay "quotes" one of the guests as writing in a letter to her lover. "He's poor as Job, but has wit and vanity enough for four. His life is said to be as strange as his person, and that's saying much. I hope we'll know the tale someday. Mme de Maupéou and I felt that between us we could guess it. 'Ugly as his face is, his eyes show that love plays a large role in his story,' she said. 'No,' I answered. 'You can tell from his nose that the chief role is vanity.' 'Well, then—both.' " (Two years after the performance of *L'Engagement téméraire* at La Chevrette, in 1750, Rousseau's celebrity was launched when his essay on progress in the arts and sciences won a contest sponsored by the University of Dijon. In his posthumously published *Rêveries du promeneur solitaire* he speaks scornfully of the entertainments at La Chevrette as "*des plaisirs de moquerie et des goûts exclusifs engendrés par le mépris.*"[8])

Nor were theatricals and Rousseau the only innovations that Francueil brought into Mme d'Épinay's life. She was invited to attend the informal dinners held by Mlle Quinault, formerly a *sociétaire* of the Comédie-Française (she was famous for her performance in the role of Phèdre) and now a bluestocking of fifty, the center of a group of intellectuals. Gathering twice a week around her table in the rue d'Anjou, or at that of her archaeologist friend, the comte de Caylus, these freethinkers overflowed with the ideas of the Enlightenment, all new and dazzling to Mme d'Épinay. In the Memoirs, to convey the brilliance of the talk—the great freedom of which shocked her at first—she presents, in skillful dramatic form, two "general conversations" that she constructs from her later reading of contemporary literature. We hear Diderot on primitive sexual customs, an exposition drawn from his essay on the explorer Bougainville; and there are passages from Rousseau, Diderot, and others on aspects of early and modern Christianity. Present at these dinners, in addition to Rousseau, were the novelist Crébillon *fils*, the dramatist Marivaux, and others of an intellectual quality hitherto unknown to Louise d'Épinay, including Charles Duclos, author both of erotic novels and works of history, and sometimes remembered today for his remark, "Those in power hate culture as footpads hate streetlights." It was perhaps Duclos' official biography of Louis XI, and his preeminently social manner—he was famed for the quantity and quality of his talk—that in 1750 won for him, through the favor of Mme de Pompadour, his appointment as royal historiographer. (Voltaire had recently resigned that post to serve King Frederick II in Prussia.)

The Memoirs tell of the compliments Mme d'Épinay received from Mlle Quinault's other guests: compliments on the questions—few, naive in tone, but well-founded—that she timidly asked during her first evenings with the group, and others that she later asked more boldly. These sessions were her "university," she says; they broke her of "the habit of judging people by how kind they were to her." They brought her—for the time being—Rousseau's esteem and won her the admiring attention of Duclos, who told her "repeatedly" that "she had a much better mind than she realized"; that "it lacked only cultivation." But Duclos was apparently not content with helping her to cultivate her mind: he did his best, although without success, to supplant his friend Francueil in her affections.

Following the death of M. de Bellegarde in 1751, Mme d'Esclavelles, who had continued as his housekeeper to the end, almost immediately moved to a Paris flat of her own. The greatest share of the old gentleman's fortune had come to Épinay as his eldest son, and life in the rue Saint-Honoré and at La Chevrette, always ample, became luxurious. Mme d'Épinay describes the new *train de vie*:

M. d'Épinay says the household staff [in Paris] is now complete. He has three footmen and I two: I didn't want more. He has given me Le Bel [her father-in-law's elderly valet]. He wanted me to take a second lady's maid, but since I wouldn't know what to do with her I held firm. As a compromise he insisted that the woman in charge of the linen help me every day with my toilette. When he is there, I send for her, but I am almost always dressed before he is up—not very difficult, since he usually sleeps till ten. The entire staff, including upper servants, maids and valets, amounts to sixteen.[9]

. . . When my husband is up, his *valet de chambre* is there to serve him. In addition, two footmen stand ready to take his orders. The first secretary brings the business letters from Brittany and Périgord. He has already opened them and written replies, and my husband need only sign these; but in this he is interrupted two hundred times by every kind of person imaginable. A horse trader has some very special mounts for sale, but they have already been spoken for by another gentleman. The dealer has come only because he promised to; even were my husband to double the gentleman's offer, he could not accept. "What is the price?" "M. so-and-so offers sixty louis." "I'll give a hundred." "Can't be done, unless he changes his mind." Of course the other gentleman does change his mind, and the deal goes through for a hundred. I witnessed that bit of business last week.

Now there's a rascal come to sing an aria: he goes off with a recommendation to the Opéra, after being given a lecture on good taste and how French should be sung. Then there's a demoiselle. If I'm still there she's asked to wait. I go out: the two footmen throw open the double doors for me—for me, who could pass through the eye of a needle; and the two of them bawl out "*Madame! Messieurs, voilà Madame!*" Everybody waiting stands up—people to sell dress goods and musical instruments, jewelers, peddlers of various sorts, footmen hoping to be hired, bootblacks, people who look like creditors—everything absurd and troublesome imaginable.

Noon or one o'clock has struck before Monsieur's toilette is completed; and the secretary, who doubtless knows from experience the impossibility of having a detailed discussion of business, brings out a little list he has made of the topics to be discussed at the meeting of the *fermiers* that afternoon. My husband glances at it, and tells him what to say. On other days he goes out on foot or in a cab, rushes back at two, has dinner with me or sometimes with his first secretary as well, who tells him how every item of expense should be kept track of, how he should delegate some of his business, etc. The only reply is "We'll see about it." After which he goes out again—people, the theatre—and if we don't have guests he stays out for supper.

On those evenings out, M. d'Épinay was not inclined to change his habits: "The elder demoiselle Fauconnier . . . the younger demoiselle de Verrières . . . [during the year following his father's death, d'Épinay installed both demoiselles de Verrières in a house at Auteuil] the demoiselle Deschamps . . . the demoiselle Briseville, to whom he has given diamonds and cheques made out to bearer. . . ." Through spies of all sorts, the Paris police kept track of d'Épinay's profligacy along with that of other rich men, and compiled their dossiers.

Rich though he now was, d'Épinay persisted in his old habits of not providing household money for his family and not paying debts. More and more "people who look like creditors" waited in the anteroom. "It is frightful," Mme d'Épinay writes in the Memoirs, "to be the wife of a man who makes you blush at every moment because he blushes at nothing."

After mourning M. de Bellegarde's death and recounting Épinay's subsequent extravagance, the Memoirs become for a time increasingly selective and fictitious. They skim the years that immediately follow and make no mention of Mme d'Épinay's second child by Francueil, a son, born 29 May 1753.[10] And her break with Francueil, which in fact occurred later that same year, is for some reason dated two years earlier in the Memoirs.

The actual circumstances of the ending of Mme d'Épinay's relations with Francueil are not known; but "Mme de Montbrillant's" account of discovering her lover's infidelity, her despair, and the subsequent scene of his repentance, and of her forgiveness and resignation, are among Mme d'Épinay's most extravagant flights in the language of *"sensibilité"*—a term that had then only recently come into use. One extract will suffice:

> . . . "Come, come to my arms," I said, embracing him. "See in me your friend, suffering a thousandfold more for you than for herself when she sees you in pain. Believe me, only by opening your heart to her will you find the consolation that seems to elude you. It is the voice of friendship appealing to you, friendship that is

pure, that longs only to hear from your lips how to
make you happy . . ."

"No, no!" he cried, tearing himself from my arms. "I
am unworthy of such a heart as yours . . ."

"Formeuse" (as the figure of Francueil is called in the
Memoirs) does "open his heart" to Mme de Montbrillant
and tells her of his affair with a young woman whom she
had thought her friend. (Mme d'Épinay learned later that
Francueil's "openheartedness" had not been complete: in
common with her husband, he had been frequenting, as well,
"les demoiselles Verrières.")

Along with the sentimentality, Mme d'Épinay's skillful
depiction of her heroine's complex emotions—her triumph
in making her lover confess and weep, her awareness of his
pleasure in doing so (one recalls that Francueil was a talented
actor)—carries the reader into the high feelings of these early
stirrings of Romanticism. Their farewell (as lovers; Francueil
will continue for some time to be a guest in Paris and at La
Chevrette) leaves Mme d'Épinay, she says, with "an empti-
ness in her soul" and "grief at having to banish forever all
hope of happiness."

It is with this device of the dramatized farewell that she
clears the stage for the man who will be her "savior."

II

Melchior Grimm
and Denis Diderot

FRIEDRICH MELCHIOR GRIMM, the son of a Lutheran pastor, was born in Ratisbon, on the Danube, in 1723. After graduating from the University of Leipzig, he was engaged to escort an adolescent German princeling to Paris. That mission accomplished, he found himself fascinated by the city and took employment as secretary to another expatriate German, the young Graf August-Heinrich von Friesen.

When Grimm and Jean-Jacques Rousseau were presented to each other in 1749 at a garden party given by yet another francophile German princeling, they discovered not only a shared love of music but also their common preference for music that was frankly Italianate—their favorite composer was Pergolesi—rather than the established, courtly scores of Lully and Rameau. (This question of musical preference was a fashionable theme of aesthetic controversy at the time.) They quickly became friends. The next year, Rousseau, expansive in the celebrity brought him by his Dijon prize, introduced Grimm to Parisian intellectual society. He took him to call on Louise d'Épinay. She had heard "great things" of him, she says, and of his wit and erudition:

> I invited him to dinner the next day. I was very happy to know him. He is gentle, polite; shy, I think, because he is too intelligent for the embarrassment he displays to have any other cause. He is a passionate lover of music, and we all—he, Rousseau, Francueil and I— played and sang for several hours after dinner. I showed him a few of my own little compositions, and he seemed to like them. If anything about him displeased me, it was his exaggerated praise.

Grimm invited his new Parisian friends to Friesen's house. Meanwhile, a particular sympathy had grown up between Grimm and Denis Diderot, the editor of the great *Encyclopaedia* since its inception in 1747. Articles by Grimm on German literature began to appear in the *Mercure de France*, and he also published pamphlets about German and Italian music. Grimm was vivacious and a polymath: "How dare this Bohemian have more wit than we?" Voltaire demanded after reading one of his essays.

At first Mme d'Épinay saw him only occasionally. She perhaps heard about an early Parisian infatuation: Grimm had "almost died of love," it was said, for an expatriate German princess who remained unaware of his very existence. And she learned of a more recent obsession. The story—or, rather, a version of it—appears in Rousseau's *Confessions*:

> After being for some time on friendly terms with Mlle Fel, the opera singer, Grimm decided that he was desperately in love with her and that she must break with [the dramatist Louis de] Cahusac. *La belle*, who prided herself on her constancy, refused to have anything more to do with this new suitor. Grimm took the affair tragically and decided he wished to die of grief. He suddenly contracted the strangest illness imaginable. He spent his days and nights in a continual lethargy, his eyes wide open, his pulse normal, but never speaking, eating, or

Melchior Grimm, by Carmontelle

moving, sometimes seeming to hear what was said, but never responding, even by so much as a sign—never displaying agitation, pain, or fever, but acting as if dead. The abbé Raynal and I took turns watching over him; the abbé, more robust and in better health than I, stayed at his side by night, and I by day; he was never left alone—one of us departed only when the other arrived. Count Friesen was alarmed, and called in Dr. Senac. He examined the patient carefully, said there was nothing to worry about, and wrote no prescription. My alarm for my friend made me observe carefully the expression on the doctor's face as he left: I saw him smile. The patient remained motionless for several more days, refusing all nourishment, even broth, except for a morsel of cherry jam that I would put on his tongue from time to time: he swallowed that with seeming satisfaction. Then one morning he got up, dressed himself, and resumed his usual way of life. Never did he mention to me, nor, as far as I know, to the abbé or to anyone else, that strange lethargy or the care we had given him.

Grimm's moonstruck behavior in this episode was much talked about, giving him something of a quixotic, romantic reputation among the ladies of Paris.

It was on a winter day in 1752 or early in 1753, as Mme d'Épinay relates in the Memoirs, that dramatic, quite unexpected news was brought to her and her mother: the news that Grimm, whom for several years she had esteemed simply as one of her friends, had been wounded in a duel he had fought in her defense. His anger had been aroused during a discussion at an exclusively male dinner given by Friesen. The subject was the current Parisian gossip about Mme d'Épinay: it was being said that following the recent death of her sister-in-law, Mme de Jully, she had purloined and destroyed some papers from that lady's desk—papers that contained the only proof of a debt owed to M. de Jully by M. d'Épinay. Grimm insisted that she could not have done so, that she was "*honnête, fortunée et généreuse*"; and when another guest began to tell offensive stories about her, Grimm invited him to "step outside." They fought with swords, and both were wounded.

The news astounded Mme d'Épinay; on hearing it she "almost fainted." She and her mother immediately sent messages to Grimm, and when he had sufficiently recovered he asked permission to call.

> I have seen M. Grimm [Mme d'Épinay writes]. I saw him at my mother's. He was announced. She went to greet him. He kissed her hand respectfully: she embraced him. I was behind her; she led me toward him. "*Ma fille*," she said solemnly, "*embrassez votre chevalier.*" "I should be very proud of that title, were I to deserve it," M. Grimm replied. "What I defended was charity —charity itself. It is true," he added, looking at me, "that never had charity been more flouted, and more unjustly."

That is the story as presented in the Memoirs. No confirmation exists, but it is certain that about this time Mme d'Épinay's regard for Grimm ripened into affection, and then into love. That spring and summer, in the rue Saint-Honoré and in the country, they saw each other constantly. Grimm became a favorite. He quickly won over her children. M. d'Épinay, who on first learning of the duel had ironically asked his wife "how she was enjoying her *gloire*," changed his tune when he learned that Grimm had fought in defense of his, M. d'Épinay's, reputation as well as hers, and thenceforward praised him everywhere.

For several weeks that summer Grimm was away, traveling in central France with one of his new friends, the baron d'Holbach, the philosopher, who was mourning the recent death of his wife. "I esteem him the more for going," Mme d'Épinay writes, "but I cannot tolerate an ambulatory life in the person with whom I have most enjoyed living. I said to M. Grimm, 'But who will be my defender, Monsieur, if I am insulted while you are away?' He answered, 'Your best defender, Madame, will be as before: the record of your past life.' "

Meanwhile, Grimm accepted a suggestion—made by the abbé Raynal, the friend who, with Rousseau, had nursed him in his lovesickness—that he assume the editorship of *Les Nouvelles Littéraires*, a newsletter that Raynal had founded some years before and had been dispatching from Paris to several German courts. Bearing a new name, *Correspondance Littéraire, Philosophique et Critique*, Grimm's first number was dated 15 May 1753. During the forty years of its existence, until the French Revolution put an end to its delivery, this monthly or fortnightly Newsletter (as it will be referred to in these pages) went out to its twenty or more royal and princely subscribers in copies handwritten by amanuenses in Zweibrücken, just over the border in the German Palatinate, thus avoiding French censorship. European courts welcomed this regular, candid, and cultural news from "the world's capital."[1] And Mme d'Épinay's participation in the Newsletter became, as we shall see, one of the joys of the new life she began to lead with Grimm. Her existence was transformed. He was her confidant, and a protector such as Francueil had never been. "He advised her"—to quote one of her modern admirers—"on the education of her children, her interests, and the proper behavior with her husband and her friends. Henceforth she would put herself into his hands. She was now approaching thirty, and her union with Grimm (a few years older) marked the end of a sterile period in her life."[2]

During those first years with Grimm, Louise d'Épinay began to read more extensively and more seriously than in the past—"to study the great men, Locke, Montaigne, Montesquieu." "If you could lend me the fourth volume of Plutarch's *Lives* you would give me great pleasure," she wrote to Rousseau in May 1754. (He replied, "Here is Plutarch, who is my master and my consolation.") She had always participated in her children's education, correcting and supplementing as best she could the foolish tutor her husband insisted on keeping for their son, and conferring with the excellent governess she herself had chosen for her daughter.[3] In this, Grimm and Rousseau now became her allies; and Francueil, still a family friend, encouraged the children with their music—until his jealousy of Grimm became unmanageable and he was asked to stay away. Stimulated particularly by Rousseau—eloquent in those days with the pedagogical ideas the world would some years later find in his *Émile*—Mme d'Épinay began to express some of her own thoughts about education, in the form of essays, *Letters to My Son* and "Letter to my daughter's governess," which were published both in the Newsletter and in separate volumes. And Grimm, encouraging her, composed a "Letter to a lady seriously engaged in the education of her children," which appeared in the *Mercure de France* for June 1756.[4] Through Grimm, Mme d'Épinay began to extend and enrich her circle of acquaintances, seeing something of the baron d'Holbach and his friends, many of them contributors to the *Encyclopaedia*, and having a first, tentative meeting with Diderot.

In 1756, at the outbreak of what was to be the Seven Years' War, which aligned Austria, France, Russia, Sweden, and Saxony against England and Prussia, Grimm accepted a commission in the French army, to serve for six months as liaison officer in the field. He and Diderot had become close friends—"You are my master: you tell me what I am thinking, and you confirm me in those thoughts," he wrote to Diderot from the field; and to Diderot, as well as to his own assistants, he confided much of the writing of the Newsletter during his absence.

Early in the morning of 27 April 1757, Grimm left for Westphalia with his company. Half an hour after his departure, Mme d'Épinay, in tears, found a letter he had left for her, full of affectionate encouragement. It was the first of a series of such letters, which, together with her replies, are to be found in the pages of *Madame de Montbrillant*—an excellent correspondence, certainly reflecting, if not precisely reproducing, for readers of the novel actual letters that passed between Mme d'Épinay and Grimm. "I beg you," he wrote from a military address that he could not divulge, "do not neglect your vocation: it is entirely in your own power to be the happiest and most adorable creature on this earth, provided you know how to be self-sufficient and don't set the opinion of others above your own."

He frequently exhorted her in this vein, and her efforts to respond can be glimpsed in a letter she wrote at this time to an acquaintance who had remarked that she seemed, nowadays, "somehow different":

> The great mistake I had been making with my friends and myself was always to give preference to *their* fancies, with no thought of what *I* might be wishing. Owing to that little system, I found that half of my "friends" were in fact my masters. To have a will of my own seemed to me a crime. I was doing a thousand unsuitable things with a willingness that was equally unsuitable. I was a perpetual victim, inspiring gratitude in no one. I examined myself closely. I began to dare to be myself. Now I have no regard for the caprices of others. I do only what I prefer, and feel marvelously the better for it.

It was Grimm's encouragement, and her loneliness in his absence, that drove her to begin *Madame de Montbrillant*.

Rousseau, who was writing the epistolary novel that would become *Julie, ou La Nouvelle Héloïse*, had asked her to read the opening chapters, and before long she was writing tentatively to Grimm:

> I am going to try to find some useful and agreeable occupation to remedy the vacuity I'm aware of these days—something that won't tire me. I don't know what, as yet, but I intend to think about it. Rousseau's book might almost make me wish to write a novel composed of letters. It seems to me that one would need only naturalness and taste to produce something good of this kind.

A few weeks later:

I have just begun to write—something that pleases me so far. It was Rousseau's novel that gave me the idea. All the letters in it are so beautiful, so perfectly written, that I find it cold and tiresome. When I finish a few chapters I'll send them to you, to know whether it's worth going on with.

She did send her first chapters, and Grimm wrote from the field in reply:

Truly, I am so angry that I cannot restrain myself. I have read the two thick notebooks of your novel, both written in your own hand. Are you absolutely determined to kill yourself, O most adorable of all possible and impossible friends? What—with no regard for your health, and no respect for my orders, you have copied, yourself, these two great volumes? I must admit, however, that since their arrival yesterday my anger has been giving way to the admiration that your writing deserves. Really, it is charming. I was very tired, very harassed, when the bundle came. [Grimm was finding life in a military encampment anything but congenial.] I glanced at it—and couldn't put it down. At two this morning I was still reading it. If you keep this up, you will certainly produce something unique. But, please, work only when you feel like it, and, above all, forget that you're writing a book. It will be very easy to connect the various parts. Such a wonderful air of truth can continue to flow only spontaneously: even the happiest imagination is no substitute. . . . If you'll take my advice, you'll show no one what you've written until it's entirely finished, because, even without realizing it, you'd worry about the work and lose your naturalness in trying to make it elegant.

She sent him further chapters; they brought more praise; and she continued to write.

But quite suddenly her health, always precarious, began

to break down: *"Ma poitrine est en mauvais état,"* she told Rousseau, who reports it in the *Confessions*. By September 1757, when Grimm returned to Paris from the field, she was seriously ill. Through Rousseau she had met, in Paris, the famed Swiss physician Dr. Théodore Tronchin, Voltaire's doctor and the author of the article "Inoculation" in the *Encyclopaedia*; Mme d'Épinay had corresponded with him after his return to Geneva. Now she resolved to go to Geneva to put herself in his care. Grimm, detained in Paris by duties connected with his military commission, could not accompany her, and she accepted her husband's unexpected offer to escort her—fully aware, she says, that he "would be happy to have her away, leaving him freer to rob her with no fear of punishment." Confiding her daughter to the care of her governess and Mme d'Esclavelles, she set out across France with her husband, their son, who was now eleven, and the boy's tutor, followed by several servants in a separate coach.

In a village in the foothills of the Jura she fell so desperately ill that Dr. Tronchin was summoned from Geneva to rescue her. By the time he reached her bedside she had been saved by one of his colleagues in a nearby town, and after a few days Tronchin accompanied her on the rest of the journey. "Aesculapius-Tronchin is attracting all the pretty women of Paris," Voltaire wrote to a friend early in November 1757. "He went to the rescue of Mme d'Épinay, who fell ill on the way from Lyons to Geneva. He will restore her to health, as he has done for others. I believe in no miracles except his."

For two years Mme d'Épinay remained in Geneva, where Dr. Tronchin, becoming "the doctor for her body and her soul," as she wrote, did indeed save her life, "as by enchantment."

And it was while she was in Geneva that some of her writings first appeared in book form. Stimulated by Voltaire, and welcomed by his friends, she was pleased to be invited by a Genevan whom she had met in Paris, M. Gauffecourt, a friend and admirer of Rousseau, to make use of his private printing press in the nearby village of Montbrillant. Her first published book, *Mes moments heureux*, a miscellany of verse, essays, and letters, dedicated to her mother and including her self-portrait and the "Letter to my daughter's governess," appeared in 1758, followed a year later by *Letters to My Son*, a work of striking candor, showing a pessimism concerning her son's future that events would prove to have been well founded. Both volumes were printed anonymously. And although Grimm's name never appears in full, one of the chapters in *Mes moments heureux* is the affectionate "Portrait of Monsieur G****"; and the dedicatory pages of the volume are clearly addressed to Grimm. "You have guided my pen," they conclude. "Now guide as well the responses of my friends, to whom alone I offer this book." Only twenty-five copies of each volume were printed. It is not known to whom they were sent. In Geneva, Mme d'Épinay says, where everyone knew of the volumes' existence, she refused all requests for them, even Voltaire's. (But Voltaire wrote her later, to Paris, telling her that pirated copies were circulating.)

Continuing to work on her novel (and appropriating the family name of her heroine's husband from the name of the village containing the printing press), she included in it a series of letters, apparently versions of those she was sending at this time to Grimm. In Geneva she was studying botany and geology, and discussing health and hygiene with Dr. Tronchin: some of her observations on those subjects found their way into the Newsletter. In her letters she described Calvinist Geneva and the Genevans, and her new acquaintances. She came to love the city: for her it was a haven, peaceful but not insipid. "Oh!" she wrote to Grimm. "If only four people could be transported here, I'd agree never to see Paris again." Her mother, perhaps; her daughter; Grimm; and—who else? Her son? One wonders.

Voltaire admired her greatly. "Occasionally I have as my guest Mme d'Épinay, the wife of a tax-farmer," he wrote to a friend. "In my opinion she is among the most intelligent of women. If her nerves were as robust as her mind, she wouldn't be in Geneva with Dr. Tronchin." And: "Mme d'Épinay is with me at the moment. She is no scatterbrain: she is a *philosophe*, with a very clear, strong mind." Continually struck by the contrast between her strength and her fragility, he called her *"un aigle dans une cage de gaze"*—"an eagle in a gossamer cage."

Among her pleasures was her attendance, in April 1758, at a ceremony of which she later wrote a lighthearted account in the Newsletter—Voltaire's arrival with his niece at his newly acquired house at Ferney, just over the French border:

> The *seigneur patriarche* drove from Les Délices [his previous dwelling in Geneva] to Ferney in a gala carriage, accompanied by Mme Denis, who wore her most splendid gown and every diamond she possessed. He wore a suit of crimson velvet, lined and trimmed with ermine, even with ermine tails; and although the costume seemed a little warm for the season, no one could fail to admire its taste and magnificence. So caparisoned, uncle and niece attended High Mass in the parish church. . . .

In late February 1759, Grimm joined her, his incongruous military duties at an end. He had been helping Diderot with the eighth volume of the *Encyclopaedia*, and now Diderot, in turn, would once again give much attention to the Newsletter. For almost eight months Grimm and Mme d'Épinay were together, seeing Voltaire (it was the year of *Candide*) and her other new friends. These were the happiest months of her life, Mme d'Épinay tells us; and she slowly gathered strength.

But Grimm, though patient and affectionate, was always ambitious; and now he accepted an appointment as diplomatic representative in Paris for the free city of Frankfurt-am-Main, at an annual salary of 24,000 livres.[5] As gently as he could, he began to prepare Mme d'Épinay for their return to Paris. One morning, she writes, after she had spent a sleepless night worrying about letters she had received both from and about her husband, they went to sit in "a little alcove at the end of the terrace":

"What?" he said. "Your husband's misdoings—you have constantly stood out against them—do you really think they can still affect your reputation and your happiness?"

"Not my reputation, I hope, but perhaps my happiness . . ."

"The happiness of someone faint-hearted and pusillanimous, perhaps, but not yours. Is it the question of money that troubles you?—the money from which you never benefited and that you see him squandering?"

"No, certainly not."

"He has forfeited the right to torment you with his chicanery, and you have won the right to take charge of your children and their education, which is what interests you the most: the right to be mistress of your own household. *Ma tendre amie*, you must prepare, now, to rejoin that household, and in the proper spirit. . . . As for me, I shall always be at your side, offering you the most tender care."

"But your work? And all my duties?"

Grimm's response, if Mme d'Épinay's rendering is moderately faithful, once again displays that other, worldly side of the northern Romantic:

"Are those things cause for anxiety, *ma chère amie*? One must follow one's vocation. And yours cannot be to live in solitary retirement with me: we must devote to each other those moments of repose that our duties allow us. Our happiness during these past months might never have been granted us: it has been a gift from heaven, and we must be grateful for it. It has been a blissful period in our lives, but we would be wrong to bewail its brevity: our duties call us away."

She was now free, he reminded her, to choose her friends, to lead the life she wished; and he hoped that she would allow him always to be at hand to second her in fulfilling the duties she owed her family, and to prove that he cherished her and would never cease to make her the object of his admiration and care.

She thanked him. Although she feared that his words might describe "only the poetry of the situation," she said, she hoped they might "intoxicate" her and make her worthy of his expectations.

Such, she writes in the Memoirs, had been their conversation. She felt calmer for this talk, she says, but could not rid herself of the dread that circumstances might prevent their having, with any frequency, other exchanges of the kind.

She and Grimm returned to Paris early in October 1759.

Seventeen fifty-nine was a black year for France. Quebec was lost, and there were defeats in Westphalia and in India; the French fleet was put to rout by the British in the bay of Quiberon; and these disasters brought an upsurge of political oppression and censorship. In March the *Encyclopaedia* was abruptly suppressed. Seven volumes were in print, through the letter G. There was a symbolic burning of the volumes by the public hangman, and the pope ordered Catholics to have their sets destroyed by a priest (an order that seems to have been largely ignored).[6]

Diderot was in distress, but the nobility and strength of his nature were extraordinary. Grimm admired him immensely. In October 1763, he wrote of Diderot in the Newsletter:

Profound and vigorous in his writing, but even more astonishing in conversation, he delivers oracles on every subject imaginable. Of all men he is the least inclined to know in advance what he will do or say: whatever he says, he is always original, always surprising. His imagination is so strong, so impetuous, that it might be alarming at times, were those qualities not tempered by his irresistible bonhomie.

Mme d'Épinay, who became Diderot's friend at this time, also pays him tribute. Because of a certain skepticism on

39

Diderot's part, it had been impossible for Grimm to bring them together before; but a chance meeting had gone well, and when they found themselves together once again at the house of friends soon after Mme d'Épinay's return from Geneva, Diderot asked Grimm to present him to both Mme d'Épinay and her mother, who was with her.

My mother replied that there were so many reasons for our being delighted to make his acquaintance that any such formality would be superfluous; and I added, "Monsieur, when two people know of each other as well as you and I do, there is no longer any question of introductions. We speak of you constantly, and are vain enough to think that occasionally you may speak of us."

Her admiration of him was "enormous." She had always known that he was a great man; and when he called on her the next evening, she and her mother were "honored":

Since that evening he has come to see me every day. . . . His conversation is ravishing: his confidence, his self-possession, an inspiration. He has stirred my mind and my soul; he—how shall I express it? It is not that he has made me happy, precisely, but he has given me a new capacity to enjoy all my advantages. I find myself more strongly attached to my duties, to everything I do. I work more easily: in short, I am more *myself* than I was. M. Grimm is so happy with all of us here! He takes pleasure in my own satisfaction and my triumph: and indeed those are real. And I myself am happy in his happiness. . . .

During the months following her return, Mme d'Épinay quite swiftly gathered around her, in Paris and at La Chevrette, a delightful company of friends—old friends as well as many now introduced by Grimm. She held no regular salon, such as those over which Mme Du Deffand and Mme Geoffrin then presided—she was never a true bluestocking —and, in the country especially, her house, always open, became known for its new and distinctive atmosphere. Diderot's letters to his friend Sophie Volland provide glimpses of life at La Chevrette:

10 September 1760. I arrived here on Monday night, after they had given me up. Grimm and I crossed each other on the way, so I spent two days tête-à-tête with his *amie.* This is what my life has been. Conversations now merry, now serious, a little card playing, walks together or separately, much reading, meditation, silence, solitude and rest. Grimm arrived on Wednesday night at eleven o'clock: we had been worried for two hours: the night was very dark, and we feared something had happened to him. So here we are, the three of us, until next Monday. What do I do? What do they do? In the morning, he works alone in his study, writing: we see each other for a moment before dinner. We dine. After dinner, a game of chess; after chess, a walk; after the walk, a nap; conversation: after conversation, supper; after supper, a little more conversation; and so ends an innocent, sweet kind of day, a day during which we have enjoyed ourselves and been busy, a day of thinking and learning, of mutual affection and esteem.

At other times La Chevrette was full of family and friends:

15 September 1760. Yesterday there was a fête here at La Chevrette. I am apprehensive of crowds and had resolved to spend the day in Paris, but Grimm and Mme d'Épinay detained me. When I see my friends look sad and pull long faces, any reluctance I feel always evaporates and I'm putty in their hands.

Beginning on Saturday afternoon, booths were set up under canvas stretched between the trees. The next morning, people from the surrounding countryside began to pour in, fiddlers tuned up, and all afternoon there were games, drinking, singing, dancing. It was a mixed crowd of charmingly dressed young peasant girls and *grandes dames* from the city with their rouge and beauty spots, carrying long reed staffs and wearing straw hats, arm in arm with their escorts. About ten o'clock the male guests at the château drove off into the country. M. de Villeneuve arrived at noon.

We were then in the rather somber but magnificent salon of the château, each occupied in his own way: a charming scene. At the window giving on the gardens, Grimm was having his portrait painted and Mme d'Épinay was leaning on the back of the artist's chair. Another artist, sitting on a low stool, was drawing her profile. (Her profile is charming and all the ladies crowded around to see whether the artist was capturing a likeness.) M. de Saint-Lambert was sitting in a corner reading the last brochure I sent you. I was playing chess with Mme d'Houdetot. Nice old Mme d'Esclavelles, Mme d'Épinay's mother, had the children around her and was talking with them and their tutors. Two sisters of the artist who was painting Grimm were embroidering, one merely holding the cloth, the other using a round frame. And a third was trying out a piece by Scarlatti on the harpsichord.

On his arrival, M. de Villeneuve greeted the mistress of the house, and came and sat beside me. We spoke a little. He and Mme d'Houdetot knew each other; from some rather bold words they exchanged I even gathered that he had once behaved badly to her in some way.

Dinner was served. Mme d'Épinay was in the middle of one side of the table and M. de Villeneuve opposite her: they presided together, as it were, in the most charming way. We dined splendidly, gaily, and were a long time at table. Ices: ah, such ices!

After dinner there was a little music. The young woman I mentioned has a marvelously light and expert touch on the harpsichord. She astonished us all: the others, by her extraordinary talent; me, by the charm of her youth, her sweetness, her modesty, her grace and innocence. The applause she received made her blush:

she was charmingly embarrassed. She was asked to sing, and she sang a song whose words were something like "My fondness carries me away: my heart is no longer my own." But I swear she didn't grasp the meaning. I looked at her and thought in my heart of hearts that she was an angel, and that one would have to be more wicked than Satan himself to entertain evil thoughts about her. I said to M. de Villeneuve: "Who would want to change anything there? All is so lovely as it is." But M. de Villeneuve and I do not have the same principles. If he encounters innocence, he likes to "instruct" it. "Instruction," he said, "is beauty of another kind."

. . . Our hunters returned about six o'clock. Then fiddlers arrived, and there was dancing till ten. We finished supper at midnight, and by two o'clock at the latest we were all in our beds. Despite my forebodings the day had been very pleasant.

A charming picture—almost a genre picture that tells a story, or several stories. The fête resembles a scene from Watteau, offered by the *châtelains* to their country neighbors, with friends and relations from the city, dressed in rustic style—among them the celebrated pair of lovers Mme d'Houdetot and the marquis de Saint-Lambert. (She was Mme d'Épinay's younger cousin Sophie de Bellegarde, whose governess Louise had shared when they were children and who was now her sister-in-law. Rousseau adored her and had her in mind when he portrayed his Julie in *La Nouvelle Héloïse*. Her husband was tolerant, and she and Saint-Lambert—he was a poet, and wrote the article "Luxe" for the *Encyclopaedia*—survived the Revolution and remained together until after 1800.) There is Grimm, virtually one of the hosts; the portraitist at work; the lovely young harpsichordist; the youthful rake Vallet de Villeneuve (who nine years later would marry one of Francueil's daughters); the conversation; the returning hunters; the dancing. And Diderot, observing it all.

•   •   •

43

In a later century, the imagination of Marcel Proust, conjuring such a scene, turned irresistibly to these very personages, this *douceur de vivre*:

> My mouth waters for the life . . . they had, each working in his little room and then, before lunch, gathering together—in a drawing room so vast that it possessed two fireplaces—for conversation of the highest order, interspersed with parlor games, the whole bringing to mind the existence depicted by Diderot in that masterpiece *Letters to Mademoiselle Volland*.[7]

Happier, self-confident, her health improving (although she would always be frail)—"a new person," as she called herself—Mme d'Épinay entertained her guests at La Chevrette. And now she would enter upon another friendship, which would remain important until her death. In the spring of 1759, an Italian had come to Paris: a worldly, witty, learned young Neapolitan abbé named Ferdinando Galiani—a new friend with whom Mme d'Épinay was destined to play a new role.

III

The Young Abbé from Naples

FERDINANDO Ernesto Francesco-Saverio Pier-Celestino Galiani was born in 1728 in the town of Chieti, in the Abruzzi, where his father, Matteo Galiani, *"un gentil-uomo,"* was a minor government official. Of his mother little is known. When Ferdinando was seven, he was sent to Naples to join his elder brother, Berardo, in the care of their eminent and scholarly uncle, the archbishop Celestino Galiani, rector of the university. There the boys attended excellent schools and profited from the company of their uncle's learned friends, and in due course they were enrolled in the University of Naples.

Berardo would become known as an archaeologist, architect, and translator into Italian of Vitruvius's *De architectura*. Ferdinando gained a reputation for brilliance, erudition, and wit while not yet twenty. A precocious specialist in monetary and social studies, he read, at nineteen, before the members of a Neapolitan learned society, the Accademia degli Emuli, a treatise, replete with quotations from ancient Greek, "On Money at the Time of the Trojan War, as Depicted in the

45

Poems of Homer," which impressed all who heard it. (The year before, he had given a similarly sophisticated "Discorso sull'amore," ranging from considerations of Plato to a discussion of heterosexual and homosexual love in his contemporary Naples.) Even earlier, at sixteen, he had translated into Italian much of John Locke's *Some Considerations of the Consequences of the Lowering of Interest, and Raising the Value of Money.* Galiani also delighted Neapolitans by publishing, in collaboration with his friend Pasquale Carcani, a burlesque eulogy of the city's recently deceased official hangman, Domenico Iannacone—a pamphlet to which the young wags attached the name of one Giannantonio Sergio, a local lawyer well known for his self-importance, a blusterer who, as it happened, had recently made the mistake of humiliating the young Galiani in public.

Two years later, in an episode which he would always leave unmentioned, Galiani was exposed by an indignant Central European scholar, the Reverend Father Boscovich, as the author of an elaborate, learned spoof recently printed in the Roman *Giornale de' Letterati* concerning the excavation, near the church of San Lorenzo in Lucina, in central Rome, of an obelisk that had been brought from Egypt by order of the Emperor Caesar Augustus. (The obelisk now stands in Piazza di Montecitorio, outside the Camera dei Deputati.) On that occasion, Galiani had used the *nom de plume* "Ernesto Freeman," a fictitious "English scholar."

Among eminent persons at Naples who became aware of young Ferdinando's precocity was the minister of justice of the Kingdom of Naples, Bernardo Tanucci. A Tuscan, Tanucci had been professor of law at the University of Pisa when the Neapolitan king, Carlo di Borbone, admiring his writings in favor of Tuscan and Italian independence, invited him to Naples and made him his trusted adviser. Tanucci was to wield great power at Naples for more than half a century. Following the burlesque eulogy of the public hangman by Ferdinando and his friend Carcani, the two culprits had thought it wise to confess in advance of their inevitable exposure; and Tanucci, knowing that even their sovereigns

Bernardo Tanucci, artist unknown

had enjoyed the farce, and yet feeling that token discipline was required, pronounced a sentence of a few days' "fasting and prayer" in a local monastery. After the malefactors' release, Tanucci kept a benevolent eye on both of them. A few years later, upon his own promotion to the rank of minister of foreign affairs, he appointed Carcani his assistant.

As for young Galiani, his translation of Locke and his learned discourses on money and love, followed by the hangman affair and the Freeman escapade, aroused curiosity as to the direction of his next move—a curiosity that was soon satisfied.

In the autumn of 1751, some months after the episode of the obelisk, a volume of 370 pages, entitled simply *Della Moneta—On Money*—was published in Naples. The author's name did not appear; the volume opened with a dedicatory letter to the king signed by the publisher. His Majesty's pardon was entreated for the author's anonymity, which was due solely to his "complete absence of ambition." "May your life be joyful," the dedication concluded, "and for our sake may it be long, in order that you may restore this kingdom to great prosperity—as in part you have already done— following its many years as an unhappy province [of Spain and Austria]."

Shortly before, on 16 August 1751, the marchese Nicola Fraggianni, the Neapolitan magistrate one of whose functions it was to transmit for royal approval, if he saw fit, the verdict of the ecclesiastical censors concerning literary works awaiting publication, had sent the king a long report on *Della Moneta*. It was couched in the elaborate style, reminiscent of the Oriental, then current in absolute monarchies:

> In humble obedience to Your Majesty's order that I present my unworthy opinion of the book entitled *Delle Monete* [*sic*], which the printer Raimondi begs permission to publish and dedicate to Your Majesty, I have not, following your sovereign command, contented myself with the extract ordered by the First Chaplain to be

prepared and sent to me by a professor at the university; but have preferred to read the entire work, even though all of it is not yet in print.

I have read it with the greatest pleasure, and I believe that it will not fail to please anyone who admires method, precision, delicacy of idea, clarity and elegance of diction. The subject of money, which is its theme, has exercised the pens of many foreign writers. But I am emboldened to say that none has shed such light upon it as our anonymous Neapolitan. Certainly, among our national writers he is the only one so far to have hit the mark, treating not only the history of money, but, what is more important, its function—and this with particular reference to our own currency. . . .

In short, the work is rich in firm principles and highly judicious maxims. And although many aspects of the subject of money may be dry and difficult—similar in that respect, one might say, to the metaphysics of political theory—nevertheless our author has known how to vary his subject, and to enrich his exposition with appropriate digressions and examples (without ever losing sight of his purpose), thus making the work pleasant and instructive. And even were it not so agreeably written, it would serve to stimulate other gifted minds (of which our nation can boast so many) to employ their talents in this field, which is of great national importance.

Unquestionably, no such accomplished a work on this theme has hitherto been published in Naples. It will do honor to our country and cause those in other lands to envy our new dignity in the field of letters—a dignity achieved under an august Maecenas, who is ever so gloriously provident in giving new vigor to the sciences and fine arts.

It is therefore my humble opinion that Your Majesty would do well to permit this work to be printed, and to accord it the honor of allowing Your Majesty's august name to appear on its opening pages as the recipient of its dedication by the publisher—the author in his modesty preferring to remain unnamed.

And because the originality and excellence of the book will excite the cupidity of other publishers and tempt them to print editions of their own, I appeal to Your Majesty in his clemency to grant the publisher an exclusivity of ten years and the right to fix the price of the volume at ten *carlini*.

Twelve days later, Carlo III gave permission for the book to be published and the price fixed as recommended.

The first chaplain, who had ordered that an abstract of *Della Moneta* be submitted to Fraggianni for further approval, was, as we have seen, young Ferdinando Galiani's eminent uncle, Monsignor Celestino Galiani, among whose titles was that of ecclesiastical censor; and the university professor charged with having the extract prepared was the seventy-year-old Tuscan Bartolomeo Intieri, a close friend of the monsignore and one of Ferdinando's most beloved teachers.[1]

In his preface to the second edition of *Della Moneta*, published thirty years later, Ferdinando Galiani—who was, of course, the anonymous author (and the author, as well, of the dedicatory letter from the "publisher")—wrote, using the third person, that

Della Moneta, which was published anonymously, was the youthful production of Ferdinando Galiani, who composed it when he was not yet twenty-one. He wrote it quite unaided, and with little help from books. He preferred not to ask anyone's assistance, enjoying writing and publishing it secretly, concealing himself from view—even from his famous uncle Monsignor Galiani, in order to give him a pleasant surprise, as in fact occurred. It was all the more extraordinary, and all the more difficult, to maintain this secrecy, since he lived not only under his uncle's rigorous care and discipline, but in his very house, where he was never unobserved. Furthermore, Monsignor Galiani, in addition to the post of first chaplain, which he so gloriously filled, exercised such great authority at the university, and over men of letters and all books printed in Naples, that it seemed impossible to hide anything of this sort from him. Nevertheless, the secret was kept, being divulged only to two young men of the author's age. These were signor Don Pasquale Carcani, whose name alone is sufficient commendation, and signor Don Pasquale di Tommasi, to whom the republic of letters owes the splendid dictionary published by the Accademia della Crusca in Naples in 1746, enriched with so many words overlooked by Florentine scholars. It was they who applied for and obtained the necessary permission for publication, who took the manuscript to the printer, and who supervised the final corrections that were required almost until the day the book appeared—tasks that the author in his chosen anonymity could not perform. The ruse was so successful that for [almost] . . . two months the author was able to listen to the impartial and sincere judgment of all kinds of readers, could watch scholars torment themselves in vain efforts to guess the author's name, and could listen to praise [of the anonymous author] from his uncle himself, to whom he was required to read the book aloud, as he read other books, in his hours of rest.

Looking again at Fraggianni's enthusiastic report to the king, we may wonder if Ferdinando Galiani, writing his preface to the new edition a generation later, did not exaggerate some of the circumstances. His uncle the ecclesiastical censor may well have been ignorant of the book's authorship when Ferdinando read it aloud to him, and "pleasantly surprised" upon learning the truth; but it is unlikely that he was still in ignorance when he had the extract prepared for Fraggianni. And though the author's identity may have been kept from Fraggianni for a time, it seems doubtful that Fraggianni (who owed his appointment as what might be called "lay censor" to Celestino Galiani) was still in ignorance when he sent the king his report—a report that scarcely sounds objective. In a note to the 1780 edition, Ferdinando Galiani explicitly assures readers that Fraggianni "could never have guessed that the author was the young Galiani he often saw in my uncle's house"; but he does not say that Fraggianni was still ignorant when writing to the king. Even the king himself may not have been kept in ignorance.

In any case, both Intieri and the first chaplain kept the "secret," having foreseen—as the former would put it, on 30 September, in a letter to the latter—what had in fact by then come to pass: "a ridiculous and shameful volte-face from some who praised the book, now that the author is revealed as being young and unknown."

In the second edition, Galiani refers scornfully to the Neapolitan policy of those earlier days: "The state preferred to fill its coffers with short-term profits instead of its subjects' stomachs with bread. No similar example exists in civilized Europe, but only in the African desert and in barbarous Tartary." And in one of his notes to that edition he makes a confession concerning certain passages written in his youth:

> Here let me warn my readers . . . that the better to conceal my identity, I thought it expedient to pretend that the author of the book was a grave man of mature years, tried and battered by misfortune, weary of a world he knew too well; and indeed that fiction, that bit of cunning, was so successful that nothing would have helped me more to ensure the book's success and to keep the author's identity a secret.

Fraggianni's enthusiasm, overflowing from the ornate frame of the official report, spoke the truth: *Della Moneta*, its rich detail eloquent of Galiani's immense, precocious knowledge, and illustrative of the high intelligence of his concepts of history and money, is a masterpiece—"one of the latest examples," it has been called, "of the literary genre whose models are *The Prince*, *The Courtier*, and [Giovanni della Casa's] *Galateo.*" The reader familiar with English literature may well be surprised and pleased as he enjoys this work written by a twenty-one-year-old Italian, with its charming eighteenth-century Italian style, to find himself reminded of passages from English writings of a century before—of Burton's *Anatomy of Melancholy* and of certain valetudinarian curiosities of Sir Thomas Browne.[2]

On 2 December 1751, shortly before his twenty-third birthday, Ferdinando Galiani set out for Rome and northern Italy on what might be called today a promotional tour, or series of personal appearances.

In Naples the jealous gossip continued. "I don't know whether you have done well to confess your authorship [of *Della Moneta*]," Bartolomeo Intieri wrote him. "There has already been a lot of malicious jabbering. Of course those people are all jackasses—*asini, asinissimi.*" Along with the local braying, Galiani received messages of praise from scholars in other Italian cities; and even Intieri, while warning him of dangers that might come from "excessive admiration," encouraged him to profit from his early fame. By mid-December he was in Rome, where he stayed until March, and where he noted the letters by "Ernesto Freeman" and Father Boscovich in the *Giornale de' Letterati,* and "Freeman's" remarks about an inscription on the Via Appia in the Florentine *Novelle Letterarie.* But by now Ernesto Freeman was part of the abbé Ferdinando Galiani's past.

For Ferdinando Galiani was, indeed, an abbé, and had been one for several years. He was a "commendatory"—that is, an absentee—abbé. The abbacy of many a monastery, together with the annual income that went with it, was in the king's gift as a sinecure—somewhat analogous to a permanent absentee professorship today. Ferdinando's uncle had secured from Carlo di Borbone the living of a monastery in Calabria for his nephew Berardo, who had had to relinquish it in 1745 when he decided to marry; the archbishop had seen to it that the title and the living were transferred to the seventeen-year-old Ferdinando. (Later, the livings of other monasteries were added.) To qualify, Ferdinando had made the necessary vow of celibacy and submitted to the tonsure—two gestures which he would never allow to interfere with his uninhibited private life. A correction to the tonsure was soon suggested by the Archbishop himself in one of his letters to his nephew in Rome: "Remember the proverb: 'When in Rome do as the Romans do': since everybody there wears a wig, even the gravest prelate, and since to go without one makes one conspicuous, I think you should wear one. Especially since a wig would make you look a little less tiny." Here his uncle was touching on an essential theme: Ferdinando had been born extremely small, and his height would never exceed four and a half feet. He would always wear the black habit and white clerical collar of his office.

In ecclesiastical Rome, the diminutive young abbé, who was now a celebrated author, received a welcome perhaps more varied than he had expected. A decade earlier, Celestino Galiani had spent many months in Rome helping to negotiate a concordat between the Holy See and the Kingdom of Naples. There he had made many friends, and those friends now greeted his nephew Ferdinando with affection, and with praise for *Della Moneta*. But in Rome, too, *asini* abounded. "Let me tell you first of all that I have more enemies than friends here," Ferdinando wrote to one of his teachers in Naples. "Envy, hatred and other ugly passions, daughters of human malice, have preceded me, and my presence has perhaps increased them. You may imagine how much I wish to remain in such an atmosphere." His welcome in the Vatican took an unexpected turn. Pope Benedict XIV and Celestino Galiani had enjoyed each other's company in Rome, and Ferdinando must have heard from his uncle that His Holiness liked a joke. But after inquiring about the archbishop's health that February morning in 1752, the pontiff surprised Ferdinando by his choice of compliment. "The pope, whom I saw on Wednesday, poured great praise on the hangman farce," Galiani wrote to a friend. "He and I seem to share a taste for such things. Of my book he said little."

After he left Rome and was traveling farther north, Galiani had the impression, amid continuing applause for *Della Moneta*, that the pope's preference for the farce was known and had even become a fashion: "I must tell you that I received more praise for *Iannacone* than for my book," he wrote, perhaps with some exaggeration, from Pisa. "I am better known for my jokes than for all my studies." He traveled steadily north, greeted by professors and prelates in Florence, Bologna, Venice, Verona, Milan, and Turin (where he discussed economics with the grand duke, Carlo Emanuele II). On 9 November 1752 he was back in Naples.

Soon after his arrival in Rome he had learned that his uncle, now in his early seventies, had suffered a pair of strokes affecting his right arm, and was under doctors' care; but Ferdinando had been persuaded, apparently by the patient himself, and by the callous egotism of youth, not to hasten his return. In the affectionate letters that his uncle valiantly continued to send, he saw the script deteriorate until it was all but illegible; and on 20 July 1753, seven months after Ferdinando's return to Naples, Celestino Galiani died.

In May 1754, a friend in Florence wrote to Galiani of a rumor that a biography of the late archbishop had been published in Naples. "No, no life whatever of my uncle has been published here," Galiani replied. "I have heard that a eulogy has been written by an abbot in Rimini called Padre Buonafede. He writes very well, and I know that he was preparing such a work—we sent him some information from here. But we haven't had the consolation of receiving any news of the outcome. Monks are monks." (The "monk" Buonafede had been one of Ferdinando's childhood teachers. He had, in fact, just finished a brief *Vita* of the archbishop, in Latin, which Ferdinando would soon receive.) "I myself would have liked to honor in that way an uncle to whom I owe so much," Ferdinando's letter continues, "but I have been blocked: the occasion is too cruel, too barbarous, too sad. I could write a *Life*, but the result would serve no purpose: I am incapable of writing anything that could be of use."

And indeed, for many months following his uncle's death, Galiani did little. The remark that he made in his preface to the second edition of *Della Moneta* many years later—that at the time of the book's first publication he had wanted to give his uncle "a pleasant surprise"—was perhaps something of a confession. He had possibly felt compelled to demonstrate to the archbishop, by a formidable show of intellectual power, that the prelate's affection and encouragement had not been misplaced. There was no need now for continued proof.

Galiani often admitted, and even perversely boasted, that he was "fundamentally lazy." Certainly years passed before he was stimulated to make an effort comparable to that which he had put into *Della Moneta*. His reluctance to concentrate his genius in enduring published works undoubtedly helped to keep his name obscure beyone his native land and outside the France he came to love. The demands of his diplomatic duties during his decade of service in Paris were to take, moreover, a heavy toll on his time for writing and reflection—as testified by the extant volumes of his official reports and commentaries. The attested brilliance of his conversation, however, was not merely sociable, often including sustained disquisitions on central questions of culture, government, and economics.

During 1753–54, following his uncle's death, he assembled, from notes made over the years by his old teacher Bartolomeo Intieri, who was now almost blind, a book on the preservation of grain—a crucial matter in those days, when crop failure meant famine. But not until the spring of 1755 did he show himself again in good spirits. On 15 April he wrote to a Tuscan friend:

Amico carissimo: Be not afraid! This is not Ferdinando Galiani's ghost who writes to you, but the man himself. . . . I am back from the very home of the devil, and bring you my news. Know then that I have been, in person, on Vesuvius, in the service of His Holiness the pope. What a contrast! I can hear you shout: *"Quae est consensio Dei et Belial?"* Indeed: what connection can there be between the pope and Vesuvius? What could I be doing, a "soul visible" (if a man may be so described), in the company of those who dwell eternally in blackest hell? The fact is that since last December's eruption I have been wanting to present the pope with a collection of Vesuvian stones, to be sent to his museum at the university in Bologna. I thought it would be a simple and easy way of showing people the strange things vomited up by the volcano. But as I collected them, I found them so extremely curious, and so intricately related, that I have decided to write a little book about Vesuvius. I flatter myself that I am more learned than anyone ever has been about the composition of the lava, and other Vesuvian secrets. I discovered various metals—not by inference, but actually existing, intact, clear, in virgin rock undamaged by fire. I found the most beautiful gems—gems resembling chrysolite, resembling topaz, beryl, rock crystal. I found talc, many rare kinds of marble, including a green variety studded with jewels, and another, white-veined, like *verde antico*. I found hard jasper, as fine as the Sicilian. And finest of all, a lava resembling porphyry, extremely beautiful. . . . I found glass—from the Vesuvian glassworks!—and other fine things. But what I have enjoyed most has been putting together a series of stones: beginning in their virgin, primordial state, one sees them progressively scorched, baked, calcined, mixed with others, vitrified, fused, and finally become lava. In this way, without using chemicals, I present an analysis of various specimens of lava, showing very clearly the elements of their composition. This museum that I have formed is now in Rome. . . .

"That collection," as one of Galiani's early biographers put it, "was packed in six cases and sent to Pope Benedict XIV,

Galiani having inscribed on one of the cases the message *'Beatissime Pater, fac ut lapides isti panes fiant'*—'May these stones be turned into bread.' The immortal pontiff, who always enjoyed a display of wit, promptly conferred on Galiani the canonry of Amalfi, and sent the stones off to Bologna."

Meanwhile, Bernardo Tanucci had been watching the young Galiani in the varied early brilliance of his literary career. For the two years that followed the archbishop's death, Tanucci left Galiani alone. However, in 1755, now elevated to the rank of minister of foreign affairs, Tanucci gave Galiani his first official assignment.

The ancient city of Herculaneum, at the foot of Vesuvius, near Naples, had been buried by the great eruption of A.D. 79 that also destroyed Pompeii. Herculaneum had often been dug into and plundered—notably, on a large scale, in the early eighteenth century when Naples was under Austrian rule—and many Herculanean artifacts were shipped abroad. In October 1738, four years after the Austrian expulsion, Carlo di Borbone ordered a systematic excavation of Herculaneum. His chosen supervisor employed local quarrymen as diggers, supplementing these with inmates of a nearby prison, as well as with Tunisian and Algerian slaves (the crews of captured privateers). Galiani reported, in a letter of November 1752 to a Florentine friend, the recent discovery of a library—probably that of Lucius Calpurnius Piso, the father-in-law of Julius Caesar: "So far, they have found almost twenty papyrus volumes, which can be read to the extent that their burned condition permits. It is said that some Latin and Greek letters can be distinguished. I don't believe that: still, it is a splendid discovery." This was the inaugural revelation in the long drama of the Villa dei Papiri at Herculaneum—a story whose denouement is still awaited today. In the following year, 1753, the Genoese antiquarian Padre Antonio Piaggio came to Naples at the king's invitation to begin the task of unrolling and deciphering these papyri with an instrument of his own invention. All the retrieved papyri, together with quantities of marble and bronze sculpture, paintings, furniture, and tools, were temporarily stored near the Vesuvian shore in the museum of the royal palace at Portici, to which few visitors were admitted.

Tanucci, who was a scholar of antiquities, had quickly seen that official publication of descriptions of the treasures, in richly bound and illustrated volumes—not to be sold, but intended as royal gifts to fellow monarchs and other distinguished personalities abroad—would bestow glory upon the King of Naples and his realm. After an early attempt at official presentation proved unsatisfactory, unauthorized accounts of the excavations began to be published, both in Italy and elsewhere. Tanucci became increasingly impatient; and, in one of his first acts as minister of foreign affairs, he persuaded the king to order, for the supervision and completion of the task, the formation of what was designated the Royal Herculanean Academy, composed of fifteen distinguished Neapolitan scholars: historians, antiquarians, numismatists, and a vulcanologist.

Tanucci appointed as one of the academicians the twenty-six-year-old Galiani, and to him was assigned the writing of an introduction to the first of what would become a celebrated series of ten large-folio volumes illustrating and describing the artifacts disinterred at Herculaneum and in its environs. Pasquale Carcani, Galiani's friend and fellow culprit in their hangman hoax, was appointed secretary of the academy; he wrote much of the text of the volumes.

The title page, printed in red and black, reads:

LE PITTURE ANTICHE D'ERCOLANO

E CONTORNI

CON QUALCHE SPIEGAZIONE

TOMO PRIMO

NAPOLI MDCCLVI

NELLA REGIA STAMPERIA

Engravings of fifty or more Herculanean frescoes are accompanied by descriptive texts written by the scholars. The texts are anonymous: all glory for the undertaking is assigned to Carlo di Borbone, whose engraved portrait, adorned with florid offerings of homage from his *"umilissimi sudditi,"* opens the volume. The *Pitture antiche* was greeted with enthusiasm by its royal and aristocratic recipients and by scholars across Europe, and the frescoes illustrated in the volume began to exert their immeasurable influence on neoclassical decorative styles throughout the Western world.[3]

The excellent introductory essay written by Galiani, however, remained unpublished and is consequently little known. The final manuscript, in a copyist's fair hand, with a dedication to the king by his *"umilissimo vassallo Ferdinando Galiani"* and dated 5 March 1756, is preserved in the Biblioteca Napoletana della Storia Patria; it is not known why it was not published. Years later, in one of his letters to Mme d'Épinay—and we are approaching the conjunction of these two—Galiani himself, chronicling his principal writings, does not explain it:

> I attained fame by way of a poetic joke—a funeral oration on the death of our then recently deceased hangman, the celebrated Domenico Iannacone. Then in 1751 I published my book on money; in 1754 the one on grain; in 1755 I wrote my dissertation on the natural history of Vesuvius, which was sent, together with a collection of stones from the volcano, to Pope Benedict XIV, and which has never been published. . . . In 1756 I was made a member of the Herculanean Academy, and did considerable work on the first volume of plates. I even wrote a long dissertation on *The Paintings of the Ancients.* . . . In 1758 I published a funeral oration on Pope Benedict XIV (this is my favorite among my works).[4]

At a New Year's party on 1 January 1759, Galiani read aloud a eulogy of the role, in contemporary Neapolitan society, of the *cavaliere servente*, or *cicisbeo*. Citing many a mock-historical precedent, he praised the socially approved, *chaste* attachment (his ironic stress of the adjective is not in the least overdone) of a married man or woman to a chosen

mistress or lover—"a noble sentiment," Galiani called it—
which enables him or her not only to endure but to transcend
carnal relations with a spouse conventionally and arbitrarily
chosen for social and financial reasons. It is perhaps not
excessive to suggest that this spirited and worldly New Year
celebration of the *cicisbeo*, coming after its equally lighthearted predecessors, the Freeman masquerade and the Iannacone farce, played a role in determining Tanucci's next
order—an order that transformed the abbé Galiani's life and
brought him within the circle of Grimm, Diderot, and Mme
d'Épinay.

In 1734, Carlo di Borbone, duke of Parma, son of Philip V
of Spain and Elisabetta Farnese, had led Spanish troops into
Neapolitan territory, expelled the Austrian occupants, and
been proclaimed by his father (actually, by his masterful
mother) king of an independent Kingdom of Naples, thus
restoring to the Italian peninsula south of papal Rome an
autonomy it had not enjoyed for more than two hundred
years. In 1744, a last Austrian attempt to regain Neapolitan
territory had been defeated by the same Carlo di Borbone
at Velletri, south of Rome.

With the help of Bernardo Tanucci, chief among his chosen ministers, the king initiated a series of political and administrative reforms aimed at reducing the power,
accumulated over centuries, of the nobility and clergy. (Both
groups, hitherto tax-free, protested loudly, the clergy pointing to a timely eruption of Vesuvius as a sign of divine
disapproval.) In other moves, Carlo employed the genius of
Luigi Vanvitelli and his fellow architects to embellish the
capital and its environs with palaces, in emulation of Versailles. (His wife, Maria Amalia of Saxony, was a woman of
taste; he himself, a grandson of Louis XIV, was reviving his
ancestor's strategy of turning nobles into courtiers.) Other
imposing public buildings were constructed, among them
the Albergo dei Poveri (a huge shelter for the poor) and the
Teatro San Carlo, a splendid new opera house, given the
name of the king's patron saint and opened on the royal

birthday in 1737. (Its repertory came to include operas by Scarlatti, Porpora, Handel, Paisiello, Pergolesi, and Piccini.) Streets were newly adorned with private palaces. Street lighting was introduced, in the form of oil lamps placed at crossroads, in front of niches containing images of the Madonna. Paintings and sculpture in the royal collections at Parma and Rome were brought to Naples, where they continue today to provide an essential part of the city's artistic treasure. The sensational excavations at Herculaneum and Pompeii were exploited. Artisans in every field were invited to the city: makers of porcelain and glass from Germany and Bohemia; tapestry weavers from Florence; goldsmiths, silk weavers, silversmiths, workers in marble, marquetry, even tortoiseshell.

Together, Carlo and Tanucci were determined to increase Neapolitan prestige—and, in the face of continued threats by stronger powers, Neapolitan security: orders were given for the construction of a fleet of battleships.

To guard the interests of the Neapolitan Borboni among their powerful Bourbon cousins in France, a special Neapolitan envoy was needed: a Neapolitan learned in history and economics; a Neapolitan to watch the very ambassador whose deputy he would be; a Neapolitan who would send to Naples regular reports of all that Naples should know; a Neapolitan who spoke French; and—a requirement that particularly narrowed Tanucci's choice—a Neapolitan capable of holding his own in a society whose chief quality, in Tanucci's view, was one that he himself found odious: *frivolity*, a quality that every Frenchman was known to possess and that was often employed, as Tanucci believed, as a brilliant gloss to cover mischief.

Only one Neapolitan, Tanucci reported to the king, was known by his works to meet all those requirements. The king agreed. The chosen paragon was appointed, intensively prepared, endowed with a suitable title, and, at the end of April, dispatched abroad. It was somewhat to his own surprise, as we know from his letters, that Ferdinando Galiani found himself, in the spring of 1759, en route to Paris as secretary

The abbé Ferdinando Galiani, artist unknown

of the Neapolitan embassy. "May Your Excellency deign to direct and instruct me," he wrote to Tanucci from Rome, "now that I find myself in a new world, snatched from a city where nobody discusses anything, bound for lands bustling with business and debate."

I V
―――――

Paris (I)

ONE AFTERNOON, WHEN the abbé Galiani
and Denis Diderot were walking at Versailles—it was some
months after Galiani's arrival in France in early June 1759—
Diderot commented on the trees in the royal park. "How
tall they are, and straight, and slender!" "Like courtiers,"
Galiani replied. One may imagine his tone. On the day of
Galiani's presentation at court by his chief, the Neapolitan
minister plenipotentiary whom he had been hired to observe,
the courtiers in attendance on the king had greeted his minuscule and provincial appearance with derisive laughter. The
scene recalls Rigoletto's *"Cortigiani, vil razza dannata."* Galiani's response—reminiscent, in its turn, of Horatio's "A
piece of him"—was reportedly instantaneous: "What you
see is but a sample of the secretary: the complete secretary
will come later." The riposte was admired, made though it
was with an Italian—worse, a Neapolitan—accent.

The pain of such an episode was undoubtedly familiar to
Galiani; and he had presumably learned to endure it, and to
take consolation in the awareness of his superior powers of

mind. Later, as we shall see, he would tolerate such allusions when they were made by friends, and occasionally he himself referred to his small size. Peter Quennell, in his biography of Alexander Pope—another diminutive figure, whose height, like Galiani's, was four and a half feet—has discussed this dichotomy of mental and physical stature. Of Pope, he has written that "the feeling that he was weak where others were powerful, and powerful where the 'tall fellows' who surrounded him were insignificant and ineffective," sought expression and compensation in "an imaginative system in which the discordant materials of life were reduced to forms of classic elegance." Some analogy may be drawn with the ability of the malformed Galiani to penetrate and dissect the disorder of human affairs, and to expose convoluted theories to the light of reason.

The slights inflicted at Versailles were compounded, at this time, by Galiani's circumstances in Paris. On his arrival in the city, he had been given comfortable quarters in the hôtel de Sens, a turreted mediaeval mansion that had become the official residence of the Neapolitan diplomatic staff; and his chief, Juan de Baeza y Vicentolo, conde de Cantillana, a Spanish grandee in the Neapolitan service, though known to be obtuse—Tanucci called him "a mere automaton"— was courtesy itself. But for a southern Italian, June in Paris was astonishingly cold and the very quality of the air seemed strange. Matters of rank and etiquette were, moreover, rigidly respected, and Naples was a second-class power. A secretary was a mere secretary; one might have had special instructions, but they could not be divulged; superior though one knew oneself to be, one was at the bottom of the diplomatic heap.

All Galiani's early reports to Tanucci—to whom he wrote each Monday—contain laments.

22 June 1759. My health isn't bearing up as I would wish under conditions here. Really, things are very hard. Bad, heavy air, poisonous water, an incredibly strange

climate . . . no fruit, no cheese, no good seafood—
everything here does violence to the Neapolitan
temperament. . . .

Last Tuesday I was taken to see the duc de Choiseul
[the foreign minister], who deigned to glance at me for
a fraction of a second. I wouldn't want to think this an
indication of the degree of attention he gives to other
business: the idea of such superficiality is alarming.

10 July 1759. . . . I am utterly disenchanted, and realize
that I am not cut out for Paris. My clothes, appearance,
character, my way of thinking and all my other natural
defects will make me everlastingly odious to the French
and to myself.

And to his brother, Berardo:

1 October 1759. My sole desire is to get out of this place
at all costs. My health worsens from day to day; the
boredom, the odium . . . ! I have written asking you to
be attentive to the abbé de Saint-Non.[1] I do not know
him personally, but the abbé Morellet, to whom I am
greatly obliged, has requested this of me. Whatever you
do for him will be more than the French do for us.

And in another letter to Berardo he called France "the most
f----- -up country to dishonor the face of the earth."

In August of that year, change had suddenly been set in
motion by the death, in Madrid, of Ferdinand VI, King of
Spain, the childless elder half-brother of Carlo, King of Naples. Carlo inherited the Spanish throne. Since international
agreement forbade the union of the Neapolitan and Spanish
crowns, Carlo abdicated the Neapolitan throne in favor of
his third and youngest son, the eight-year-old Ferdinando.
And after appointing a council of regency to govern Naples
for the duration of the new king's minority, he set sail for
Spain, on 6 October 1759,[2] in an elaborate ceremony of em-

barkation recorded by contemporary writers and painters. Tanucci, as first regent, was now virtual ruler of the Kingdom of the Two Sicilies. (He would mail regular, respectful reports to Carlo—now Carlos III of Spain—in Madrid until Ferdinando came of age.) Galiani, sending assurances of loyalty to Tanucci and their new king, billed Tanucci for the expensive suit of mourning he had been obliged to buy in Paris.

At the end of his first French winter, Galiani appealed strongly to Tanucci:

> *10 March 1760.* Signore, it is impossible for me to remain in Paris. Ten months of fever are the least of my sufferings. Not even an ambassadorship, a cardinalate, a seraglio—none of these would tempt me to remain here.

Tanucci, who from the beginning sent frequent soothing messages to Galiani, replied this time that to leave his post would be "*poco decoroso*," and reminded him that by resigning he would forfeit all chance of advancement in the foreign service. Then, a few weeks later, Cantillana took an unexpected leave of absence from Paris to attend to pressing family matters in Spain, and Galiani suddenly found himself appointed by Tanucci chargé d'affaires at the embassy, with an increase in salary. And on 28 April 1760, Tanucci reported to Carlos: "Galiani now wishes to stay in Paris."

The unexpected prospect of independence and authority, temporary as Galiani knew them to be, had tipped the scale. But even before this sudden promotion, sunk in what he felt to be near-anonymity, he had been attracting the attention of Parisians. His sallies, to him as natural as breathing, were being enjoyed and repeated. In Naples he had become friendly with a witty Frenchman, a fellow abbé, André Morellet, a Lyonnais graduate of the Sorbonne who had been touring Italy as tutor to a wealthy young Parisian. Since then, Morellet had become a free-lance writer in Paris, a pet of fashionable hostesses, who enjoyed his sharp tongue: Voltaire called him *"l'abbé Mord-les"* (*"Bite 'em"*).[3] Introduced by Morellet into one salon after another, the newly arrived Italian had surprised the ladies and their guests—Academicians and Encyclopaedists among them—with his wit and learning.

So much has been written about the Parisian salons of the mid-eighteenth century that a mere listing of Galiani's hosts and hostesses will indicate the tenor of his life in Parisian society at this time. The most celebrated trio of bluestockings was constituted by the blind Mme Du Deffand (Horace Walpole's friend) in the rue Saint-Dominique; Mme Geoffrin in the rue Saint-Honoré, renowned for interrupting long-winded guests with a tart *"Voilà qui est bien"*; and Mlle Julie de Lespinasse in the rue des Petits-Champs, beloved by Jean d'Alembert, Diderot's collaborator in the early days of the *Encyclopaedia*. There was also Mme Helvétius in the rue Sainte-Anne; her husband, Claude-Arien Helvétius, a great lover of Shakespeare, was the author of *De l'esprit*, a philosophical work that had been condemned as heretical by the Parlement and burned by the public hangman in the courtyard of the Palais de Justice. The baron d'Holbach, in the rue Royale, whom we have already encountered with Grimm, was the author of articles on metallurgy, mineralogy and other sciences in the *Encyclopaedia* and of atheistic books published under pseudonyms; for him, atheism was "the basis of all virtue." Holbach was a lavish host, famed for his good dinners: Galiani called him *"maître d'hôtel de la philosophie."* Later the catalogue came to include Mme Necker, wife of the financier. (As Suzanne Churchod she had been wooed, in Geneva, by Edward Gibbon. Mme Necker's small daughter, Germaine, the future Mme de Staël, would sit beside her, obediently silent, listening to the guests.) All these and many more welcomed the abbé.

Gibbon, who saw Galiani at these salons during his visit to Paris in 1763—we may think of the two men together, both under five feet tall—likens him, in his autobiography,

to Democritus, "the laughing philosopher," and character-
izes the society in which they both moved:

> When visiting a capital like Paris, it is necessary and
> proper that you be furnished with letters of recommen-
> dation, to distinguish you from the crowd. But as soon
> as the ice is broken your acquaintance multiplies, and
> your new friends make it their pleasure to find you
> friends still newer. Such is the delightful result of the
> easy, charming character of the French, who in Paris
> have attained to a grace and freedom in society that were
> unknown in the ancient world and remain so even today
> in other countries. In London one must learn to make
> one's way; houses are very difficult of access; a host
> thinks of himself as one who gives pleasure to an invited
> guest. Whereas a Parisian considers that the pleasure is
> his.

Casanova, in his memoirs, recounts his meeting with Galiani in Paris, illustrating the abbé's wit with an example in
which geniality, philosophy, and straight-faced preposter-
ousness combine:

> I made the acquaintance of the abbé Galiani, secretary
> of the Neapolitan embassy. . . . [He] was a man of wit.
> He had a knack for making the most serious subjects
> appear comic; and being a good talker, speaking French
> with the ineradicable Neapolitan accent, he was a fa-
> vorite in every circle he cared to enter. The abbé de La
> Ville told him that Voltaire had complained that his
> *Henriade* had been translated into Neapolitan verse in
> such a way that it elicited laughter.
> "Voltaire is wrong," said Galiani, "for the Neapolitan
> dialect is of such a nature that it is impossible to write
> verses in it that are not laughable. And why should he
> be vexed? He who makes people laugh is sure of being
> beloved. The Neapolitan dialect is truly a singular one;
> we have in it translations of the Bible and of the *Iliad*,
> and both are comic."

"I can imagine the Bible would be, but I should not have thought that would have been the case with the *Iliad*."

"It is, nevertheless."

When Cantillana returned from Spain in September and the chargé d'affaires resumed his former rank, Tanucci made a compromise in the matter of salary; and although Galiani, knowing himself fitted for a superior post, chafed and constantly complained, his popularity amid the attractions of Parisian intellectual society was now an increasing compensation.

It was at this time, as three of Galiani's new acquaintances became his particular friends, that he met Louise d'Épinay, later to be a singular and consoling presence in his life.

As representative in Paris of Frankfurt-am-Main, Melchior Grimm was among Galiani's diplomatic colleagues. With Grimm, Galiani felt a quick sympathy, and with Grimm he found himself welcomed into the intimate atmosphere of Mme d'Épinay's château de La Chevrette and in the rue Sainte-Anne in Paris, where she had taken an apartment for herself, with a room on the upper floor for Grimm.

It is from Denis Diderot—who had often written "we three" when speaking of Mme d'Épinay, Grimm, and himself—that we hear, most notably in his letters to Sophie Volland, of the Italian newcomer now welcomed as a fourth.

Early in their acquaintance, Diderot had a moment of hesitation. "Like you, I am in a bad mood," he wrote to Mlle Volland on 20 September 1760 from La Chevrette. "The abbé Galiani has just arrived. His stories don't amuse me as they used to. . . . He displeased me greatly by confessing that he had never wept in his life, that the loss of his father, his brothers, his sisters and his mistresses had never cost him a tear." (The abbé liked to tease. He had indeed lost his father, but his only brother and his five sisters were alive and well in Naples. Nothing is known of his Italian mistresses.) Along with his formidable intelligence and imagination, the warm-hearted Diderot was known for an engaging naiveté and for *la larme facile*, and he must have wondered whether friendship would be possible with such a monster of insensitivity.

However, only ten days later he wrote differently to Mlle Volland about his miniature fellow guest: "The abbé is endlessly clever and amusing, a treasure on rainy days. I told Mme d'Épinay that if the people who carve chessmen were to make some pieces in his image, everybody would buy one to take home." Soon thereafter, following the departure of an unpleasant visitor from Mme d'Épinay's Paris apartment, "in came the abbé Galiani, and with him gaiety, imagination, wit, nonsense, merriment and everything that enables one to forget life's displeasures."

The two men saw each other frequently in the houses of friends, and Diderot enjoyed having Galiani accompany him on his visits to the Paris salons of painting and sculpture, on which he "reported" for the Newsletter. (Remarks by Galiani on the exhibits frequently found their way, always properly attributed, into Diderot's text.)

In another letter to Mlle Volland, Diderot tells of walking with the abbé in the gardens of La Chevrette, where a few days earlier Galiani had teased Mme d'Épinay's swans and been forced to flee: "Now the swans hate the abbé. As soon as they see him, even at a distance, they flap their wings, rush toward him, necks outstretched, beaks half-open, squawking: he doesn't dare go near them." One pictures the little Neapolitan running from the angry swans on his short legs.

And again to Mlle Volland:

Apropos of the inimitable abbé, some time ago he delivered himself of an apology for Tiberius and Nero. Yesterday he did the same for Caligula. He claims that Tacitus and Suetonius were a sorry pair who stuffed their works with the gossip of the marketplace. I much prefer fun like that, which reveals brilliance, intelligence, the mind of a scholar, to flat, disgusting drivel about J.C. and his apostles.

(Although no believer, Diderot was bored by the atheistic chatter of the day.)

Later, after his return to Naples, Galiani was to write Mme d'Épinay of the days at La Chevrette, when "my wig was always in the air and my cheeks were on fire." His meaning becomes clear when we read in Morellet's memoirs that "after dinner the abbé would sit in an armchair cross-legged like a tailor; and because of the heat of the fire he would hold his wig in one hand while gesticulating with the other." And Diderot, writing to Galiani in Naples about certain verses of Horace: "I would much rather be speaking with you of these things than writing. I think how we used to talk beside the fire, you with your wig off, your head steaming; how you would take up a subject, pursue it, delve into it, casting light, as you went, into the most obscure corners of literature, antiquity, politics, philosophy and morals."

It was the great rhythm of Paris, in contrast to the languid intellectual tempo of Naples.

But Galiani had been sent to Paris to work.

When, as mere secretary, he had been presented by his chief to the French minister of foreign affairs at Versailles, the duc de Choiseul had "deigned to glance" at him "for a fraction of a second." Since then, during Cantillana's absence, Choiseul had been obliged to deal with Galiani as the Neapolitan chargé d'affaires. Very soon Choiseul seems to have sensed a threat in Galiani, this underling so much sharper than the ambassador he was temporarily replacing, and also so admired by Parisian intellectuals. He began a campaign of seduction.

It opened with his offer to put at Galiani's exclusive service, as a token of his esteem, one of the ministry's official carriages: the streets of Paris were often muddy and always unpleasant, even dangerous; besides, the carriage of the Neapolitan embassy was often crowded when it made its way to and from Versailles. (As Galiani wrote to Tanucci: "Ministers of foreign powers are not permitted to live in Versailles. Everything there exists under a veil of secrecy.") The offer of a carriage was declined—politely, but on the clearly implied ground of official impropriety: Galiani had recognized it as a gesture that could have been made only to a representative of a lesser power. Choiseul seems to have been made to realize, as well, that his allusion to Galiani's small size was another mistake. He changed his approach, and his success was immediate.

Galiani to Tanucci [Versailles, Sunday–Monday], 15 August 1760. . . . I couldn't be happier about my most recent audience with the minister, last Tuesday. About myself he spoke in terms that would have turned my head had I not realized that he was simply being his genial self. He told me he was sorry that I was leaving the ministry, and asked what post was to be given me. (He shares the opinion of everyone here, that I cannot remain under Cantillana after having been advanced to a higher rank.) In short, he paid me a hundred compliments. In this connection I suspect that Your Excellency is not fully aware of the great favor you have done me. Your Excellency has made me, to all intents and purposes, a minister, since, in this court, a chargé d'affaires and a minister are exactly the same. I am on equal footing with the ministers of Portugal, Sweden, Russia, Mainz, the Palatinate, etc. I have my own seat in the royal chapel at Versailles. In short, I am the equal (who would believe it!) of Prince Galitzine. To return to Choiseul, after he had paid me those compliments I was able to talk business with him as hitherto I would never have dared. When our time together was about to run out, I asked whether he would see me again before today. He kindly suggested that I dine with him on Sunday (yesterday). [This was part of Choiseul's flattery: Sunday dinners were fashionable at Versailles.] Today being a great holiday (the feast of the Assumption), and tomorrow the day I see the king, I have remained here overnight.

Now it is late: I am sleepy, and very tired from having

gone to see the fountains in the royal park: Sunday is the only day on which they play.

In October, soon after Cantillana's return to Paris, Choiseul, well aware of the abbé's discontent, wrote to M. de La Houze, the French ambassador in Naples: "If the marquis Tanucci could give the abbé Galiani a ministerial post in the Kingdom of the Two Sicilies, I believe the abbé would consider himself very fortunate; and should M. de Cantillana remain here alone, I would assist him in taking charge of the affairs of His Most Serene Majesty." That suggestion, again an impertinent show of French condescension toward a lesser power, was ignored by Tanucci.

"I haven't seen M. de Choiseul for some time," Galiani reported to Tanucci in another of his weekly letters, in which he again begged that his post at least be reclassified: perhaps he could be called *royal* secretary and in consequence be better paid. "But the duke and I send each other a thousand *belle cose* via common friends—*amici ed amiche*." Galiani went on to report to his chief that Choiseul had told him again that in Parisian diplomatic circles his demotion by Tanucci was unanimously considered insulting. Choiseul had assured him of his own hope that Galiani would remain in France, so that he, Choiseul, could deal with him as often as possible instead of with Cantillana, who spoke incomprehensible French. ("Cantillana," Galiani reminded Tanucci, "because of his lack of teeth, cannot articulate French sounds. He habitually mixes Italian and Spanish, coming out with a third language, very difficult to understand.")

Galiani to Tanucci, Paris, 5 January 1761.

On Tuesday, Saint Louis's Day, I went to Versailles and dined with M. de Choiseul. [Choiseul received the diplomatic corps at dinner every Tuesday.] It so happened that I saw him before we went to table, and I must tell Your Excellency what passed between us. He began by kindly regretting that I don't call on him more often. (This was an expression of his habitual courtesy, which I must not abuse. I adhere to my resolution not to attend court except when I have some important and obvious reason.) The duke then immediately asked how I stand financially, and whether I still receive the higher salary. When I replied with a sad "No" he asked, "Why don't you let me write to Naples about it?" But I declined. . . .

It is so rare, and so difficult, to have an opportunity of talking with Choiseul that although our conversation wasn't a long one, it nevertheless astonished many of those present, and I was applauded and congratulated by several of the ministers on the duke's having honored me with a private conversation on a day when almost no one could get a word with him.

I never cease to admire and praise Choiseul.

Tanucci, knowing as he did that Choiseul would have liked nothing better than to have Galiani removed from France, may have been surprised that the abbé, with all his intelligence, could be so easily seduced by the minister's flattery; and perhaps Tanucci's awareness of Galiani's increasing fascination with Parisian society helped him ignore these pleas for improvement of title and salary.

Galiani's excellent weekly reports told Tanucci much that he wanted to know. A depiction of daily concerns and national preoccupations in mid-eighteenth-century France, they covered countless aspects of the Parisian scene, and of the European scene as viewed from Paris, including whatever Galiani thought would interest his astute chief. A sample of matters treated, in letters written between May 1759 and Galiani's first departure from Paris, on leave, in November 1764, suggests the diversity of themes.

Throughout, there is the progress, especially in Westphalia, of the long, bloody conflict with England and Prussia. The outrageously prolonged imprisonment at Marseilles of "innocent Neapolitan fishermen" who disembarked "unaware" at various Provençal ports is a matter of concern: France calls them smugglers; Naples says that they merely offered, in all innocence, to barter a few Neapolitan-made trifles—"cotton and woolen caps, blankets, stockings." Parisian enthusiasm for the volumes on the Herculaneum antiquities and their immediate effect on French decorative styles are mentioned. We hear of the Parisian sect of religious fanatics called *convulsionnaires* and learn diplomatic news of England, of Portugal, of Turkey.

Exiled Protestants and Jews are being invited to return to France. All Jesuitical schools in France will certainly be closed: the Jesuit order has become far too intrusive politically. Carlos, Galiani hears, has banished pigs from the streets of Madrid; Naples should follow that example, he suggests, for it is high time to forget about pigs being "sacred to Saint Anthony": "I have seen one of those sacred pigs bite the hand of a poor child who was sitting on his doorstep holding a piece of bread." (At that time a chapel in the Teatro San Carlo contained a statue of Saint Anthony, protector against fire, accompanied, as always, by his pig. The saint's feast day, 22 January, was celebrated with illuminations and fireworks.)

In 1763 and 1764, crop failure and the hoarding of grain by speculators bring famine and epidemic to Naples and its countryside: thousands die. Tanucci's letters to Galiani contain dramatic and desperate reports of the disaster: denunciations of profiteers, of the inefficient and indifferent officials of the food office, of the callousness of the rich; and they report his attempts, continually frustrated despite his high position, to import grain from abroad. Galiani to Tanucci: "The corpses in the city!" (A new cemetery had been hastily opened, each day's fatalities filling a fresh common grave.) "The famine and the deaths weigh heavily on my heart. I know the struggle you are waging. May God give you strength, and a heavy cudgel."

In Paris, Galiani tries to have grain shipped to Naples from Marseilles: when that attempt fails, he can send only sympathy and suggestions, the latter including the immediate importation from the north, and the cultivation near Naples itself, of potatoes, turnips, and other vegetables locally unknown. The first planting of these, Galiani suggests, should be made by the royal gardeners in fields surrounding the palaces of Capodimonte and Portici; the produce can be sold to the many English inhabitants of the city, who are accustomed to such fare, and thus introduced among Neapolitans, who will spread the news of these unfamiliar vegetables. "The well-to-do will not eat them; but the poor, and the peasants in the surrounding countryside, will find them delicious." But Tanucci replies that although he will order a little potato planting throughout the kingdom if Galiani will send him tubers, he is sure that such an experiment will be useless in Naples itself. "Here nobody wants anything foreign except vice, luxury, and perdition. Capodimonte and Portici are to be kept either wooded for pheasants or as pleasure gardens: sacred territory, not to be profaned by anything so commonplace and rustic." Unexpected news about potatoes in southern Italy comes to Galiani from some *zampognari*—bagpipe-playing shepherds from the Abruzzi—whom he meets in Paris. (It was, and to a certain extent still is, the custom of these shepherds to travel to distant cities during the holy seasons and play their reedy regional music in the streets.) Galiani writes to Tanucci on 30 April 1764:

Let me tell you that a few days ago there arrived here in Paris several *zampognari* who are making their usual rounds in Europe. I advised them to buy potato seed in England and sow it when they returned home. They told me that several of their compatriots had already taken some home with them last year and sown it with success. I cannot tell you how pleased I was to hear this. . . . In only forty years this vegetable, imported from America, has already covered the fields of Ireland, England, Germany, Switzerland, and most of France. If you consider that during this time there have been published more than a thousand dissertations on the administration of the grain supply, it must be said that a single potato is better than any theory.

Even today there are parts of Italy where the potato is scorned. W. H. Auden wrote to Igor Stravinsky in 1949 from Forio in Ischia: "Forio thinks us crazy because we eat potatoes which are to them a mark of abject poverty."[4] In Naples a particular dish survives from the era when it was necessary to make potatoes palatable to skeptical Neapolitans: outsiders who have eaten the delicious *gattò*—a baked concoction in which the potato component is nearly overwhelmed by cheese, ham, and other ingredients—will find reason to †hank Ferdinando Galiani for his persistence. The name of the *gattò*, italicized from the French *gâteau*, presumably reached the Neapolitan bourgeoisie together with another imported phenomenon: the French cook who was traditionally, in Bourbon times, a member of the well-to-do Neapolitan household, and who was known, in his turn, as *il Monsù*.

Not only the current economic and political crisis but the intellectual events of the day are discussed in the letters. In a postscript to his letter of 19 October 1764, Tanucci, who had been reading essays by D'Alembert, asks several questions:

> You have never spoken to me about the *Enciclopedia alfabetica*, which D'Alembert mentions so often. What is it? What is said about it? How many volumes? How valuable is it? D'Alembert is a learned man: a pity that he isn't more open-minded. No enemy of Italy can be truly open-minded—that is, anyone who doesn't take Italy into account, even if only to demonstrate that he's not ignorant.

> *Galiani to Tanucci, 12 November 1764.*
> You ask me about the *Encyclopaedia*. This dictionary is an enterprise headed by M. Diderot, who is responsible for its form and content. Of all the French writers I know, Diderot is the most accomplished. He reads Latin and Italian easily, and loves both languages. His greatest passion is for metaphysics: in this he might be likened to Genovesi, whom he greatly resembles in ap-

pearance, voice, etc. He has written excellent dramatic criticism and two mediocre plays. In this he resembles Gravina.

D'Alembert is responsible for all the articles in the fields of geometry and mathematics. He somewhat resembles the late Don Pietro di Martino, but he is more jovial, more humorous, even at times something of a buffoon. He is a good friend of Italians, and esteems them highly. If he makes no reference to them, it is because allusion of that sort is not in the French tradition, especially among mathematicians. One cannot reproach those who merely follow the customs of their own country.

As I said, there are seven or eight principal editors of the *Encyclopaedia*, but many contributors have written articles on their specialties—art, science, etc. Seven volumes had appeared when the project encountered obstacles. The booksellers raised a clamor. Three million lire had been invested; there were 4,300 subscribers (incredible!); it was the most costly and most profitable enterprise since the invention of printing. Many sovereigns offered to have the remaining volumes printed in their countries—the Prussians, the Tsarina, Sweden, etc. But the last thing the French lose sight of is the financial side of things: they may be atheists, but they are never obtuse. Religious considerations thus had to give way to pecuniary ones. The work is being printed here, but in secret. As a precaution [against piracy], all nine remaining volumes are being printed simultaneously, and all will appear next year. There are also six large volumes of plates illustrating all the arts, crafts, etc. In all, twenty-two volumes, which will cost 22 louis d'or.[5]

Tanucci to Galiani [early December 1764].
I have been minister of justice for twenty-five years, and I say frankly that I prefer D'Alembert to all those

French scribblers who have come to my notice. I know nothing by Diderot in either Latin or Italian. For the life of me I cannot picture the kind of man whose leading passion is metaphysics. To me metaphysics seems only one element and an instrument. As for drama, I believe that rules count for little: rules will never make a good play, as we know from Gravina. Heart, and sensibility, and imagination, and whatever excellent language that expresses heart, sensibility, and imagination as it tells its story—those seem to me the components of the drama, as they are of so many human endeavors. "Jovial, humorous, a buffoon"? D'Alembert seems to me far from all that, in what I have read of his, especially the "Essai sur la société des gens de lettres, etc.," and his preface to the third volume of the *Encyclopaedia*, which I gather is being attacked by the Church. D'Alembert seems not to be hostile to the Jesuits[6]—an extraordinary thing in a great man who seems to be such a friend of the human race.

In the autumn of 1759, in Geneva, Grimm had reminded Mme d'Épinay, as they prepared to return to Paris, that she was now free to choose her friends and to lead the life she wished. As the reader will recall, she thanked him for his encouragement, but she tells us, in her Memoirs, that she feared his words might describe "only the poetry of the situation."

Nor were her fears unfounded. For a year or more after their return, her life in Paris and at La Chevrette was indeed "poetic" in that happy sense. In 1761, however, d'Épinay's extravagances brought him to the verge of bankruptcy, and despite Grimm's opinion that it would be "faint-hearted" and "pusillanimous" of Louise to be afflicted by her husband's predictable chicanery, the crisis was a real one. Following a family conference, d'Épinay's debts were paid, and he consented to be put temporarily on a modest allowance, the remainder of his annual income going to repay the advance. Incorrigibly feckless, he now incurred large new debts, some of them resulting from harebrained speculations in real estate; and in January 1762 the Treasury, displeased by mounting scandal, stripped him of his post as *fermier-général*. Complicated legal and financial negotiations with her husband's successor in that position (who was himself temporarily short of funds) resulted in Mme d'Épinay's being allotted, in return for an investment, a share of the new *fermier*'s income from his post. La Chevrette was rented; and in April 1762, with Grimm, she moved into a smaller house, called La Briche, in the village of Épinay, which had been another part of her husband's inheritance. There, on a more modest scale, she continued to see her friends.

Diderot, who visited her at La Briche for the first time the following September, wrote to Sophie Volland about it:

> I hadn't known about this house. It is small, but everything around it—ponds, garden, park—has a wild look: it is certainly a more livable place than the depressing, magnificent château de La Chevrette. The ponds are enormous, their steep banks dense with swampy growth, and there is a mossy old ruin of a bridge. No gardener has ever invaded the thickets; the trees are untrimmed, growing in their natural disorder; springs gush out here and there. The space isn't vast, yet one can lose oneself in it: that's what I like. I saw the little apartment that Grimm has chosen for himself: it looks out over courtyards and a vegetable garden, with, far off, a view of a splendid building.

In Geneva, Mme d'Épinay had worked sporadically on her novel, somewhat distracted by the pleasure of having her shorter pieces appear in print. On her return to Paris she had been too happy, and then too agitated, to write. Now, at La Briche, she returned to the manuscript. But, as the book's modern editor puts it, "Her inspiration, her verve, had deserted her," and the last chapters of *Madame de Montbrillant* lack the quality of the earlier portion.

For a time, the manuscript again lay fallow.

Madame d'Épinay, by Carmontelle

While Galiani was sending Tanucci his letters bearing French news of particular meaning for Naples, the handwritten numbers of Grimm's Newsletter were being delivered to royal and princely subscribers throughout Europe. Grimm continued to do most of the writing; Diderot was a frequent contributor; Mme d'Épinay, glad of this relief from domestic troubles, reviewed many plays, always anonymously. From time to time the Newsletter speaks of our various protagonists:

1 August 1760. M. l'abbé Morellet has been arrested and imprisoned in the Bastille.

The abbé Morellet had recently made an unfavorable reference in print to the political ideas of the princesse de Robecq, apparently forgetting that she was, or had been, among the many mistresses of the all-powerful Choiseul. Morellet would be released about two months later. His memoirs, written after the Revolution, include an account of the "excellent treatment" extended to him in the Bastille. During his incarceration he read "eighty novels from the prison library," as well as "all of Tacitus, including, twice, the *Life of Agricola*," and Hume's philosophical essays and the "six quarto volumes of his *History [of England]*." He was provided with writing materials and was well fed. "Except at mealtimes I read or wrote, with no other distraction than that resulting from my urge to sing and dance by myself, which I did several times daily."

Newsletter, 13 June 1762. The storm that began to gather on the publication of *Émile*, M. Rousseau's book on education, has swiftly burst into full fury. Following the author's indictment by the public prosecutor, the Parlement ordered that he be arrested and his book burned. That decree was issued on the 9th of this month. M. Rousseau had fled the country during the previous night. His destination is said to have been Switzerland.

On 15 February 1763, the great news was the signing of the Treaty of Paris—the end of the Seven Years' War—which cost France Canada and most of her possessions in both the East and West Indies. But "peace at any price" had long been the prevailing Parisian sentiment; and on the night of 21 June, the traditional Midsummer Night's fireworks, with "Vive le Roy" in lights reflected in the Seine, resembled a gesture of thanksgiving that the war was over. Paris was flooded with British visitors. Mme d'Épinay, reviewing a now-forgotten play in the Newsletter for April 1763, had noted only that the performance, at the Comédie-Française, was followed by a few "*divertissements au sujet de la paix.*" Diderot, on 1 July, merely referred in passing to the "*fêtes de la paix*" in an article celebrating the inauguration of two splendid Parisian monuments: the newly constructed Place Louis XV (today the Place de la Concorde) and the "grand, superb" equestrian statue of the king by Bouchardon at its center.[7] Galiani, who in a letter of 23 February 1763 to Tanucci had written eloquently about the arrival of the statue,[8] on 27 June merely mentioned "*le feste de la scorsa settimana,*" expending his energy in a plea that Tanucci "do something" about the ridiculously provincial tone of the principal Neapolitan newspaper, *La Gazzetta di Napoli*, which was constantly causing merriment abroad.

Galiani to Tanucci, Compiègne, 18 July 1763.
Before replying to Your Excellency's *veneratissima* letter of the 25th, I want to burn a bit of incense to myself. This *Re Cristianissimo,*[9] catching sight of me on his first day at court here in Compiègne, at once went up to Cantillana, who was standing by a window, and pointing to me said "*On me dit qu'il a beaucoup d'esprit.*" No one contradicts a king, so Cantillana and Grimaldi [the Spanish ambassador] were obliged to say "*Oui, Sire,*" and to cover me with unmerited praise. Those royal words (almost certainly due to something said to the king by the duc de Duras and the duc de Grissac, both

of whom are fond of me) immediately made the rounds: kings never speak without effect. Consequently I found myself the target of a salvo of compliments and praise, and am now enjoying quite undeserved celebrity. I should not write you this, but reading the letters of St. Paul has taught me that in a letter one is permitted to praise oneself when truth demands it.

Tanucci to Galiani, Naples, 6 August 1763.
Stimatissimo Sig Abate: Your letter makes me happy, for the praise conveyed by His Most Royal Majesty's words is a compliment not only to you personally, but also to you as a representative of the Two Sicilies. In my heart of hearts I can imagine nothing more pleasing than a supreme sovereign who has the humanity to praise a private citizen powerless to do him good or evil; a sovereign who speaks the truth, who values men of wit, whose gratification and esteem have not been extinguished by pride or envy, or by convoluted considerations of politics. Therefore I congratulate you, and myself as well, for reasons we both appreciate.

Newsletter, 15 July 1764. M. l'abbé Prévost, the celebrated author, died late last year. . . . He was born with a great talent [his novel *Manon Lescaut* had been published in 1731, when Prévost was thirty-one], but his disorderly life kept him in constant pawn to his publishers. He liked wine and women, and knew how to spend everything he earned.

[*Footnote in the Newsletter*] The abbé Prévost died on 23 November 1763. As he was crossing the forest of Chantilly he was suddenly stricken with apoplexy. His apparently lifeless body was discovered by some peasants, who carried it to a nearby rectory. The authorities were summoned, and with undue haste ordered an autopsy. No sooner was the first incision made than a cry was heard. It was too late: recalled to consciousness by the pain, Prévost opened his eyes only to realize the horror of his fate, and immediately expired.

The Mozart family arrived in Paris on 18 November 1763, lodging with Graf van Eyck, the Bavarian minister. They had brought with them a letter of introduction to Grimm.

Newsletter, 1 December 1763. True prodigies are so rare that a discovery of the kind merits mention. A *maître de chapelle* from Salzburg, named Mozart, has just arrived in Paris with two of the most charming children in the world. His daughter, aged eleven, plays the harpsichord brilliantly: she executes the longest and most difficult pieces with astonishing precision. Her brother, who will be seven next February, is a phenomenon, so extraordinary that one can scarcely believe what one is seeing and hearing. It is nothing for this child to play, with complete accuracy, the most difficult pieces, with hands that can barely stretch over six keys of the octave: what is incredible is to hear him improvise for an hour on end, abandoning himself to the inspiration of his genius. One ravishing melody after another pours out: there is no confusion, never a lapse of sensibility.

The most consummate *maître de chapelle* could not be more proficient than he in his mastery of harmony and his unending invention, always in the best of taste. He is so at home with his instrument that even when a napkin is laid over the keys he plays with the same rapidity and precision. Apart from his ability to execute whatever is put before him, he writes and composes with marvelous facility, quite without having to test his inventions on the keyboard. I myself jotted down the melody of a minuet, and asked him to compose the bass: the child took up a pen and immediately did so, without going near the harpsichord. You may be sure that it is nothing to him to transpose and play any melody presented to him, and in any key requested. But I witnessed something else, something that passeth understanding. A woman asked him the other day if he would accompany, by ear, without seeing any notes, an Italian cavatina that she knew by heart. She proceeded to sing:

the child tried a bass that was not completely exact, because it is impossible to prepare in advance the accompaniment of a song one does not know; but when the song ended, he asked the lady to begin again, and this time he played—not only, with his right hand, the entire melody, but with his left a perfect bass. After which he asked her, ten times, to begin again, and each time he changed the character of his accompaniment: he would have done it twenty times had he not been deterred. My fear is that I might lose my wits were I to listen to this child very often: it makes me suspect that exposure to the prodigious might lead to madness. It no longer surprises me that Saint Paul should have been in a trance after his strange vision. Monsieur Mozart's children have been admired by all who have seen them. The Emperor and the Queen-Empress [of Austria] showered them with kindness, and they were given the same welcome at the courts of Munich and Mannheim. It is regrettable that musical knowledge is at such a low ebb in this country. The elder Mozart plans to go from here to England, and then to take his children to other parts of Germany.

Grimm was able to make arrangements for two concerts at Versailles by the Mozart family, and two in a private theatre in Paris. On 1 April 1764, Leopold Mozart wrote from Paris to Lorenz Hagenauer in Salzburg:

> . . . But now you must know who this man is, this great friend of mine, to whom I owe everything here, this M. Grimm. He is secretary to the duc d'Orléans, and he is a man of learning and a great friend of humanity. All my other letters and recommendations brought me nothing. . . . M. Grimm alone, to whom I had a letter from the wife of a merchant in Frankfurt, has done everything. He took our business to the Court. He arranged for the first concert and paid me on his own account eighty louis d'or, that is to say, he disposed

of 320 tickets. In addition, he paid for the lighting, as more than sixty large wax candles were burnt. Well, this M. Grimm secured permission for the first concert and is now arranging for the second, for which a hundred tickets have already been sold. So you see what a man can do who has good sense and a kind heart. He comes from Regensburg. But he has been in Paris for over fifteen years, and knows how to launch everything in the right direction, so that it is bound to turn out as he wishes.[10]

A few weeks earlier, on 22 February, Leopold Mozart had written to Hagenauer:

> Do you know what people here are always wanting? They are trying to persuade me to let my boy be inoculated with smallpox. But as I have now expressed sufficiently my aversion to this impertinence, they are leaving me in peace. Here inoculation is the general fashion. But, for my part, I leave the matter to the grace of God. It depends on His grace whether He wishes to keep this marvel of nature in the world in which he has placed it, or to take it to Himself. . . .
>
> Monsieur d'Hébert, Trésorier des Menus Plaisirs du Roi, has handed to Wolfgang from the King fifty louis d'or and a gold snuff box.[11]

Among Galiani's friends in Paris was Dr. Angelo Gatti, a Tuscan-born physician, formerly professor of theoretical medicine at the University of Pisa and now practicing in France. Gatti was an early proponent of inoculation against smallpox, and had been among those members of the profession who persuaded Louis XV to sign a decree permitting it. On 4 October 1762, Galiani had written to Tanucci on the subject:

> The King [of Naples]'s decision not to go to Piedigrotta[12] because of fear of smallpox makes me think it practical to tell Your Excellency that Dr. Gatti . . . is

continuing his inoculations here with wonderful success. More than thirty persons of distinction have been
inoculated this autumn, most of whom have had scarcely
a single day of fever. This *Re Cristianissimo* displays great
curiosity about every case, and is most desirous that his
grandsons be inoculated; but the dauphine is not in
favor of it, remaining unpersuaded even by the example
of the duc d'Orléans. May heaven hasten the day when
the usefulness of this practice is universally recognized.
It should be a political consideration as well—the means
of safeguarding large numbers of the human race.

In the Newsletter for 15 May 1764, Grimm's sketch of one
of Galiani's Parisian hostesses ends with a now-familiar anecdote:

Mme Du Deffand is celebrated in Paris for her quick
wit and for the company she gathers around her. She
lost her sight about ten years ago. . . . She had been an
intimate friend of the famous marquise Du Châtelet.
After the latter's death, a nasty pen-portrait of her made
the rounds, attributed to Mme Du Deffand. It lost her
no friends: M. de Voltaire continued to correspond with
her, and M. d'Alembert and many other well-known
persons at court and in Paris remained faithful. Her most
famous *mot* is her remark concerning the miracle of St.
Denis, who (as everyone knows) after being beheaded
in Paris walked from there to the site of the present
abbaye de Saint-Denis, carrying his head in his hands.
"*Eh bien*," Mme Du Deffand remarked, "*il n'y a que le
premier pas qui coûte*"—"It's only the first step that
counts."

The end of a review (possibly by Diderot) in the Newsletter for 1 July 1764 of the latest volume of Buffon's *Natural
History* echoes a conversation among these friends:

. . . Let us conclude with a fact probably unknown to
M. Buffon since he does not mention it—a detail I have

from M. l'abbé Galiani, who has had it confirmed by excellent authority. The rhinoceros has two separate tongues, one lying above the other: the lower tongue extends to the front of the throat, as with other animals; the upper, covering what might be called the rear half of the lower, extends with the first back to the root. To understand the mechanism, it must be remembered that the rhinoceros, having an excessively short and rigid neck, would be unable to procure its food without a very long snout, at the end of which the upper lip, protruding far beyond the lower, enables it, like an elephant with its trunk, to take up its food and carry it on its first tongue. This transfers the food to the second tongue, which does the swallowing. Our human tongue acts in a similar way. It is raised in the middle, like a bridge: and it is this bridge that carries the food, after mastication, into the process of swallowing. It would seem that the rhinoceros's first tongue lacks the resilience of the human tongue because of its great length; in order to acquire a bridge the animal needed a second tongue to take up the food and carry it to the rear of the mouth. Splendid subject for an essay by partisans of final causes![13]

About this time, Francesco Algarotti (1712–64), author of *Neutonianismo per le dame (Newtonianism for Ladies)* and a friend of Voltaire's, had died at Pisa.

Newsletter, 15 July 1764. . . . He ordered that his tomb be inscribed *Hic jacet Algarottus, sed non omnis* [Here lies Algarotti, but not all of him]. This epitaph is probably devoutly Christian, referring to Algarotti's soul: not, I think, as has been elsewhere suggested, a boast about the immortality of his literary works. The abbé Galiani suggests that the phrase would be more appropriate on the tomb of Farinelli, Caffarelli, or Salimbeni. [Galiani and his music-loving friends were admirers of these great Italian castrati.]

Newsletter, *1 August 1764*.

Epitaph of Madame la Marquise de Pompadour,
who died on 15 April 1764

Ci-gît d'Étoile et Pompadour,
Qui charma la ville et la cour;
Femme infidèle et maîtresse accomplie:
L'Hymen et l'Amour n'ont pas tort
Le premier, de pleurer sa vie,
Le second, de pleurer sa mort.

And another epitaph:

Ci-gît qui fut vingt ans pucelle,
Quinze ans catin, et sept ans . . . [maquerelle].

In the late autumn of 1764, Grimm published in the News-letter a long, impassioned essay he had written expounding to his foreign subscribers the errors of the Church. He depicted the horrors of its history, the tragedy of its evolution from primitive poverty and piety to pitiless mediaeval omnipotence, the desperation of its waning power as personified in "that frightful St. Dominic who knew very well what he was doing when he founded the horrible tribunal of the Inquisition." Since those days, Grimm continued,

things have greatly changed. Civil power has regained its rights; reason has superseded blindness and superstition: today the weakest and most bigoted prince would not tolerate the least of the many insults suffered in silence by the powerful and enlightened Frederick II. Yet we must agree that throughout Europe, Christianity and its ministers retain, despite their decline, a substantial remnant of their former power. The three most important civil documents are still under ecclesiastical control: the certificates of baptism, marriage and death are relics of ecclesiastical legislation. In every Christian country the authority and testimony of the priest determines the very existence, and the status, of its citizens. . . . [Furthermore,] legions of priests have the right to climb into pulpits every morning at eleven and preach to the people. What a terrible instrument that would be, in hands that knew how to exploit it! Fortunately for the tranquillity of empires, the Church, in entrusting the priesthood to so many idiots, has contributed to its own decline. Its continued abuse of the spoken word has vitiated its power, and the eloquence of the pulpit has become as puerile in its effects as in its form. Yet in the narrowness of its morality, incompatible with the duties of civil life, it remains a menace. . . .

Nor, Grimm adds, in a contemptuous reference to a certain "advanced" form of Christianity fashionable in his day, is there much to be said for so-called deism as expounded by Locke, Hume, and Rousseau—a concept of divinity that rejects revelation and affirms the possibility of "knowing God" through reason alone. And he closes by asking his readers to reconsider the concept that "God is merciful." What can such a comment do, he asks, but open every barrier to those who wish to commit atrocities—"to all hearts," as he puts it, "born to crime"?

This essay had resulted from Grimm's conversations with Diderot and Galiani. The latter had apparently made no great defense of his church, saying merely that Christianity had been compelled toward authoritarianism by the lawlessness of the times; and the next number of the Newsletter, that of 1 December 1764, gives its subscribers a fuller picture of the abbé:

The man best suited to write the true history of the Church would be M. l'abbé Galiani. This diminutive individual, born at the foot of Mount Vesuvius [sic], is a true phenomenon. Behind his bright, penetrating glance there lies a vast and solid erudition; and he combines with the insights of a man of genius the vivacity and charm of one who seeks only to amuse and please. He is Plato with the verve and gestures of Harlequin:

93

he is the only man I have ever known to be diffuse and yet remain ever an agreeable companion. What a pity that such a fund of rare, fertile, original ideas should be shared only with a few philosophers, or evaporate in the conversations of a frivolous circle: that our little Neapolitan should be so indolent—or so wise—as to prefer tranquillity to renown, repose to fame! Despite the friendship one feels for him, one would have to be virtuous indeed not to wish that he might shed his indolence, and give his genius free rein; that he might produce works of public benefit—at the risk of encountering the hostility and persecution suffered by all who have dared to enlighten their century. Whatever vanity I may be guilty of has a single source: the knowledge that my ideas accord with those of the two rarest men I have had the good fortune to know—Galiani himself and Denis Diderot. Recently the three of us were talking, beside the fire, about the church of Sainte-Geneviève,[14] which we had been visiting together. This led us to the subject of the primitive form of Christian churches, and thence to the spirit of Christianity. I had been saying that in our day only the Herrnhuters [Moravians of Saxony] had sought to re-establish and reproduce the true government of the Church. The abbé took the occasion to demonstrate that the spirit of the Church has always been that of a government rather than a religion. The philosopher confined himself to raising objections that forced us to explore our own arguments more deeply; and this served, as always happens when one at last glimpses the truth, to make our conclusions manifest and irrefutable. If in what I have said on this subject there are some ideas worthy of your consideration, it is to those two men that all credit must be given: my only merit is to have suggested the discussion and committed it to print.

Newsletter, 1 May 1765. It can scarcely be said that this philosophical century has favored the fortune of philosophers. The next generation may be more just in this regard: recognition and gratitude have always been posthumous children. The philosopher Diderot, after producing works of literature for thirty years, found himself obliged to sell his library in order to pay for the education of his only daughter. He had been vainly seeking a buyer for four or five years when I suggested that I offer the library to the Empress of Russia through the good offices of General Betsky, whom I had the honor of knowing during his stay in France. He has just replied as follows:

The generous protection, Monsieur, which our august sovereign constantly accords to everything related to the sciences, and her particular esteem for scholars, made me decide to give her a faithful report of the circumstances which, according to your letter of last 10 February, oblige M. Diderot to dispose of his library. Her tender heart could not fail to be moved by the thought that this philosopher, so renowned in the republic of letters, should find himself obliged to sacrifice, to his fatherly affections, the object of his delight, the source of his labors and the companions of his leisure. Therefore Her Imperial Majesty, as a token of her benevolence and to encourage him in the pursuit of his career, has ordered me to purchase this library on her behalf for the sum, suggested by you, of fifteen thousand livres: on one condition only—that M. Diderot retain the library for his own use until it should please Her Majesty to ask for it. Orders for the payment of sixteen thousand livres have already been sent to Prince Galitzine, her minister in Paris. The extra payment, to be renewed annually, is yet another proof of my sovereign's appreciation of the attention and care he will continue to give to the formation of this library. The matter is thus attended to. Be good enough to tell M. Diderot how flattered I am to have been able to serve him in some small measure.

I have the honor to be, etc.,

Signed, J. BETSKY

That letter of April 1765 commemorates an enlightened gesture on the part of supreme authority. No royal favor can ever have been more wisely, or more gracefully, bestowed.

The liberalism of the privately distributed Newsletter was in great contrast to official attitudes prevailing in eighteenth-century Europe:

Tanucci to Carlo III, Naples, 1765. Owners of Voltaire's *Dictionnaire philosophique portatif* are to be sentenced to two years in prison: if they are members of the nobility, the sentence will consist of two years' confinement to their estates.

Newsletter, 1 April 1765. The Parlement has at last decided to order the burning of the portable *Dictionnaire philosophique* and, in the same decree, that of [Rousseau's] *Les Lettres écrites de la montagne.*

But even the Newsletter was slow to report one of the most celebrated cases of the century: the tragedy of the Calas family in Toulouse. Jean Calas, as the *Oxford Companion to French Literature* succinctly explains,

a Protestant cloth merchant of Toulouse, was executed (broken on the wheel, exposed, and then strangled) in 1762 on the false charge that he had murdered his eldest son because the latter wished to become a Roman Catholic. The truth was that the son had committed suicide (on the family premises) and the father found the body. At this time suicide was a crime. The father tried at first to make out that his son had been assassinated. He could not substantiate this and almost immediately gave the true story, which was not accepted but from which he refused to depart throughout an interrogation and trial conducted by the Parlement of Toulouse with the utmost fanaticism and brutality. After the execution the Calas family removed to Geneva, where Voltaire heard of the case and took it up with such vigour that in 1765 the verdict was quashed and Calas's innocence established by the Conseil d'État. The case excited public sympathy at home and abroad.

Only after the posthumous rehabilitation of Jean Calas by the Conseil d'État and the quashing of all charges levied against the family by the authorities at Toulouse was the case mentioned in the Newsletter, in its issue of 15 March 1765. On 15 April it printed an account of the sequel:

The entire unfortunate Calas family has been presented to the king and the royal family. The king has awarded them the sum of 36,000 livres, to be distributed as follows: 18,000 to the widow, 6,000 to each of the daughters, 3,000 to the son, Pierre Calas, and 3,000 to the maidservant. The comptroller general has told Mme Calas that he will pay that sum over a period of three years, at the rate of 12,000 livres a year. That arrangement greatly diminishes the efficacy of the royal grant. We learn that a subscription has been opened in England for the benefit of these unfortunate persons. We wish to follow the generous British example, and only regret that our means are far below our intentions. M. de Carmontelle . . . a pleasing and fluent draftsman, . . . has made a drawing of the entire Calas family. The widow is seated: her face bears the imprint of her misfortune. Her elder daughter [Rose], very pleasing in appearance, sits beside her, her head against her mother's arm. The younger daughter [Nanette] stands behind her mother, leaning on her chair. This young woman's appearance is particularly pleasant and interesting: she resembles a Virgin by Guido Reni; misfortune has touched her natural grace with poignancy and tenderness. These three persons—all three likenesses are perfect—have their

LA MALHEUREUSE FAMILLE CALAS.

La Mere, les deux Filles, avec Jeanne Viguiere leur bonne Servante, le Fils et son ami le jeune Lavaysse

La Malheureuse Famille Calas,
engraving by J. B. Delafosse,
after a drawing by Carmontelle

eyes fixed on young Alexandre Lavaysse, who faces them
and is reading to them the report written by Élie de
Beaumont. [Beaumont, a celebrated lawyer engaged by
Voltaire, had obtained the reversal of the verdict. Lavaysse, a family friend, and Jeanne Viguière, the Calas
maidservant, had refused to testify against them despite
threats of torture by the Toulouse authorities, and had
been imprisoned with them.] Pierre Calas stands behind
Lavaysse, reading over his shoulder. Between them and
the mother and daughters we see their elderly servant,
erect and attentive. Pierre Calas is the member of the
family who seems most embittered by misfortune: he
will not easily regain peace of mind. His companion in
misfortune, Lavaysse, has a mild, agreeable face. Thus,
the entire picture is interesting in every way. Our intention is to have it engraved, and to present the plate
to Mme Calas. We must reserve to ourselves and a few
friends the privilege of bearing the expense of the plate;
but we intend to open a subscription for the sale of the
engraving—this to benefit the family, so deserving of
the interest of all Europe.

Grimm saw to the publication of an eleven-page "Projet
de souscription pour un ouvrage tragique et moral," which
was distributed to five thousand potentially interested par-
ties, including the subscribers to the Newsletter. The Calas
project was the occasion of a generous movement of humanity throughout Europe. Subscribers were numerous in
France and abroad, and represented every social stratum.
Historic names appear together with those of artisans:
Catherine of Russia (who subscribed for 50,000 livres), the
duchess of Saxe-Gotha, the princesse Palatine, the princess
of Hesse-Darmstadt, Horace Walpole, Leopold Mozart
("*maître de chapelle du prince-archevêque de Salzburg*"), the
marquise de Polignac, the comte de Schomberg, M. and
Mme Necker, Mme Geoffrin; Voltaire (twelve copies), Dr.
Gatti, Helvétius, Diderot, and many more.

Everything promised well, when the Parlement of Paris

suddenly ordered subscriptions suspended. "I foresaw it all," Diderot wrote to Mlle Volland. "I said so to Grimm, but he laughed at me." As the Newsletter reported on 15 August, the Parlement based its opposition on three grounds: Voltaire seemed to be the instigator of the project; the engraving was injurious to the Parlement of Toulouse; Protestants would benefit. A compromise was reached: the authorities would close their eyes to the subscription on the condition that there be no publicity and that the engraving be sold only to subscribers. These conditions were promptly ignored; the engraving soon found its way to shops and enjoyed a wide sale.

The Parlement played a larger and far more sinister role in another celebrated case—that of the Church versus the young chevalier de La Barre.

Newsletter, 15 July 1766. There is much concern in Paris over the recent frightful episode in Abbeville. So far, accounts have been confused. All Europe would have reacted with indignation and pity had those responsible for the tragedy not silenced the partisans of innocence and humanity with threats of retribution. The known facts must be kept in mind, as an example of horrible cruelty occurring in the middle of a century that prides itself on its philosophy and enlightenment.

On the night of 8–9 August 1765, a wooden crucifix standing on a bridge in Abbeville is mutilated by blows from a sword or hunting knife. Blind superstition, rampant as ever, cries Scandal. The bishop of Amiens, one of the most fanatical bishops of France, leads a procession of clergy to the site, to expiate the so-called crime by a series of superstitious rites. Admonitions are posted, in an effort to discover the person responsible. (This ecclesiastical practice of troubling timid consciences and inflaming weak minds by ordering everyone to discuss matters of no concern to them or risk eternal damnation is one of the most baneful abuses in French criminal jurisprudence.) More than one hundred twenty fanatics or dupes testify. Not one can identify the person or persons responsible for the desecration . . . but all report rumors and scraps of gossip accusing the most prominent young people in the city of impious remarks, supposed profanations, improprieties of one kind or another meriting, at most, parental reproof. These young scatterbrains are ordered to stand trial. The mutilated crucifix is no longer the prime topic: up for judgment are the so-called crimes revealed by the monitoring.

It is easy to imagine the consternation of a city where five children of the most prominent families, all of them minors, find themselves implicated in criminal proceedings. Their parents had arranged their escape, but the very animus involving them in this cruel affair ensured that the authorities were informed of their flight. A search was instituted and, of the five, two were captured: the young chevalier de La Barre and a seventeen-year-old youth named Charles-François Moisnel.

At Abbeville, last 28 February, one of the young men, Gaillard d'Estalonde, was sentenced by the court [in absentia: fortunately he had escaped to England, with two companions similarly charged] to apologize, to have his tongue cut out and his hands cut off, and to be burned alive. . . . By the same court, Jean-François Le Fèvre, chevalier de La Barre, was ordered to apologize and sentenced to have his tongue cut out and to be beheaded, his body then to be reduced to ashes. Suspended sentences were given to the other three—one of them, Moisnel, being in prison with the chevalier de La Barre.

Criminal sentences must be confirmed by parliamentary decree in the district concerned. The unfortunate young men had had statements printed in their own defense, hoping in this way to arouse public sympathy; but maître Le Fèvre d'Ormesson, a good criminologist, a close relative of the chevalier de La Barre, after having been shown the entire Abbeville proceedings, was of the opinion that the Parlement would not uphold the sen-

tences, and had forbidden publication of the statements. He hoped that the young men, after being quietly
acquitted, would be grateful to him for having thus
quashed publicity. His confidence proved fatal: publication of the statements would unquestionably have
aroused public indignation, and the Parlement would
not have confirmed the Abbeville sentence. On 4 June
the Parlement did confirm it, and after many attempts
to obtain a royal pardon had failed, La Barre was executed at Abbeville on 1 July. He died with unexampled
courage and calm.

He had been found guilty of the following offenses:
of having passed within twenty-five paces of the procession of the Blessed Sacrament without removing his hat
and kneeling; of having uttered blasphemies against
God, the Holy Eucharist, the Blessed Virgin, and saints
both male and female as listed at the trial; of having
sung two impious songs; of having spoken "with respect
and adoration" of certain lewd and filthy books; of having profaned the sign of the cross and the usual bene-
dictions of the Church. That is what brought about the
decapitation of a heedless, undisciplined child, in the
heart of France and in the mid-eighteenth century. Even
in countries where the Inquisition exists, those crimes
would have been punished by a month in prison, followed by a reprimand.[15]

V

"The Hot Baths on Ischia"

GALIANI was in Paris throughout the years of the
Calas tragedy, but by the time of the execution of young La
Barre he was in Italy, on leave. He had never ceased to find
the Parisian climate trying, and in the spring of 1765 the
Neapolitan council of regency granted his request for six
months' respite, "to benefit from the hot baths on the island
of Ischia."

Galiani's request served Tanucci well.

Choiseul had for some years been promoting a series of
international agreements known as Family Pacts, designed
to unite the regal and princely members of the house of
Bourbon against constant threats of alliance between England and various Continental powers. Tanucci was opposed
to Neapolitan participation in such agreements, fearing that
they might involve Naples in costly and dangerous wars.
Using various excuses—the famine and plague of 1763–64,
the minority of young King Ferdinando—and with support
from King Carlos in Madrid, he had been able to ensure, at
least for a time, that Neapolitan adherence to the pacts re-

mained vague, tentative, and noncommittal. Now, with Ferdinando approaching majority on his sixteenth birthday, steps were required to counter French impatience. Tanucci's method of playing for time was to seek, or to pretend to seek, as a preliminary to ratification, the solution of certain details currently affecting Franco-Neapolitan relations, with particular reference to matters of commerce and contraband.

Galiani, now the veteran of several years' experience in dealing with Choiseul and French bureaucracy, was thus *persona gratissima* to Tanucci; and, at first from the hot springs and mud baths of Ischia, and later—his stay prolonged—in Naples itself, he helped the minister to improvise tactics of delay.

As this work continued, the French ambassador in Naples was advised that treaties of commerce and navigation "and other matters" were being discussed behind closed doors at the highest governmental level. Such proceedings are invariably time-consuming, and it was not until May 1766 that a document was dispatched to Choiseul and a public announcement made. To deal with Franco-Neapolitan affairs, a special council had been formed consisting of the minister of finance, the president and secretary of the Commercial Court, a Neapolitan businessman "elected by the people," the professor of commerce and economics at the University of Naples (the celebrated economist Antonio Genovesi), and Galiani, who had just been appointed councillor at the Commercial Court, his term to begin whenever he might return to Naples permanently from Paris. What was not announced was the fact that this special council, though "formed," had not met. It would never meet: Tanucci and Galiani had never intended that it should. But France was aware that the body formally existed: it conveniently fulfilled a familiar, if farcical, bureaucratic purpose.

It was Galiani who polished into its final form the long official document that Tanucci sent to France—a document redolent with Neapolitan complaints, in themselves designed to prolong matters.[1] Predictably, France found it unsatisfactory. In ensuing years it was to be followed by further documents, all of them leading to further, Jarndycean discussions that would continue for decades, long outlasting Galiani, Tanucci, and Choiseul, and terminating only with the irruption of the French Revolution.

Despite Galiani's repeated requests to be allowed to return to Paris once his Neapolitan task was completed, Tanucci detained him several months. Only in September 1766 did the regents vote permission for his departure. Tanucci, having himself arranged the matter, cast the only dissenting vote—an elegant indication of his refreshed awareness of the abbé's qualities.

Carrying with him "simple instructions to do everything possible to ensure that Franco-Neapolitan relations appeared, if they had not indeed become, less strained than in the past," Galiani reached Paris on 17 November 1766, after visiting friends in Rome, Genoa, and Milan. On 24 November he wrote to Tanucci:

> I must do this justice to the Parisians: that they have welcomed me back with such loving-kindness as to make me realize how much more loved I am in Paris, to speak generally, than in Naples. For so much love, I can forgive the eternal fogs of this climate, and the lack of appetite, the nervous tension and headaches, from which I suffer here. To be loved is the greatest happiness in life.

On the same day, to his brother: "Here, I have been welcomed so affectionately and festively, that without exaggeration or vanity I can say I am more loved in Paris than in Naples."

On 8 December, to Tanucci: "Paris considers me a naturalized citizen."

And on 23 February 1767, after Tanucci wrote that he "marveled" at Galiani's love of Paris, he replied, quoting a law of physics: "Each body finds its proper place: I fell into place in Paris, and here I hope to stay forever."

VI

Paris (II)

THE PERIOD of more than two years that followed Galiani's joyful return to Paris appears, with hindsight, to proceed inexorably toward the blow that was to determine all his future life.

Choiseul's welcome to him, in that winter of 1766–67, was effusively cordial, in bland diplomatic contrast to the indignant messages he was simultaneously sending to Tanucci in Naples—messages fulminating against the document that had, as Choiseul well knew, largely been concocted by the abbé.

> *Galiani to Tanucci, Paris, 12 January 1767.*
> I spent two hours with Choiseul at the Spanish ambassador's last Friday, enjoying the most pleasant conversation imaginable. . . . Rest assured that he could not be more sincere, or more kindly disposed toward us. . . . I am convinced that there are no two people in the world better suited to love one another than Your Excellency and Choiseul. . . . I was pleased with everything he said

that evening, and I see that his intentions toward us are, in every way, the very best. . . .

A month later, Galiani assured Tanucci, who had written him dryly about the affronts he had been receiving from Paris, that the situation resembled that in Plautus's comedy *Amphitrion*: "There are two Choiseuls. The Choiseul I talk with is one; the Choiseul who writes to Your Excellency is another." In fact, Galiani assured his chief, the indignant messages reaching him could only have been hastily *signed* by Choiseul after being written by someone else—probably a minor official, some "badly brought-up young fellow who imagined he was displaying astuteness." Choiseul, overworked, and ailing into the bargain, could not be blamed for signing routine documents in haste:

> Does it seem to you that a man who is frantic with nephritic pains can have any great desire to read? The duke has the War Ministry—an immense responsibility: three hundred lieutenant generals, four hundred regimental sergeant majors, five hundred brigadiers: simply to remember their names would be the work of a man's entire life. In great empires, the interior is the most important: the duke must think of the army and the navy. Abroad, there are London, Vienna, Madrid: regarding each of which, the situation speaks well of his work. . . . Games and dinners with the king; constant travel; long meetings, consultations, everything to be handled in a conciliatory way; his duties as colonel of the Swiss Guards. . . . His private affairs (a man's usual duties—one might call them the terrestrial side of his divinity—and they have not been few this year). . . . You will agree it is prodigious that he can do what he does.

Tactless, surely, to insist to Tanucci, overworked in his provincial capital, on the duties of his opposite number in the great metropolis. Little tact: and, one might ask, how much sincerity?

Was Galiani really misled by Choiseul, the latter playing,

in his wily way, on Galiani's very evident pleasure at being welcomed back by his Parisian friends—welcomed as a "naturalized citizen" of Paris? Or were the abbé's words to Tanucci a defense thrown out to prolong the delightful present, to protect those Parisian friendships, now more precious than ever when contrasted with his recent months in Naples? He had written to Tanucci on 5 January:

> In Naples there is no affection I can count on absolutely except that coming from Your Excellency. The other people who were fond of me there, or said they were—was it Galiani they loved, or Tanucci's friend? A direct ray, or its reflection? All those relatives, friends, acquaintances, etc.: was it *I* they loved? or the commercial councillor and their own prospects? Was it *I* whom all those nice people were fond of, or was it the nephew of that Monsignor Galiani who had created them bishops and professors? In Paris *sono tutto io*: I am entirely myself. And that self has no influence. Therefore, if people love me, and there are many here who do, I no longer have to find an answer to those questions—an answer that in Naples I shrink from discovering.

From Versailles, throughout these months, Choiseul was keeping a watch on Galiani as before. Author of the formal Neapolitan complaints, and now in greater favor with Tanucci than ever, Galiani was under constant scrutiny by Choiseul's spies.

Ferdinando IV was the first native-born Neapolitan sovereign in several centuries, and his coming of age at sixteen was the occasion for celebration.

> *Galiani to Tanucci, 12 January 1767.* Today the king reaches his majority. May God render it as fruitful and happy as we all desire: a wish that, to my mind, is the same as saying "May God keep Your Excellency in good health, and willing to stay at the helm."

Tanucci was indeed needed at the helm: he had done nothing to help prepare young Ferdinand to rule—determined,
with the consent, and even the collaboration, of Carlos in
Spain, to share his administration only with Madrid. As Gibbon wrote of another regent: "Though he uniformly behaved
with tenderness and regard to his infant colleague, he gradually confounded . . . the office of a guardian with the authority of a sovereign."[1] None of his seven fellow regents,
nor the boy's tutor, had raised any notable objections; and
Ferdinando, whatever his latent intellect may have been, had
come of age an uneducated dolt, a good-natured clown, recognized as such by his often embarrassed familiars, loved as
such by the Neapolitan populace, regarded with astonishment by visiting foreigners.

Soon Galiani, in Paris, was busy buying wedding presents.
A Neapolitan rapprochement with Austria was desired by
both governments, and it had been agreed during Ferdinando's infancy that he would marry one of the many daughters
of Empress Maria Theresa and Emperor Francis I. The first
of the chosen archduchesses died very young of smallpox;
the second succumbed to the same disease the day before
she was to have left Vienna for Italy; the third, Maria Carolina, survived to become Ferdinando's bride and Queen of
Naples in May 1768. She was seventeen, Ferdinando a year
and a half older.[2] Two years later, Maria Carolina's youngest
sister, Marie Antoinette, would marry Louis, dauphin of
France—a union hailed in Grimm's Newsletter for July 1770
as "an event on which rests the happiness of the future generations of a great kingdom."

In the autumn of 1767, Galiani, in Paris, congratulated
Tanucci on the expulsion of the Jesuits from the Kingdom
of Naples. (A special medal bearing Tanucci's portrait was
struck by the Neapolitan mint that year in commemoration
of his leading role in the event.) And in December, Galiani
wrote from London, where Tanucci had given him permission to accept an invitation from his friend the marchese

Domenico Caracciolo, Neapolitan ambassador to the Court of St. James's.[3]

Galiani to Tanucci, London, 8 December 1767.

At this moment I am an Albionite; but I shall not abuse Your Excellency's kindness, and a week from now, God willing, I shall be back among the Gauls. My greatest thanks to you for allowing me to see this country— a land very well worth seeing, and which I have found quite different from descriptions given me by others. A full account of my impressions would be far too long. Speaking generally, I find England quite similar to Italy and infinitely unlike France. One is impressed by the newness of everything, and by the short time it has taken the English to become so remarkable.[4] One sees that they have moved in the proper direction, and that they will outstrip the French and become what Italians were in the days when we were all citizens of the same nation—and what we shall be again when we resume our destiny as a united land. However, the English will never really be what the Italians were and could be again. The climate is against that, and the fertile soil, and the population, which is now nine million at most and never can be more: that is, a third less than Italy. This country's great disadvantage, on the other hand, is the constant expense of shipping, needed to obtain essential foreign products, such as wine, certain foods, silk, oil, etc.

Their present strength reminds me of the qualities that used to characterize the Jesuits: their diligence, their capacity for taking pains, their great frugality, their enthusiasm, their love of their state and their religion; their endless exertion, their hatred of waste and empty show. Thunder rather than lightning: durability rather than flair. Of this country it can be said that *plus hic boni mores quam alibi bonae leges.* Nowhere have I seen greater energy, greater vigor. This shows that the apparatus is new. Time slows all action, slackens all holds: here, that relaxation has not yet come to pass.

On 18 January 1768, back in Paris, replying to Tanucci's habitual questioning:

Eccellenza: My saying that England resembles Italy was not profound metaphysical speculation: it merely expressed my automatic physical sensation of imagining myself in Italy when I was in the heart of London.

The climate, milder than that of Paris, the Italianate architecture of the houses, many of them of brick, with few stories, and with façades directly on the street; the men corpulent, their hair roughly combed, no perfume, no horrible hats, no swaggering; the ladies without rouge, richly but badly dressed, always wearing a hat or other head-covering. In short, these things remind me of Italy; not of all Italy, but of those parts that have a republican tradition, either alive or extinct—Tuscany and Lombardy. All these external aspects of England I found reminiscent of Italy. Manners are certainly unlike ours, except for the general seriousness that seems to prevail in both nations—that is, in London as in Venice and Genoa. . . .

Galiani may also have noticed another contrast with Paris: the dearth of a conversational tradition in which the sexes mingled to intellectual profit. Even had he, a wit, not been at a disadvantage with the English language, he would have suffered from a lack of that charm and stimulus in educated discourse which was the greatest joy of his Parisian life. In England, at that period, discussion flourished in the male haven of the coffeehouse. Two centuries and more after Galiani's English visit, Anthony Powell would pronounce, through fiction, on the deficiency: "There have never been any real salons in England. . . . Everyone thinks a salon is a place for a free meal. A true salon is conversation—nothing to eat and less to drink."[5]

III

In 1764, fearful lest her husband plunder the dowry of her daughter Angélique, Mme d'Épinay had arranged the girl's marriage, at the age of fifteen, to an honorable provincial vicomte of thirty-five, Dominique de Belsunce. His château was far distant, at Méharin, in the foothills of the Pyrenees, where he was *bailli*, the local magistrate. Two sons were born to them, and—apparently in March 1768—a daughter, Émilie. Mme d'Épinay seems not to have been particularly interested in her grandsons, one of whom was destined to meet a tragic end; but the education of Émilie was to become the subject of her best-known book.

The Newsletter for July 1766 printed an account of the Mozart family's brief visit to Paris, after eighteen months in England and six in Holland, where both children had, as usual, everywhere "astonished the connoisseurs." In London, Johann Christian Bach had taken Wolfgang, then nine, "between his knees, and together they improvised on the same piano for two hours in the presence of the king and queen. . . . This child is the most lovable creature imaginable . . . and his cheerful disposition reassures those who had feared that one so precocious might not live to maturity."

Six months later, there was further news of Diderot and his library:

> *Newsletter, 15 January 1767.* In 1765 the Empress of Russia bought M. Diderot's library for the sum of fifteen thousand livres without having seen its catalogue, stipulating that the philosopher should retain the books until she might ask for them. Her Majesty further ordered that M. Diderot be paid an additional sum to cover the expense of caring for the books and adding to them; and the money for the first year was paid in advance as a supplement to the purchase price. In 1766, this annual sum not having been paid, General Betsky was ordered to add the following postscript to one of his letters to the Russian embassy in Paris:

Her Imperial Majesty, having been informed in a letter sent to me by Prince Galitzine, that M. Diderot has not been paid the sum due him since last March, has ordered me to tell him that she most particularly does not wish his library to suffer as a result of bureaucratic negligence; and for this reason she wishes M. Diderot to be paid, for fifty years in advance, the sum she has always destined for preservation and increase of his library; and she adds that on the expiration of those fifty years she will take further measures. For this purpose I send you the enclosed bill of exchange.

This postscript by General Betsky was dated 30 October 1766, and was accompanied by a bill of exchange for twenty-five thousand livres payable to M. Diderot. I recommend the arrangement to the attention of the editor of *La Gazette du Commerce*: he may never in his life have occasion to report a similar transaction. M. Diderot sells his library but continues to enjoy full use of it, while having acquired a sufficiency beyond any expectation. Thirty years of labor having brought him no reward whatever from his own country, it has pleased the Empress of Russia to discharge France's debt. In the space of eighteen months Her Majesty has given this philosopher more than forty thousand livres. I suggest that historians comb their archives for the names of sovereigns who have rewarded merit so magnificently and with such tact and grace.

A lady recently remarked to M. Diderot that he was fortunate in having pleasant things happen to him. . . . A few years ago, when the philosopher was visiting Greuze, the latter drew his profile. For some time thereafter the philosopher kept expecting that the artist would offer him the drawing as a gift, but it was not forthcoming; and on subsequent visits M. Diderot did not see it in the studio. At last, one fine day, the drawing was delivered to him, together with a plate made from it and the first 100 proofs made from the plate. Greuze had lettered the etching simply "Diderot." The engraving was done by Saint-Aubin, and is a masterpiece of the genre. Unfortunately Greuze's portrait is far from being a likeness. A certain journeyman "artist" named Garand, in the Place Dauphine, drew me a profile of M. Diderot that resembles him far more.

VII

Recalled

THE PASSION for general enlightenment that had carried Diderot through the long labor of the *Encyclopaedia* was expressed in a characteristic "Note to the Reader" he wrote to be printed at the head of Volume VIII. In it, Diderot announced his hope that "education of the public may advance at so rapid a pace that, within twenty years, scarcely one in a thousand of our pages will be remote from common knowledge." It was Diderot's crusade for the extension of knowledge—knowledge as an aid to judgment—that would now engender Galiani's best-known work, *Dialogues on the Grain Trade*.

The genesis of this lively—and, improbably, delightful—treatise is revealed in two letters sent by Diderot to Mlle Volland in November 1768. In these, Diderot records two conversations with the abbé on a matter with which all Europe was seized and with which Galiani had himself become acutely familiar during and after the Neapolitan famine of 1764: the supply and storage of grain. In that same year,

Louis XV, acting on the advice of officials in favor of free trade, had signed an act permitting the free exportation of grain from France. The price of bread had immediately risen; famine and profiteering followed; rioting broke out. In subsequent years these disorders would recur, particularly in Normandy and Brittany; and abroad there was famine in Rome and Tuscany, and in Madrid.

The abbé Galiani explained himself clearly. If anything in public policy is demonstrable, it is this: free exportation of grain is madness. I swear to you that no one, until now, has spoken a rational word on this subject. I begged him, on bended knee, to publish his ideas.

Here is but one of his principles:

"What do you mean, to 'sell' grain?"

"It means exchanging it for money."

"You don't know what you're talking about: it means exchanging grain for grain. At the present time can you ever advantageously exchange the grain you have for grain that people will sell you?"

He showed us all the implications of that law: they are immense. He explained the cause of the present high prices, and brought us to understand what no one has ever perceived. Never in my life have I listened to him with greater pleasure.

Diderot did not bend his knee in vain.

Galiani, always a prolific writer, had nevertheless, for almost twenty years—since the appearance of *Della Moneta* in 1751—written little that could be called his own. The unpublished introduction to the Herculanean volumes had been a set task; his reports to Tanucci occupy many hundreds of pages; and there is the lengthy list of Neapolitan grievances sent to Choiseul. Galiani and Paris had been enjoying each other; but we are able to share in that enjoyment chiefly through letters exchanged among his friends or published in the Newsletter. Now, while lamenting that there already existed "a thousand books" about grain supply, and despite the satisfaction he often took in deploring his own "indolence," Galiani was fired by Diderot to write; and in a few months he completed the eight *Dialogues sur le commerce des blés*. These form a small masterpiece, instructive, admonitory, and attractive. The work is both narrative and sermon, its lightness of tone skillfully employed to emphasize seriousness of theme. Socratic in form, the "dialogues" are presented as a series of conversations between Galiani himself (the "chevalier de Zanobi" in the text) and his foil the "marquis de Roquemaure" (resembling his Parisian friend the marquis de Croismare). The first dialogue sets the scene and plunges straight into the matter:

THE MARQUIS
Did you have a pleasant time in Italy?
THE CHEVALIER
No.
THE MARQUIS
"Leave Paris and life stops," as the saying goes. Your native land had lost its charm for you?
THE CHEVALIER
It wasn't that, but I'd chosen a bad time to return there. In Rome there were food shortages. The news from Tuscany, and especially from Naples, intensified the horror. In Naples, it was no mere matter of shortages, but of a cruel and terrible famine. Thousands of miserable, starving people were eating grass and dying of hunger, and the outbreak of an epidemic completed the catastrophe.
THE MARQUIS
It must have been frightful. I see you are still shaken by the memory. To what do you attribute such famine?
THE CHEVALIER
To human error. . . .

And it is human error—including the hoarding of grain by profiteers, the lack of control over exports, and the fraudulent shipment of damaged foodstuffs in those days of slow transport, all vivid in Galiani's mind since his months in Naples in 1765–66 and repeatedly deplored in his letters to Tanucci—that the *Dialogues* proceed to chronicle and analyze. It is for these mistakes that remedies are proposed. Despite the grim subject, the tone is swift and sociable. Led by François Quesnay, the "physiocrats," or "Economists" (the dogmatic free-traders of the day, opposed to interference with "natural law" and adopting the maxim of "laissez-faire," or *"laissez agir la nature"*), did not fail to deplore Galiani's "frivolity," but his lightness is of the Socratic kind. For a summary of the *Dialogues* we may turn to Fausto Nicolini, writing in 1931:

> Galiani maintains that economic questions, unlike philosophical ones, can be resolved in a hundred different ways, according to the varying contingencies of time and place; and that therefore unlimited trade in grain, advantageous in such and such a country in such and such a year, can become harmful in the same country in a different year, and, in fact, in the same year in a different country. This thesis is recognized as unobjectionable today, but the physiocrats deplored it as anti-libertarian.

Or, as Diderot put it: "The Economists advanced general principles with the most marvelous intrepidity. But not a single one of these is immune from an infinity of exceptions in practice."

While Galiani was writing the eighth and last of the *Dialogues*, he received a sudden command that broke his heart and determined his future life:

> *Portici, 6 May 1769.*
> *Signor don Ferdinando Galiani*: It is the king's wish that Your Most Illustrious Lordship should, within four days after receipt of this dispatch, leave Paris for Naples, there to assume your post as councillor at the Commercial

Court. I send this order in the king's name, for execution as stated.

Bernardo Tanucci

Galiani had been careless. Worse than careless: he had been guilty of the capital diplomatic crime: indiscretion.

He had gossiped in such a way as to endanger the Family Pact, that display of Bourbon solidarity conceived and promoted by Choiseul. Tanucci had been withholding from the crucial document the signature of the Bourbon king of Naples, indicating to Choiseul that ratification would be forthcoming only if certain Franco-Neapolitan differences were resolved—differences that Galiani had eloquently listed for Tanucci in Naples. Recently, there had been an upsurge of French difficulties with Denmark, one of the countries, together with Russia and England, against which the pact was designed as a bulwark. And Galiani's offense had been to repeat to his friend the baron de Gleichen, the Danish ambassador in Paris, something he had learned on this theme from Tanucci himself. Their conversation had been overheard, as Galiani later learned, by a Dane on Gleichen's staff who was a spy in the French pay and who reported it to Choiseul: "The abbé Galiani, secretary to the court of Naples and close confidant of the marquis Tanucci, informed the baron de Gleichen that the King of Naples . . . would *never* accede to the Family Pact."

It was the opportunity Choiseul had been waiting for, and he struck at once. Bypassing Tanucci, he reported the slip directly to his opposite number in Madrid, the Spanish foreign minister, for transmittal to Carlos; and it was Carlos, embarrassed and angry, who ordered Tanucci to send Galiani the order of recall.

Galiani had been expecting news of some kind:

Galiani to Tanucci, Paris, 29 May 1769.
An angry letter concerning myself, couched in very general terms, sent by the duc de Choiseul to [the marquis de] Castromonte [the title recently inherited by the former comte de Cantillana] about two months ago,

caused both my ambassador and myself to fear that about now—considering the length of time it would take for the letter to reach you and for a reply to be received here—we should be hearing further. Neither he nor I, however, expected what has now come.[1]

Since there are two ambassadors here who are fond of me—and who are so to speak my natural judges, able to vouch for my every action—I had imagined myself immune to disaster. I was mistaken: and only death itself could be worse than this blow I have received. If I have deserved it, I comply; if I have not, may God forgive the person responsible—who is certainly not Your Excellency. Though I have had no letters from you concerning this matter, nothing will ever convince me that I have lost your esteem and affection. Such treasures are not lost by one who is innocent. Nor even by one who is guilty, unless the guilt be proven. Nevertheless I shall blindly obey the king's command. . . .

On the day I learned the news, I could eat neither dinner nor supper. That night I had a fever, with violent convulsions. The next day I forced myself to go out, to complete a commission given to me by the prince of Belmonte—I believe, by order of the queen. I am now somewhat better, but still weak: I still do not sleep, and this is my fourth day without appetite. Yesterday I was feverish again, with renewed convulsions during the night. What alarms me most is a numbness in my right side and leg. To make things worse, Dr. Gatti, the only doctor I trust, is away, at Chanteloup.[2] Meanwhile, I have attended to my affairs as best I can. I have sold my horses and carriage and done my packing.

Tomorrow I shall force myself to call on the duc de Choiseul: on learning of my recall he expressed great surprise and regret.[3] After which I shall give more thought to travel plans than to my health. Concerning my health, I shall put my trust solely in God; and, concerning my fate in Naples, solely in Your Excellency. If God chooses to prolong my life, the consolation of once again kissing Your Excellency's hands will be my calm after the storm. If I die, I shall die an unhappy victim of my most constant and faithful devotion to Your Excellency.[4]

As in that letter, so in his next to Tanucci (which would be his last from Paris), Galiani becomes, in his anguish, martyred, hypochondriacal, and self-applauding:

Paris, 3 June 1769. Last Tuesday, even though I was very ill, I went to Versailles. What the duke said to me there consoles me greatly. He spoke very frankly and openly, my ambassador was with me, and later we were joined by the Spanish ambassador. The duke assured me that he had nothing personal against me, and spoke repeatedly of his friendly feelings toward me: I have no cause to feel regret or shame for any of my actions. He promised—and I have no doubt he will keep this promise—to give similar assurances to Your Excellency and to the marchese Grimaldi. He thought it proper that I should take leave of the king; and the ceremony was most handsomely performed and brought me considerable distinction. I have received the greatest expressions of affection and regret from the duchesse de Gramont, from the archbishop of Albi, and indeed from the entire court. None of this surprises me: I have been loved here. I think I may be honored by being presented with the king's portrait, if a way is found to circumvent the rules of etiquette: so far, only one exception has ever been made. . . .

The duke's remarks to me were brief, cut short by his having to welcome Walpole and by his being obliged to set off for Chanteloup directly after dinner. He was anxious that I not depart before his return. Therefore I have stayed. . . .

But now, whatever I may feel, I must leave this land. . . . Along with all joy in living, I have lost every attachment to life. I hope that Your Excellency may obtain His Majesty's consent that my return to Naples not appear unseemly. That I do not deserve. And I hope he may allow me to take up residence in some city in Italy or Provence, where I may complete whatever life might be left to me—a life which destiny has made a sacrifice to my friendship for Your Excellency.

If you wish to honor me with a reply, you may direct the letter to Genoa, where, if God spares my life, it will find me.

Before departing, Galiani asked Dr. Gatti to pay twelve francs a month to a certain Mme de La Daubinière in the rue Saint-Honoré, "the mother of an infant child"; and in mid-June he set off, taking with him a French manservant. In Genoa he found a degree of consolation in the form of a letter signed by Tanucci and headed "The Palace, 27 June 1769," fulfilling the promise made in Naples three years before: his appointment by King Ferdinando, generously made retroactive to that June 1766, as councillor of the Neapolitan Supreme Court of Commerce.

In Paris he had taken leave of his friends. "*Le petit abbé nous a dit adieu*," Diderot wrote to Mlle Volland. Grimm was away, traveling in Germany and Austria. A farewell letter, without date, salutation, or signature, said to have been sent by Galiani to Jean d'Alembert, appears in several French and Italian scholarly volumes:

I have not had the courage to take leave of you in person. It is a terrible thing for an affectionate man to separate himself from his friends and from those he has loved, esteemed and honored—from all who have made my life in France a joy. *Adieu, mon cher ami!* I will write to you, and I hope you will sometimes send news of your well-being and keep me abreast of developments in the sciences, so that I may believe I have not yet completely left this world. Farewell, dear friend: remember me when you are among the charming people I have known: my heart will always retain the sweet and tender memory of so worthy and admirable a friend.

Galiani had left in Paris heart, friends, mistress, and child. He had also left the manuscript of the *Dialogues sur le commerce des blés*, complete except for the last half of the final dialogue: the conclusion would always lack the form he had intended to give it. As he departed, he entrusted the manuscript to an official who was a friend and admirer of all members of the group—Gabriel de Sartine, lieutenant general of the Paris police, a country neighbor of Mme d'Épinay. Sartine was to read it with an eye for possible difficulties with the censor, suggest advisable changes, pass it to Diderot and Mme d'Épinay for a final polishing, and license it for printing. They were all aware that the censor's office was beleaguered by hostile free-traders in high places who had got wind of the book and hoped for its suppression. Of that campaign Sartine could keep them informed. It was agreed that publication would be anonymous.

The abbé had not told his friends what lay behind his departure. That it had been essentially an expulsion was bound to become known; but, for the time being, the innocuous phrasing of the recall, and now the news of his promotion, which he could send from Genoa, were sufficient. Nevertheless, the Parisian friends to whom he wrote from Genoa wondered why he lingered there.

He had what he imagined was good reason. Remaining near the French border, he was cherishing, silently and all but secretly, the illusion that Choiseul, if properly approached, might be induced to relent. To Chanteloup he had sent a letter addressed to the duke in Gatti's care, begging to be recalled to Paris. From June until the beginning of the autumn he waited in Genoa.

In late September he had his answer.

After repeatedly putting him off, Gatti wrote, Choiseul had finally allowed him to present Galiani's petition; and with no hesitation whatever he had given a reply that was brief and brutal: "Monsieur the abbé Galiani is very witty, but he is not quite straightforward, and I do not think he is right for affairs of state." When Gatti persisted, reminding Choiseul of Galiani's love of France, and especially of Paris—"the café of Europe," Galiani had called the spirited city—Choiseul was unmoved. The abbé's offense was unforgivable: the leaking of a state secret to the ambassador of an unfriendly foreign power was a supreme diplomatic crime. And Choiseul closed the conversation by quoting a drastic French saying about what had happened to a man who had talked too much. "*Il s'est noyé dans son crachat*"—"He drowned in his own spittle." No message could have been clearer: in the world of diplomacy, Galiani was a castaway.

Now without hope, he left Genoa and visited friends in Rome. In a letter headed "Naples, 18 November [1769]," he wrote to Mme d'Épinay: "As you see, my travels have ended. I have been graciously received by the king, and that is all I can tell you. I would be deceiving you were I to say what I expect to do in the spring. I shall certainly spend the winter in Naples."

In one of his letters from Genoa, Galiani had begged Mme d'Épinay for news:

> I am well, and there is nothing wrong with me except my grief at being far from you and Paris. That grief weighs on me so heavily that I wonder whether I can bear it. Please encourage everyone to write to me. Would the marquis de Croismare [their friend whom he had portrayed in the *Dialogues* as the "marquis de Roquemaure"] be a good correspondent?

Mme d'Épinay's reply, dated 9 September 1769, had opened with an immediate offer: "You can count on a letter a week from *me*, as long as there are things to say that might interest you." And then:

> The marquis is charming as always. We see each other often, and always speak of you: he regrets your absence even more keenly than I, if that is possible. He came to see me one morning recently, just as I was going over a page of your manuscript. I gave him a book to read while I continued what I was doing. When I had fin-

ished, he asked: "Is that some writing of your own?" "No, marquis, it's not by me"; and it was on the tip of my tongue to add "It's by you." That would have petrified him. I was afraid of being indiscreet, and of his probably questioning me, so I didn't make that little joke. But when the book is published he'll not get off so easily. I'll make him read it aloud, and show him plainly that one of the speakers has exactly his tone, his way of seeing and saying things, and that those passages must originate with him.

As to your inquiry, I do not think, my dear abbé, that the marquis would be a suitable correspondent for you. First of all, he is almost blind: he no longer reads or writes except when absolutely necessary. However, I repeat that it would give me the sweetest satisfaction to accept that commission myself; and you will see that, woman though I am, I know how to keep my word, and am quite capable of demonstrating my affection to absent friends just as faithfully as I do to friends present. I shall have more time to myself when our friend the traveler returns—and he will return at the end of this month. (Why can't one say the same of you, my charming abbé?) Tell me in general what direction you would like our correspondence to take, and you will be served with all the zeal that affectionate friendship can display. A woman of my age [forty-three] can discuss subjects of every kind. Besides, I don't mind what people may say: I shall be writing to my friend, and as long as I am satisfied with what I write, and he is too, all will be well. . . .

Galiani accepted immediately, in a reply that opened with a phrase familiar to all his Parisian friends: " 'Voilà qui est bien, madame.' Write me regularly," he went on, "even if there is nothing to say. I will reply in similar fashion, even when I have no news; and the result will be an interesting correspondence." He added, "I long for news of the *accouchement* and delivery of my posthumous child," and ended with, *"Mille embrassements au grand et au petit philosophe"*—his greetings to the tall Diderot and the smaller Grimm.

It was the beginning of a correspondence between Paris and Naples that was to continue for a dozen years.

PART TWO

THE CORRESPONDENCE

VIII

The Publication of the *Dialogues*

IN PARIS, Sartine delivered Galiani's manuscript of the *Dialogues* to Mme d'Épinay and Diderot, together with discreet and valuable suggestions. Now the two friends set about preparing it for the printer.

At this time, Mme d'Épinay was giving up La Briche, the country house with the ponds that Diderot had preferred to the palatial La Chevrette, and where Grimm had often lived with her. Her son, Louis-Joseph d'Épinay, erstwhile subject of her pessimistic *Letters to My Son*, now twenty-five and holding a nominal degree in law, had been obliged to resign his post with the Parlement of Pau, which had been found for him by M. de Belsunce. Incessant gambling had brought him to disgrace. Several times his parents had paid his debts, and now, united in desperation if in little else, they obtained a *lettre de cachet* (a move perhaps facilitated for them by Sartine), and Louis-Joseph was sent to debtors' prison at Bordeaux. He would remain there two years, receiving severe letters from the father on whose extravagance he had patterned his own and who, in Paris, was continuing to wreak his habitual havoc. These events combined to drive Mme d'Épinay from La Briche, and, at times, to drive her to distraction.

Madame d'Épinay to Galiani, La Briche, 4 November 1769. . . . I think I told you, my dear abbé, that I am giving up La Briche, being forced to that economy by endless delays in the payment of my income. M. d'Épinay has canceled my lease and put the house up for rent. As I write to you I'm busy dispatching the pieces of furniture I don't want to sell.

Ten days ago I was in the large salon, drawing up just such a list. My son-in-law was sitting in one corner of the fireside, his face contorted by toothache, while his wife was in the other, suffering from colic. The abbé [Mayeul, her secretary] stank because he had been out shooting, and our fat little curé was walking about farting, having overeaten. A lady unknown to me was announced, come to see the house. She was a tall, beautiful woman, very elegant, very scatterbrained, the kind of person who looks without seeing and talks of twenty things at once. She finds everything charming, delightful, the garden too, and so on. "Madame," she says to me, "there are fish in the pond? And the furniture? The house is to let furnished, I assume?"

I reply, quite unaware of what I am saying: "No, Madame. The pond is for sale, and the furniture is fished out every third year. . . ."

The following day, Grimm, just returned to Paris from four months in Germany, wrote to Galiani, now the sole missing member of the quartet:

Paris, 5 November 1769.
Cher et charmant abbé: Although I had time, in Germany, to accustom myself to the idea that I would not find you in Paris on my return, I am nevertheless as unhappy as though the news had been unexpected. Paris now seems to me a solitude.[1] You know that we consider

only two men among our acquaintances worthy of being listened to—even if, outside our circle, the rest may be thought veritable eagles. Well, now I find only one: the other has abandoned us. Everybody is desolate, but no one more than I. I'm sure that you must feel somewhat the same way, since it would be impossible not to miss such persons as ourselves; but your feelings are less acute to me than my own longings for your return. Tell me, for God's sake, what our hopes or fears may be, and rest assured that I will forgive you your desertion only if I am convinced that you are happy.

Here, I have not yet had time to know what or where I am. I have been traveling widely; I have met a great number of princes, all of them men of merit. . . . One misfortune I shall never cease to regret is to have been in Vienna while the emperor was in Italy. [Joseph II had been in Naples, visiting his sister and brother-in-law, Maria Carolina and Ferdinando.] I had been misinformed as to the duration of his journey. However, I made a conquest of the prince von Kaunitz, and enjoyed a brilliant success in Berlin and Potsdam. The King of Prussia detained me three days, and each day we conversed for about two hours. It was he who persuaded me to stay an extra day, begging me a second time to do so. As parting gifts he gave me a beautiful snuffbox and a letter of recommendation to his sister, the duchess of Brunswick. I assure you that he could hold his own in any company, and, apart from you and the Philosopher, there is no one I would rather listen to. The hereditary prince of Saxe-Gotha sent you a thousand kind greetings, the prince of Brunswick did not forget you, either, and I spoke a great deal about you with the prince von Kaunitz.

But when will you come here and talk with us? I am reading your book with delight, but your book is not your person. I beg you to let us know what hopes or fears we may have about seeing you. And I strongly advise you, unless you choose to be guilty of gross injustice, to think of me as the most affectionate, and most grief-stricken, of your friends.

Mme d'Épinay to Galiani, Paris, 11 December 1769. . . .
Your book is at last in print. We meet next Thursday —the Philosopher, the Prophet and myself—to read it from beginning to end, to ensure that there are no capital errors, and to prepare the proof for immediate publication. I don't think we'll find anything essentially wrong. Small misprints are inevitable. They will certainly not be the fault of the Philosopher: he went through incredible torments, urging accuracy on the accursed printers. Printers are incorrigibly squalid beasts.

From Naples, which he found so depressingly provincial after Paris, Galiani sent only complaints of boredom and nostalgia: no news—he said he had none to send. "This city, condemned to idleness since the time of Virgil and Horace —*et in otium natem Parthenopem*—will give me as much leisure as I could wish, and still more. Plants become denatured with a change of soil, and I am a Parisian plant." He remembered a few words he once had in Paris with Laurence Sterne: "The only good thing said to me by that boring Mr. Sterne was that one would rather die in Paris than live in Naples." And as he awaited word of the publication of the *Dialogues* he begged Mme d'Épinay to arrange with their friend Jean-Baptiste Suard, editor of the Paris weekly newspaper *La Gazette de Paris*, that the journal be sent to him regularly. She did so; and, knowing him to be thus provided with French public news, she seems for a time to have been uncertain as to how to keep her epistolary promise. Rather timidly, she had told him in a New Year's letter that Diderot had been praising a new translation of Virgil's *Georgics*.

Galiani to Mme d'Épinay, Naples, 20 January 1770. . . .
The subject of the *Georgics* is no longer one for poetry in our age. An agricultural religion would have to be practiced by a farming people, before one could write

grandly about bees, leeks and onions. What can be done with dreary "consubstantiality" and "transsubstantiality"? There are two kinds of religions: those of primitive peoples are lively, being concerned with farming, medicine, athletics and human existence; those of developed peoples are dreary—being nothing but metaphysics, rhetoric, contemplation, elevation of the soul; these inevitably lead to the abandonment of agriculture, to a decrease in population, and to the lowering of general health and the joy of living. We're growing stale.

In this way, somewhat haltingly, the correspondence between Mme d'Épinay and Galiani began.

Suddenly, even before Galiani had written those words about the *Georgics*, his *Dialogues on the Grain Trade* appeared, unannounced, in the bookshops of Paris. Their publication had been abruptly cleared by changes in state policy: Galiani's ideas were given official support, and, to make the moment still sweeter, Choiseul was dismissed.[2] Now Mme d'Épinay did have news to send: the *Dialogues* were selling. They were being commended on all sides, except by the Economists, who attacked them vociferously. Grimm and Diderot were sounding Galiani's praises throughout Europe by means of the Newsletter. The *Dialogues*, Diderot wrote in the January 1770 issue, "recall the Dialogues of Plato, enhanced by the special, dazzling talent of a charming 'humorist,' to use a British term." Elsewhere, Diderot prophesied that Galiani's book, "a model of the dialogue form," would remain beside Pascal's *Provincial Letters* long after the persons and subjects treated by those two men of genius ceased to be of concern.

This good news—and, in due course, a copy of the book itself—reached Galiani in Naples, exceptionally delayed by bad winter roads and high seas.

Galiani to Mme d'Épinay, Naples, 3 February 1770.
I have at last received the book that is causing such an uproar in Paris, and have read it most eagerly, having

almost forgotten its content. *Foi de connaisseur*, it's a good book! . . . I found few changes, but those few make a very great effect. *Un rien pare un homme*. I thank my benefactors. . . . But I beg you to tell everyone—everyone who knows I am the author—the lamentable history of this unfortunate work. As I wrote the last chapter, I was sobbing. . . .

He was not prepared for the praise that poured in. Diderot had sent a copy to Voltaire, not revealing the name of the author; and from Ferney came an immediate and enthusiastic reply: "It's as though Plato and Molière had joined forces to compose this work! . . . No one has ever argued better or more agreeably." Two days later, Voltaire, still ignorant of the author's identity, wrote to the economist Turgot:

> *12 January 1770*. . . . It's the only book of its kind that's lively and delightful. How is that possible, on such a subject? The author has discovered the secret: he makes us read as we read a good play. . . . He doesn't argue. He expresses himself as a man of the world—sometimes, indeed, like a statesman. It's as though Molière had returned from the other world. . . .

But Turgot, a physiocrat, replied that he could praise "only the excellent style" of the *Dialogues*.

On 25 July, D'Alembert, in Paris, wrote to Voltaire:

> Have you read a book entitled *Dialogues sur le commerce des blés*? It's causing great excitement here. In certain respects its tone is inappropriate, yet it seems to me full of wit and good thinking. I only wish that the author wrote less favorably about despotism: I have almost as much aversion as you to despots, from shop clerks to publishers.

D'Alembert, in this letter, did not mention the author's name, which he almost certainly knew—for by now the secret was out.

Voltaire to the comte d'Argenson, Ferney, 24 January 1770.

I have read the abbé Galiani's book. What a witty man! Never did anyone present sober facts so amusingly. It takes a Neapolitan to show us Frenchmen how to deliver truth with a light hand. This man could make even our legislators laugh, but I doubt they're capable of learning from him.

Voltaire also wrote to two ladies about the *Dialogues*.

Voltaire to Mme Necker, 6 February 1770.

I have read the abbé Galiani. No one has ever been so funny about famine. This amusing Neapolitan knows our country very well—knows that it enjoys being entertained even more than being fed. Only the Romans needed *panem et circenses*. We have suppressed the *panem*: for us *circenses* suffice—*l'esprit comique*.

Voltaire to Mme d'Épinay, 6 November 1770.

How can you say that I don't know the abbé Galiani? Haven't I read him? Therefore I have seen him. He and his work are alike as two drops of water, or rather two sparks. Isn't he lively, brisk, full of good sense and humor? I repeat: I have indeed seen him: I could paint his portrait. . . .

There was praise from Duclos, from Mme du Deffand, from Holbach and Helvétius, from Catherine of Russia, from Frederick of Prussia, from German princes who were readers of the Newsletter—from many quarters. Cheered at the outset, Galiani came to find the applause maddening: to be so far from Paris—to be in provincial Naples—while his book was the talk of enlightened Europe, was intolerable. A letter from Mme d'Épinay was intended to console, but did not:

Paris, 2 April 1770.

You would laugh if you could see us when we get one of your letters. As soon as it arrives, I read and reread

it, and then wait for the elect to assemble. They arrive, obviously with the one thing in mind. Grimm says:
"Is there a letter?"
"Yes."
The marquis [de Croismare]: "Is it good and long?"
"No."
"Damn! No matter: let's have it anyway."
If it *is* long, shouts of joy. Who's to read it? Spectacles come out of pockets, and then, whoever reads, there are shouts of Grimmian laughter, exclamations from all about the abbé—he is divine, sublime, glorious . . . in short, having your letters to read is the most splendid present imaginable.

Adieu. Tell yourself how much I love you and you'll not be saying the half of it.

"Here in Naples I'm bored to death!" Galiani wrote to the baron d'Holbach on 7 April. "I'm like Gulliver in the land of the Houyhnhnms, with two horses as his only company"; and in a letter to Suard, he called Naples *"ce petit théâtre héroï-comique."* Torn from his beloved Paris, he could perhaps not be expected, at this time, to "be fair" to Naples, but he was by no means living in a backwater. The city, embellished by Carlo III early in the century, continued to develop under Tanucci's regency. Naples was, furthermore, a goal of artists from the rest of Europe, and a principal halt for foreigners on the Grand Tour. The historian Lucio Villari has written of this Naples in his *Settecento Adieu*:

These years, up to the threshold of the 1780s, are the greatest moments in the history of the Neapolitan Bourbons. Government posts were occupied by Illuminist intellectuals; there were many projects of agricultural, economic, and administrative reform. The culmination was perhaps the experiment of San Leucio, the silk-manufacturing village outside the city. Here conditions were egalitarian and progressive, both socially and culturally—a program supported by intellectuals, by the court, and by the king himself. It was a Rousseauistic idyll that had few counterparts in pre- and post-Revolutionary Europe. Before 1789 it gave rise to many reformatory hopes and illusions, and it bequeathed to the subsequent Bourbonic reign, and to the life and thought of many Neapolitans, an elegance and intelligence that remain supreme today.

Galiani, who had loved Naples in his youth, eventually recovered some of his feeling for the city. But now, chafing in what seemed to him provincial and absurd isolation, he seized on any news that came to him from Paris; and he greeted much of it, whatever its subject might be, as an opportunity to discuss his own book.

> *Mme d'Épinay to Galiani, Paris, 13 April 1770.*
> The rue Royale Sundays, the rue Saint-Denis Thursdays (not mine), and rue de Cléry Fridays have launched a project of erecting, by subscription, a statue to Voltaire, to be placed in the new theatre of the Comédie-Française, now under construction.[3] Pigalle has been given the commission. He asks ten thousand livres and two years. Panurge [the abbé Morellet] took immediate charge of the project, and has drawn up financial arrangements for its execution. The first stipulation is that in order to subscribe one has to be an *homme de lettres* and published; and he has set the terms of subscription at two louis, ten louis, and two thousand livres. D'Alembert will be in charge of soliciting subscriptions and of the money as it comes in, and Panurge insists that subscribers' names and the amounts of their contributions be kept confidential. And, to crown his despotism, he has made a list in which he arbitrarily sets down what each person in the group should pay. So, my dear abbé, if you care to participate tell me your wishes or write direct to d'Alembert. . . .

And in her letter of the following week: "The inscription will read: *À Voltaire de son vivant par les gens de lettres ses compatriotes.*"

Galiani to Mme d'Épinay, Naples, 5 May 1770.
I will subscribe to the statue of Voltaire only on a re-
ciprocal basis: one must be erected to me, in that fine
circular entry of the new Grain Hall. I'd be wonderfully
well off there, among the sacks of flour and all those
Parisian girls who hang about nearby. I would have
everything necessary for my nourishment, and for the
increase of the population as well. . . . I want the figure
to be colossal, to conceal my true size from posterity.
The tutelary genius of France must be shown crowning
me with a wreath of wheat. . . . In a medallion, an Economist will be shown crouching in adoration before the
god of gardens, showing his behind, which the god,
very irritated, will be striking with his venerable instrument as he utters the words *Priapo vindici.* . . . In another
medallion the Economists will be shown crouched before a rustic altar, sacrificing their miserable writings to
Harpocrates, god of silence, sleep and oblivion; and the
god, in gratitude, would be showering them and their
volumes with poppies, over the inscription *Nocte aeter-
nae.* I don't know what the devil I'm saying, but anyway,
consider it a poem written on the spur of the moment,
and show it to Grimm and the baron. . . .

D'Alembert and Mme Necker, as members of the com-
mittee, had written to Ferney about the proposed statue and
inscription, and had the following replies:

Voltaire to D'Alembert, Ferney, 27 April 1770.
There isn't a shred of evidence, my dear Philosopher,
my dear friend, that Voltaire is *vivant*: the inscription
should be *À Voltaire mourant*, for I'm no longer up to
anything, and for the past few days have been feeling
at the end of my rope. In the splendid project you speak
of, I regard myself as your proxy. The intention is to
erect a monument against fanaticism, against persecution. It is to you, it is to Diderot, that the statue should
be erected. I consider myself merely the scaffolding.

Voltaire to Mme Necker, Ferney, 21 May 1770.

My fitting modesty, Madame, and my common sense, made me think at first that the idea of a statue was a good joke; but since the matter is a serious one, let me speak seriously.

I am seventy-six years old, and am barely recovered from a grave illness that wreaked havoc with me, body and soul, for six weeks. M. Pigalle, I am told, is to come and model my face; but, Madame, for that I must *have* a face; whereas my face is in fact difficult to find. My eyes have sunk inward three inches, my cheeks are pieces of old parchment glued to some bones that are themselves attached to nothing. The few teeth that remained to me are now gone. What I am saying is not at all coquetry: it is pure truth. No one has ever sculpted a poor old man in this condition. M. Pigalle would think we were making mock of him; and, for my part, my pride is such that I would never dare appear in his presence. . . .

I remain very philosophical about the matter. But since I am even more grateful than philosophical, I give you over what remains of my body that same power you have over what remains of my soul. Both are in great disorder; but my heart is yours, Madame, as though I were twenty-five, and all three go to you with my very sincere respect. Pray assure M. Necker that I am his humble servant.

The sculptor Jean-Baptiste Pigalle arrived at Ferney early in June. "When the people in my village saw Pigalle wielding some of the instruments of his art," Voltaire wrote to Mme Necker, "they said: 'Look! They're going to dissect him! This will be fun!' "

The Newsletter for 15 July 1770 carried an account of the sculptor's visit:

Phidias Pigalle has made his visit to Ferney and is back, after a week's stay. The day before he was to leave

Ferney he had still accomplished nothing, and had decided to abandon the enterprise and return to Paris with the news of his failure. The patriarch had granted him a daily sitting, but during it he was like a child, unable to remain still an instant. Most of the time he had his secretary beside him and dictated letters while the artist worked; and, as is his habit while dictating, kept puffing out his cheeks and grimacing, making things difficult for the sculptor. Pigalle was in despair, and felt that he must either leave Ferney or fall sick with fever. Finally, on the last day, the conversation turned, by lucky chance, on Aaron's golden calf; and the Patriarch was so delighted when the sculptor told him that such a creation would require at least six months, that for the rest of the sitting the artist was able to do exactly as he pleased, and luckily completed the model to his satisfaction. He was so afraid of spoiling what he had done that he had the mold made at once and left on Friday clandestinely, early in the morning, taking leave of no one.

Pigalle portrayed Voltaire nude except for a bit of drapery; in Paris a desiccated old soldier posed for the body. Only Diderot praised the completed work: everyone else found it displeasing, even macabre. But Pigalle refused to change it, and it was never installed in the theatre of the Comédie-Française.

Voltaire himself was unperturbed about being portrayed nude. "Nude or clothed makes no difference to me," he wrote to a friend. "I'll not inspire the ladies with any improper thoughts, however I'm displayed to them. M. Pigalle must be left absolute master of his statue."

Today there is a bronze cast of the statue in the Louvre, and a preliminary clay model in the Musée des Beaux-Arts at Orléans.

The commissioning of a tribute to Voltaire was not the only event that Galiani made relevant to the *Dialogues*.

During the month of May 1770, Paris and Versailles were constantly *en fête*, celebrating the marriage of the sixteen-year-old dauphin, Louis XV's grandson, and his Austrian princess, Marie Antoinette, a year younger. Mme d'Épinay wrote to the abbé in late April that already "the talk is of nothing but festivities, illuminations, etc." Parisian celebrations culminated on the evening of 30 May with a double fête: a display of fireworks and illuminations in the Place Louis XV and a row of illuminated holiday booths, a kind of fair, set up at the north end of the rue Royale, on the Boulevard (close to the present Place de la Madeleine). The rue Royale, the street connecting the Place Louis XV and the Boulevard, had not yet been completed. It was paved only in the center; and deep ditches, dug to hold sewer pipes but at that moment containing rainwater, were open along both sides, with flimsy protective barriers. The upper reach of the street was at that time narrower than the rest. Although the twin buildings on the north side of the Place, whose terraces had that night been reserved for the elite, and the Place itself were decorated and illuminated, the rue Royale was dim.

Some of the fireworks in the Place went awry; decorations began to blaze; pumps were called for, which had to approach down the rue Royale. Meanwhile, hundreds of spectators, on foot or in coaches—some of these drawn by six or eight horses—had begun to leave the Place and go up the rue Royale in order to visit the fair; at the same time pedestrians and carriages were descending the rue Royale from the fair, to see the illuminated Place. Into these opposing crowds came the fire pumps. Soon the dark and intensely congested rue Royale became a screaming and neighing chaos. Pedestrians were felled by horses and by each other: the barriers along the flooded ditches gave way, and many who were pushed in were drowned, or suffocated by those who fell onto them. It was a scene of horror. Hundreds of corpses were retrieved, and laid out the following day for identification and burial. As Diderot put it in a letter to

Galiani: "All necessary precautions had been taken to make this unheard-of catastrophe inevitable."

Mme d'Épinay to Galiani, Paris, 1 June 1770.

Truly, my dear abbé, I don't know whether I shall be able to write to you, I'm so sick at heart over the disaster that followed the celebrations and fireworks given by the city the day before yesterday. The congestion, the crowd, the confusion were such that more than five hundred persons were killed or injured. All of our friends are well: none was hurt. Up to now the only well-known persons injured are M. d'Argental, with a dislocated arm, but he is better and out of danger; Mme Berthelot, for whom there is little hope, though she is still breathing; and M. de Boulogne, the *fermier-général*, who is in serious condition from being bruised and trampled on. A Russian gentleman whose name I don't know was killed; a businessman from Bordeaux, smothered. As for the people,[4] those who died have been taken away in carts and placed where they can be identified and claimed. Paris looks like the day after a battle. Fortunately all our friends [on the terraces], seeing the confusion begin, remained where they were until midnight.

Galiani to Mme d'Épinay, Naples, 23 June 1770. . . . The Paris disaster and the horrible massacre in the rue Saint-Honoré [near the rue Royale] made me shudder. Poor Mme Berthelot! I accuse the Economists, Madame. They have done so much preaching about property and liberty, they have been so hostile to the police, to order, to regulations, they have talked so much about the beauty of unbridled nature finding its own equilibrium and functioning well, etc., that each person now believes he owns the right of way, feels free to push ahead, and does so. We now see the fine outcome of their interminable preaching. Truly, were I in Paris and had my usual verve, what happened that night would supply me with sufficient answer to the Economists. I would point out that the news need only spread that in a specified place liberty will be unlimited, and that place will consequently become packed with people: upon the word, those monopolists of watches and snuffboxes, the pickpockets, will appear, conspire, and profit from the *bagarre*. What I say is no joke. Think about it, and you'll discover the absolute truth of the comparison. . . .

Galiani had asked that he be sent from Paris all reviews of the *Dialogues*, hostile ones included. In some of the latter, written by Economists and their partisans, he found such distortion and misrepresentation that he asked Sartine, through Mme d'Épinay, about the possibility of prosecution for libel. Sartine advised against that, saying that such a step would only draw attention to the adverse articles, which were for the most part going unnoticed. And Galiani had learned that a high-ranking member of Choiseul's staff, after reading a prepublication copy of the *Dialogues*, had at once ordered the preparation of a refutation, commissioning for the task a ready hack—none other than the abbé Morellet, Galiani's first sponsor in Parisian society. (It was Galiani who had baptized Morellet "Panurge," taking the nickname from the Greek πανοῦργος, "Willing to do anything"—perhaps via Rabelais, who had given that name to Pantagruel's knavish companion.)

Morellet was now in the pay of the government. Grimm reported in the Newsletter for 1 July 1770: "Morellet wrote his reply so madly fast, and with such concentration, that his little finger was quite worn away from being rubbed against his desk." On learning of Morellet's commission, Galiani sent him a brilliant, biting letter—an essay on economics, too long to reproduce here—urging him to become aware of the defects of the party with which he was aligning himself. Morellet nevertheless persisted. However, when Choiseul was removed from office and Galiani's views were officially adopted, publication of Morellet's own book was prohibited; and a pamphlet that Diderot had written in Galiani's defense, now considered unnecessary, remained unpublished. Morellet's book, *Réfutation de l'ouvrage qui a pour titre Dialogues sur le commerce des blés*, finally appeared in 1775, when the line had changed yet again. It found few readers. "Just now I half-opened Morellet's book," Galiani wrote to Mme d'Épinay on 3 June of that year. "I yawned, and it fell from my hands." Nevertheless, the book preoccupied the abbé, and he often referred to it in his letters to Paris.

The empress Catherine of Russia, Diderot's admirer and benefactress, had been presented with a copy of Galiani's *Dialogues* by Grimm, with whom she was now in frequent correspondence; and Grimm encouraged the abbé to send his *hommages* to her in St. Petersburg. A draft of Galiani's letter to the empress that survives in Naples is fragmentary and largely illegible, but its contents can be deduced from messages Catherine sent to the abbé in one of her letters to Grimm.

Catherine II to Grimm [St. Petersburg, n.d.].
Here we are at the foot of Vesuvius—that is, face to face with a letter from the abbé Galiani, who begins by describing you as a facetious, scolding monster. I find it a very bad letter, since it reeks of being addressed to a Very Sacred Majesty. Tell him that the Sacred Majesty has received his letter; that she loves persons of merit with all her heart; that, together with that quality, he is said to be a person of much wit; that she greatly admires his *Dialogues sur le commerce des blés*; that she had never read Horace and will probably never read Horace until the abbé writes a commentary on him, and that we must absolutely have a translation of Horace by the abbé; that my curiosity is already aroused concerning his book on money, that I do not ask him for it but shall make it my business to obtain it as soon as it appears.

Catherine's phrase "as soon as it appears" refers to a French edition of *Della Moneta*. Although there was talk, at the time, of a French translation (by the unabashed Morellet), none would appear for almost two centuries. The *Dialogues*, on the other hand, which were published in St. Petersburg in 1776, had already been translated into German, and, over the years, other German editions were printed.

On 30 June 1770, Galiani replied to a letter from his admirer Gabriel de Sartine, one of those who had read the manuscript of the *Dialogues* with an eye for possible difficulties with the censor. Sartine had come to feel that certain controls of the grain trade were necessary; Galiani, in his reply, reveals a moderation of his own earlier opinion:

> . . . If you interfere *too much* with the distribution of grain in France you will change the form of the constitution and of the government. . . . Now a change of constitution is a very fine thing once it's done, but a very nasty bit of business in the doing. It completely upsets two or three entire generations and benefits only posterity. Posterity is a hypothesis, while we are a reality. Must the actual so inconvenience itself for the hypothetical as to make itself unhappy? So: keep your government and your grain. . . .

"It completely upsets two or three entire generations": Galiani's words were an unknowing prophecy of a time that was approaching more rapidly than he realized: a time he would not live to see or grieve ever.

IX

Madame de La Daubinière

EVEN WHILE Galiani had been lingering in Genoa hoping for favorable news from Choiseul, Dr. Gatti had replied to his request that in his absence from Paris, twelve francs a month be paid to a lady in the rue Saint-Honoré, "the mother of an infant child."

> *Dr. Gatti to Galiani [in Genoa], Paris, 1 August 1769.* . . . I have done as you asked concerning Mme de La Daubinière. I called on her the other day, and will see her from time to time. . . . No need to give yourself the trouble of sending me the small sum I'm to give her each month. You can repay me some day when we meet in Italy.

The story continues:

> *Dr. Gatti to Galiani [in Naples], Paris, 26 February 1770.* . . . More than two months ago I called on La Daubinière and, tempted by the opportunity of the mo-

Dr. Angelo Gatti, by Carmontelle

ment, I became a relative of yours. She thinks she is pregnant as a result. I find that difficult to believe; but, on the chance that she really is and that I am responsible, I have agreed to pay her two and a half louis a month, in addition to your twelve francs, and have promised her something more for her delivery. How much I might say on this theme!

Paris, 6 May 1770. . . . Let's talk about me and my affairs, or rather my misfortunes, all of which may be traced to you. You alone are the cause of my supposed, or actual, paternity with La Daubinière. I called on her to please you; I felt friendly toward her because I saw that she felt that way toward you; once, only once, *io lo mettai*, and now I am becoming a father for the first time after twenty-five years of exercising my generative faculties. You used to laugh about that and make fun of me. But knowing my own weakness I felt both panic and pity when she announced her pregnancy, and decided to give her three louis a month throughout that period and a more considerable sum *pour ses couches*. I have kept and will keep my word; but I have not seen her again, nor shall I until her child has been sent to the foundling home.[1]

But the damage you've done me does not stop there. One morning a fortnight ago, while I was still in bed, there came to see me—I don't remember her name—your girl from the rue de la Verrerie, whom I had not seen since you left, and who now deigned to undress and come into bed with me—because, as she said, I was "a friend of the abbé Galiani." Four days later I found myself with a white discharge, now turned green, which makes me heartily curse the person who was the effective and immediate cause. She had come two days before, and, not finding me, had called on Nicolai [a member of the staff at the Neapolitan embassy], who has since grown thin and pale and drinks great quantities of water but will confess nothing.

Such is my news, my dear abbé, and despite it all I love you more, and miss you more, each day.

Galiani to Mme d'Épinay, Naples, 8 September 1770. . . . I must tell you that from sentiments of humanity, I promised to have twelve livres a month paid to a woman in Paris for the support of her child, begotten and abandoned by an unnatural father. This lady is named Mme de La Daubinière, rue Saint-Honoré, opposite the little hôtel de Noailles. Gatti has been making the payments. Would you be good enough to reimburse him what he has spent, and take charge of continuing to help this person? She will call on you: I recommend her to you very strongly. After you, she is the dearest to me of all persons I left behind in Paris. She does not deserve her unhappy fate, and decidedly merits your protection. Please give her only twelve livres at a time—otherwise she would be tempted to spend it all. . . .

Mme d'Épinay to Galiani, 6 November 1770. . . . I will send a message to the person you recommend, saying that she may come and see me. You may count on me to do, gladly, whatever you wish.

Galiani to Mme d'Épinay, Naples, 8 December 1770. . . . I am plunged into the deepest grief. The person I recommended to you so warmly—the person I loved because she loved me—is, at this very moment of my writing to you, perhaps no more. Only you are in a position to appreciate how this affects me. The rest of the world credits me with more wit than heart, and would to God it were so! But I am in no state to write. If death has spared her, and if she faces a long and painful illness, I recommend her to you as fervently as I can: do for her, on my behalf, what I'd have done were I in Paris. Nicolai will speak to you about her. He has paid her 60 livres, which cover five months. Be good enough to reimburse him. Adieu, *ma belle dame.* Death is a wretched business. I am conscious, these days, of the

*Madame d'Esclavelles playing chess with her
grandchildren's tutor, by Carmontelle*

terrible difference between absence and death. Those ancient philosophers who say that death is of no importance talk drivel, believe me. . . .

Mme d'Épinay had already learned of the lady's desperate condition and, on 18 November, had written the abbé that she knew he, too, had been told:

> I cannot write with any gaiety to you today, *cher ami*. Nothing I might say could alleviate the sorrow that the news of Mme de La Daubinière's sad state must be causing you. The poor woman is very weak: there is little hope. I have sent her various things that she may need: you can be sure that she will want for nothing. I have asked Nicolai to tell me of anything she may require.

On 13 December, Galiani replied: "I hasten to answer you, knowing that tomorrow I may receive sad news that will put me into such a state that I'll be able to do nothing and write to no one." Nor was Mme d'Épinay the only Parisian to whom he revealed his feelings. "My heart is heavy and I am much afflicted," he wrote to Suard, at the *Gazette de Paris*. "The reason is in Paris. Gatti and Mme d'Épinay know what it is, and I do not blush for it."

On 9 December, Mme d'Épinay wrote that she had sent the patient, with beneficial result, "a bottle of calabash syrup from the West Indies," and had offered to visit her; but, at some time during the following fortnight, Mme de La Daubinière died. The exact date is not known, nor the fate of any children who may have survived her.

> *Mme d'Épinay to Galiani, Paris, 20 January 1771.* . . . Nicolai has been ill with pneumonia. He is well now, but because of his illness it was only yesterday that he told me of the death of the poor woman about whom you were so concerned. I assure you that I share your grief, but I shall not write you the commonplaces usually offered on such occasions. It is for time and your friends to console you in your sorrow and to convince you by their friendship and sympathy that all is not lost.

On 19 January, ignorant of the event, Galiani had written: "A thousand thanks for sending the syrup. If the patient is still alive, you could perhaps do her a great service by asking M. de Sartine whether he could have her admitted to the shelter run by the Dames Hospitalières. Nicolai will speak to you about this." Then, on 2 February, having learned the news from Nicolai: "I thought that 'those who are unhappy never die'; but I see that they die like everyone else." And a week later: "My heart tells me not to let my thoughts dwell on Paris. Every day I'm made to realize that I'm more vulnerable than I thought. And I have had another loss, in Genoa. There is no replacing these friends. It would seem that the race of lovable men and women is becoming extinct, as far as I'm concerned."

"How much more loved I am in Paris . . . than in Naples. . . . To be loved is the greatest happiness in life." "The person I loved because she loved me. . . ." These are glimpses of a loneliness that is beyond the power of sociability, or even of genius, to assuage. In a contest of intellect, Galiani could assert his superiority well enough, and among friends, he might amuse and enlighten. But in the realm of close affection and of passion, we cannot doubt that this diminutive man—whose position as a cleric in any case precluded marriage or an overt liaison with a woman of his own circle—yearned and suffered. There is a suggestion, too, that his lively role, his talent to amuse, sometimes seemed paradoxical to a man familiar with solitude and pain: "The rest of the world credits me with more wit than heart, and would to God it were so!"

Anxiety and sorrow had not been the only content of the abbé's letters throughout these months. Nor had Mme d'Épinay written him only of the patient. She herself had been living through difficult days: she was suffering, and would continue to suffer, from *"des accès d'étouffement et de toux alternativement avec des coliques d'entrailles,"* perhaps persistent symptoms of her old marital infection: her husband was still going his own wretched way, and her son was in con-

finement ("One is not a *mère de famille* with impunity: believe
me, abbé, never become a *mère de famille*").

As though by common consent, however, she and Galiani
continued to discourse on other matters. It was a time of
governmental crisis: the Parlement had been disbanded and
absolutist rule confirmed—all of which would bear bitter
fruit eighteen years later. One day she was inspired to send
him what would today be called a feminist manifesto:

Mme d'Épinay to Galiani, Paris, 4 January 1771. . . . I
am a very ignorant woman. My entire upbringing was
directed toward the development of certain agreeable
talents for which I no longer have any use. All that
remains is some slight acquaintance with the arts, and
common sense—a rarity in our day, I agree, but not
worth the trouble of being flaunted. A reputation as *une
femme bel esprit* [a woman of sense and wit] seems to
me mere persiflage invented by men in revenge for our
usually having more attractive minds than they: especially since they usually add another epithet—*une femme
savante* [learned]; and in their opinion the most *savante*
of women does not, and cannot, possess anything beyond very superficial knowledge.

I am suddenly seized by a desire to expatiate pedan-
tically on this. Let's see how it goes. We'll laugh later,
if only about what I'm going to say now. Where was I?
Oh yes—superficial knowledge.

I say that a woman, because she is a woman, is not
in a position to acquire a fund of knowledge sufficient
to make her useful to society: and it seems to me that
the ability to be useful is the only thing one can be
proud of. In order to employ one's knowledge usefully
in any field, one must be able to add practice to
theory—otherwise one is left with very defective no-
tions.

We are excluded from so many things! Everything
that touches on the science of administration, on politics, on commerce, is alien to us and forbidden. With

those matters we cannot and must not have anything to do. And those are almost the only great fields in which men of education and sense can truly be of use to their fellows, to the state, to their country. What remains for us are *belles lettres*, philosophy, the arts.

In *belles lettres*, we are still prevented, by our occupations, our duties, and our frailty, from engaging in any profound and extended study of ancient languages—Greek, Latin, etc. So French, English and Italian literature are our portion.

With philosophy, not having read the ancients, or knowing them only through translations that are usually mediocre or downright inaccurate, we can have but a slender acquaintance; and when we attempt to reason, speculate, etc. we are checked at every step by our ignorance. I speak here neither of metaphysics nor of geometry. Metaphysics is applicable to everything and never useful. I would say the same for geometry. Judge, then, whether we shall conquer the realm of the arts, and to what extent we shall be able to devote ourselves to them.

The mechanical arts cannot as yet be our field. In the congenial arts, I see us still obliged to renounce sculpture and even painting. The impossibility of travel, of seeing the masterpieces of foreign schools, the "decency" that excludes us from studying the human form, everything in our ethos opposes our progress. I feel it pointless to speak of architecture. Thus we are limited to music, dance, and banal versifying. Meager resources, which lead nowhere.

Thus we may conclude that a woman is quite mistaken, and only exposes herself to ridicule, when she sets herself up as a *savante* or a *bel esprit* and hopes to maintain a reputation as such. Yet she is absolutely right to acquire as much knowledge as possible. She is absolutely right, once her duties as mother, daughter and wife have been fulfilled, to devote herself to study and work, because that is a sure means of becoming self-sufficient, of being free and independent, of consoling herself for the injustice of fate and men—and one is never more cherished, more highly valued, by men than when one no longer needs them. However it may be, a woman who with spirit and character acquires some tincture of those things whose deeper study she must renounce will nevertheless be someone very rare, very agreeable, very highly esteemed—on condition that she renounce all ambition.

So! Are you asleep? Wake up! I have finished my harangue. Just be grateful that it hasn't been longer. I have a great deal more to say on this theme.

Galiani responded with a dismissal of "this theme" that sounds like an unconscious confirmation of what his friend had said about the delegation of women, by men, to a sphere of insignificance.

Galiani to Mme d'Épinay, Naples, 2 February 1771. . . . Is it possible that you should amuse yourself with such a discourse on the merit and studies of women at a moment so critical for France? You want to know from me what a woman should study? Her native language, so that she may speak and write correctly; poetry, if she has a taste for it. She must always cultivate her imagination, for the true merit of women and their society lies in their always being more original than men; they are less artificial, less spoiled, more natural, and thus more *aimables*. As regards morality, they must always, and very seriously, study men, and never women. They must study and come to know all the ridiculous aspects of men—never those of women.

Whatever the abbé may have meant by those last words, Mme d'Épinay ignored them, and sent him news of interest to a classicist.

Mme d'Épinay to Galiani, Paris, 25 February 1771. . . . Something quite strange happened recently at Langres [Diderot's birthplace, in Champagne]. To provide a living for the poor, the administrator of the province had obtained eight to ten thousand livres from the government for their employment on public works, and he set them to cleaning and beautifying the public promenade. Men, women and children were busy digging, when one of the women felt her pick strike something hard. She gave a sharper blow, and found that she had broken a large earthenware jar, out of which poured a quantity of small gold coins, the size of a louis, all of them ancient, representing the heads of various emperors and extremely beautiful heads of women. The workers all fell on the treasure and ransacked it. The total value of all the coins has been estimated at 60,000 livres, of which the city has been able to rescue only 3,000, the rest having been made off with. What is remarkable, really most extraordinary, is that the coins are pristine, and seem never to have circulated. There are heads of Nero, Galba, Augustus and Tiberius, as well as those of women. But would you believe it—all the coins recovered by the city, and some of those taken by citizens, have been melted down! We have a few ourselves, and we shall certainly not have them melted. Such barbarism! The abbé Grimod claims that he has never seen anything as beautiful as the two, of Galba and Nero, that have been acquired by M. Diderot. . . . He bought them for the price of the gold. There are endless speculations as to how this treasure happened to be buried at Langres. M. Diderot presumes that it was army money. It could scarcely have belonged to an individual, since all the coins are new. Perhaps they were buried the day before a battle. The general, or the paymaster, was killed, the battle lost, and the treasure left waiting for us. If you come up with any better idea, tell us.

The abbé was not always merciful to his correspondent when her spirits were low. "Why, *belle dame*, have your letters been so depressed of late?" he wrote her at about this time. "It won't be enough for you to admit this: you must repent, and change your style. It's only priests who imagine that it's enough to confess one's sins, without making some effort to correct them." She was quickly ecclesiastical in return shortly thereafter, when Galiani rashly, and quite unjustly, blamed her for the scarcity of mail from Paris. "It's not my fault if others don't write to you: you mustn't try to pick a quarrel with me on that account, or I'll answer you as the nun answered the priest: 'Well, father, if you're not satisfied with me, go and sleep somewhere else.' " Touched when he afforded her unaccustomed glimpses of his heart, as in his letters about Mme de La Daubinière, she sometimes responded with gentle raillery:

> *Paris, 1 March 1771.* . . . I have just had your reply to my number 41. [Because of the irregularity of the post, she had taken to numbering her letters.] There is an undercurrent of sadness and desolation that distresses me. What has given you the idea that there are no longer any lovable creatures on this earth? You have *amis* everywhere, as many as you could wish. As for *amies*—ah! *mon Dieu*, Paris is aswarm with them. Have you given up the idea of coming back to us? Tell me not so, for that would plunge me into the very despondency I've just been preaching against. Let 1771 go by, and come back to us in 1772. Despite what you say about yourself and your teeth [the abbé had been bewailing dental losses], you'll flit from conquest to conquest, and we'll sing you a song:

> > *Il est certains barbons*
> > *Qui sont encore bien bons;*
> > *Ils n'ont pas le caquet*
> > *D'un jeune freluquet;*
> > *Ils ont je ne sais quoi*
> > *Qui vaut mieux, selon moi.*

> Those words are from a comic opera by Grétry,[2] and are very moral. It's the slogan of the day. Nobody is singing anything else. Come, and we'll sing it to you. . . .

By the time he answered her next letter, written on 8 March 1771, in which she complained of insufferably high taxes imposed by the new comptroller general, Terray—her income, she says, might be reduced to a hundred écus; she might have to give up her house—it was Galiani who was in a position to console, and in his manner of doing so, he sounds more like his usual self.

Naples, 6 April 1771.
Your letter of 8 March leaves me shattered. What! You may be reduced to poverty! A hundred écus! Not a penny more? No: the only risk you run is that of perhaps having to move to Naples. Do you have enough to pay for the trip? Perhaps by selling a few sticks of furniture? I speak seriously: I'm not joking. Come, just come, and don't worry about the rest.[3] Do you know, truly, I begin to like the idea. . . . Buy a carriage—you, Grimm, Schomberg[4] and Diderot: in another, your maid, a valet, and two other servants. Set off, arrive; you'll send back two of the four, the choice being yours, or theirs. It seems to me that Grimm is an asset anywhere. He'll continue sending news north, using exclusively material provided by you and me. How marvelous it would be, I and the abbé Terray bringing Paris to Naples! Such are my dreams. Still, your letter saddens me. . . .

Adieu, my poor pauper. These days I have no time for anything. I was busy all last week introducing Naples to auctions, so familiar in Paris but unknown here. They've been a marvelous success. People paid crazy prices for the stock of a big merchant gone bankrupt, whose formal petition will have the honor of being heard by me. I'm the magistrate in the case. I've done my country quite an important service in this matter, eradicating a number of abuses. Good night: until next week.

In her reply of 25 April, after telling him that he would soon be receiving a copy of the *Gazette de Paris* containing a splendid article Diderot had written about him, and that a charming and distinguished gentleman introduced to her by the abbé—the chevalier de Magallon, secretary of the Spanish embassy, a Knight of Malta—had taken a place in her twice-weekly box at the Opéra, and that her daughter had been presented at court, Mme d'Épinay adds:

> Our dear marquis [de Croismare] has appeared in a two-act comedy that would make you die of laughter. It's like him—which says everything. The good man had a severe onset of hemorrhoids last week, and was ordered to bathe his behind in milk. If you could have seen the trouble he had getting into the milk! There was never anything like it. First he filled the biggest earthenware crock he could find, and settled himself therein. He was wearing an elegant new redingote. Suddenly the crock broke, and the marquis was inundated. He didn't give up. He took his barber's basin and filled that with milk; but he miscalculated the space needed to accommodate his behind; the milk flew up, splashing everything, including his face and his nightcap—everything except his rear. He says that such things happen only to him. And I well believe it.

The abbé replied on 18 May:

> Verily, *ma belle dame*, if your letter, which should have gone by special courier and which came, it would seem, by ordinary post—if your letter had been opened, both of us would have been sent to the Bastille. Who the devil would imagine that, with things as they are in France, you would take the occasion to send me a long story about the posterior of our charming marquis who wanted to make *c--- au lait* ices—that you would send it simply as a story, without a hidden meaning? If I were an inquisitorial censor, I'd be sure that the marquis's *c---* signifies Parlement, that the hemorrhoids mean the *remboursement des charges*, that a redingote clearly refers to a Prince of the Blood.

Monsieur and Mademoiselle de Croismare, by Carmontelle

A dozen more hidden meanings were adduced by the abbé as he pretended to think the letter was in cipher. At such moments, Galiani recaptured what one of his modern admirers calls his *"arte segreta di rendere seria la frivolezza"*— his secret art of making frivolity serious.[5] It was an art he shared with Swift and with Voltaire.

During that summer of 1771, Mme d'Épinay and Grimm visited friends at Le Bourgneuf, exchanging "the din of Paris for the sound of nightingales and warblers," as she put it, in Horatian mood, in her letter of 28 June to Galiani. They had with them the volumes of Voltaire's *Dictionnaire philosophique*, and to the abbé Mme d'Épinay sent a summary of the article on Cicero, along with a request: "If you happen to find a really excellent melon, send me the seeds." Then, on 4 July, she wrote to him:

From here I can send you only local news. If it isn't as interesting as the Parisian variety—of which I never speak to you: it's too sad—at least it's funnier. Besides, in my humble opinion it conveys a moral: let's see what you think.

There is a police commissioner here who is crazy about the police in the same way that we in Paris are crazy about Grétry's music—or about redingotes, if you recall the significance you attributed to that garment in the story about our charming marquis's behind. In any case, this commissioner was charged with enforcing an order, issued by the local magistrate, that all cafés must close at 10 p.m.; should they be found open later, all customers and the owner would be fined six livres. A week ago, said commissioner's barber—he is the magistrate's also—and his helpers, all of them dying of thirst at 11 p.m., ordered a bottle of beer from the owner of a café across the street. They went in and sat down. Their bottle had just been opened when in the distance they saw the commissioner and the constable coming their way. In a panic, they ran down into the cellar with their bottles, forgetting to blow out their candle. The commissioner, coming along the other side of the street, caught sight of them through an open basement window, and stood listening to them joking about their cleverness in avoiding him. Then he suddenly plunged through the window, followed by his constables, the three of them falling like so many bombs into the midst of the barber's party. The latter, recovering from their surprise, rushed up a narrow stair leading from the café basement into the shop of a woman dealing in soft cheeses. Unfortunately, she had left a considerable assortment of these on the stairs to drain overnight. That didn't stop the fugitives. They rushed straight through the cheeses, falling and getting up again; the commissioner followed, stumbling, catching his feet in his long gown, smearing himself from head to foot with cheese. They all found themselves together up in the cheese shop, looking like freaks and laughing like lunatics. They gave each other a friendly wiping-off. The commissioner didn't lose his head, however: he thanked them for cleaning his gown but summoned them to appear in police court and pay the fine. In court, the owner of the shop wanted the commissioner himself held responsible for ruining her cheeses, but it was the poor barber who was made to pay for everything, even promising the magistrate to give him a particularly good curl the next time he had the honor of serving him.

You'll admit, I think, that during the past year Paris hasn't come up with anything as agreeable as this little episode.

It was during these summer weeks in the country, when she sent Galiani, in quick succession, her summary of Voltaire's "Cicéron" and the saga of the trampled cheese, that Mme d'Épinay perfected her role as the abbé's correspondent. As a francophile, he relished the Bourgneuf slapstick, and as a classicist, he delighted her and Grimm, and no doubt their hosts as well, by listing, in the form of a dissertation at once lighthearted and authoritative, works by six seventeenth- and eighteenth-century Latinists whom Voltaire had unquestionably pillaged for his "Cicéron." And shortly thereafter, when Mme d'Épinay spurred him again, sending this time a passage from the article "Curiosité," he responded with equal verve: "I admit that Voltaire's piece on curiosity is superb, sublime, new and true. I admit that he is right about everything, except that . . ." And here again followed lighthearted erudition—the erudition of the monologues that friends had listened to beside the baron d'Holbach's fire, the monologues that Diderot had said enabled him to "forget life's displeasures."

Although he felt free to complain to Mme d'Épinay about the high postage sometimes due on her letters (she was not always able to use a diplomatic pouch), Galiani just as frequently thanked her for helping to combat his boredom and frustration. The same Neapolitan officials who had rewarded him for introducing auctions were now rejecting, one after another, his further suggestions for stimulating the city's affairs. The nostalgia for Paris never waned. "All but eight of my teeth have gone—my worst loss since losing Paris"; "Thank you for the antiscorbutic wine you sent. If you have an antiboredom wine, send it to me at once"; *"Je suis au milieu d'une nation endormie"*; *"Ah, Madame, quel affreux désert que cinq cent mille Napolitains!"*

The correspondence of these two, between whom there was no amatory bond, is nevertheless essentially the exchange between woman and man. From that foundation it derives its flavor, its pungency and poignancy, its freedom and surprise; its brief antagonisms, and its best humanity.

X

The Prodigal's Return, and
Stories Exchanged

IN AUGUST 1771, Grimm traveled to London, leaving
the composition of the Newsletter to his new assistant,
Jacques-Henri Meister, a young Swiss from Zurich, and to
Diderot and Mme d'Épinay.

Mme d'Épinay to Galiani, Paris, 14 September 1771. . . .
You ask me with whom M. Grimm is traveling—I
thought I had told you. He is with [Prince Ludwig] the
son of the landgrave of [Hesse-]Darmstadt. After London, the young man must see only France and Italy, to
complete his travels. Having already toured Germany
and Holland, he is now in England, where our friend
has gone to join him: they return to France in November. They will tour this country, and go on to Italy in
February. That is their plan. Mine, as always, is to be
as useful to M. Grimm as possible. Otherwise, I think
I would lose my courage completely. . . . I am beset by
difficulties, and others loom. I know that you feel for

me, abbé, and can put yourself in my place. Comfort me, I beg you, as best you can. . . .

Why Grimm's absence at this moment was undermining Mme d'Épinay's courage, while a particular event threatened her peace, she made clear in a letter to Galiani of the following week. Her scapegrace son, whom she had not seen for over two years, was about to be released from confinement at Bordeaux. Many months before, she had written to Galiani: "The family wants my son officially declared incompetent. I shall not oppose that, but it breaks my heart to discuss it." Galiani replied on 19 January:

> *Ma belle dame*: I pity you, I grieve for you, and I long to console you and advise you: and yet I am sure that you stand in no such need.
>
> What diabolical madness persuaded you to have children by M. d'Épinay? Didn't you know that children take after their fathers? You saw that M. d'Épinay was a wastrel. You should have had children by my ambassador, the marquis de Castromonte, who was in Paris at the time you conceived your son; he would have put your family affairs in order. [Castromonte's miserliness was legendary.] Were you ever so deluded as to believe Rousseau and his *Émile*? To believe that upbringing, maxims, preaching, had anything to do with the formation of minds? If you believe that, take a wolf and make a dog of him, if you can. . . . I have never been a mother, but I have perhaps been a father a couple of times, and I know that such procedures have no effect whatever.

She replied that his view was quite right, that his letter had made her laugh, and that she would dwell no more on the matter were it not for the thousand "*vilains petits détails minutieux*" that the situation obliged her to attend to.

Louis-Joseph had not, after all, been declared incompetent; and now, in the autumn, he returned from Bordeaux.

Mme d'Épinay to Galiani, Paris, 21 September 1771. . . .
Mon ami, I am not myself. My son arrives today. You
can imagine the state of my feelings, and how impossible
it is to control them. I need all my strength and all my
courage. . . . *Bonsoir, mon ami.* Ah, what a day for me!
How my heart is throbbing!

Galiani to Mme d'Épinay, Naples, 26 October 1771.
No letter from you this week. I have been waiting
impatiently for one, to learn about the arrival of your
son—or, to put it more accurately, M. d'Épinay's
son. . . .

Galiani to Mme d'Épinay, Naples, 2 November 1771.
I have received two charming letters from you. . . . I
was wildly impatient to learn the details of your reunion
with M. d'Épinay's son. You don't say a word about
him. One would think you hadn't seen him. . . .

Mme d'Épinay to Galiani, Paris, 9 November 1771. . . .
You're surprised that I should have written you quite a
long letter on the very day of my son's arrival. In fact,
I had far more leisure then than now, when I'm having
to move heaven and earth to make a captain of him.
And for an invalid like me to move heaven and earth
isn't exactly easy. Fortunately, our friend [Grimm] arrives about the 20th, and during the three weeks he'll
be here I'll see that he bestirs himself for me—rallies all
his lady friends—marquises, princesses, etc. . . .

*Mme de Belsunce to Galiani, Paris, Friday, 22 November
1771.*
My mother, who—with all deference to you—says
that I am very definitely her daughter as well as my
father's, asks me to explain that she cannot write to you
herself, being still too weak from her recent attack. She
says that this world is not to her liking, and that anyone
who would remove her from it would be doing her a
great service. But I can assure you that she clings to it

more firmly than she realizes, because—for all her de-
termination, before my brother's return, not to be
upset—she said she was quite sure of herself—Ah! *mon
Dieu*, if you had been there to see that meeting, monsieur l'abbé—. . . . The sound of the coachman's whip,
which she heard a good hour before the coach was anywhere near! She felt ill, and thought she would faint.
And indeed if it hadn't been for that false alarm, a blessing in disguise, I think she would have been in a desperate state. She feels things so keenly! She is so very
much a mother! She is so loving! But all ended happily.
Tears were the language we spoke, and many were
shed—the evening was half gay, half solemn—there is
so much to say at such a time. Our travelers [Louis-
Joseph had apparently been escorted from prison by his
old tutor, Linant] and I stayed up alone with *maman*.
What happened then? Again she felt ill—I was terrified,
but only briefly—she revived, and I was reassured. Now
we are making a musketeer of him—and what will become of him after that? Perhaps he will die a general—
he has a vocation. May God preserve him from misfortune! In any case, it is splendid to die for king and
country—an honorable death, preferable to any other.
But these are fine sentiments to have in peacetime! . . .

Galiani to Mme de Belsunce, Naples, 4 January 1772.
. . . So you are turning the ex-lawyer into a musketeer.
But for heaven's sake, why not let him be simply M.
d'Épinay? It's the rage in France to "make something"
of one's children. Here they are made simply their father's heirs, and it's my belief that that's the best thing
one can do for them. . . . There's no business about their
"occupying an honorable post," or sleeping their last
sleep on some stately catafalque. Here we sit on chairs,
and sleep in our beds.

Nothing could be more normal than a mother's violent
feelings as she awaits her son's return from more than two
years' detention—a detention that she herself had helped to

La Vicomtesse de Belsunce, by Carmontelle

bring about. Then, having had him with her for two months, she is again prostrated. No details are known. She casts about to find him a regimental post. And the young man's sister, with them in the house, declares: "It is splendid to die for king and country." Galiani, with his reiterated "M. d'Épinay's son," recalls old difficulties and foresees new ones.

New ones were not long in coming. As early as 19 December, three months after her son's return, Mme d'Épinay was writing to Galiani: "I have just learned that Grimm will again delay his return by several weeks. Just when I have greatest need of my friends!" And during the following February, six months after his release from prison, young d'Épinay fought a duel. His adversary's name is not known. His mother assured the abbé that the circumstances were "honorable," but: "The moment of crisis was the cruelest that I have lived through in my entire life."

That is all we know about the young man's first months at home. His mother's relief, her anguish, and perhaps a longing for escape are evident in the mistaken heading, and in the content, of her next letter to the abbé:

> *Naples* [*sic*], *16 May 1772*. . . . I have just obtained a place for my son in M. de Schomberg's regiment. My friend does me a great service in accepting him, and I am very grateful. . . . Abbé, do come here and live with us—I will shelter and nurture you. . . . Oh, such fantasies!

On 20 June, she announces her son's departure for Schomberg's regiment of dragoons, at Nancy. A month later, he has already run up new debts: "*Mon malheureux fils me désole et ruine*. Now I think he really will have to be declared incompetent, and sent to the islands." (Martinique, Guadaloupe, and other parts of the West Indies were then a repository of profligate young Frenchmen.) For a time she finds solace in the house that her daughter and son-in-law have rented for the summer at Boulogne-sur-Seine, then a hamlet outside Paris: "Oh, abbé, how delicious everything is here, the Bois de Boulogne, the Bois de Saint-Cloud! Why aren't you here to stroll with us?"

Galiani to Mme d'Épinay, Naples, 22 August 1772.
I am desperately sorry about the wretched time your son is giving you. But since he is more M. d'Épinay's son than yours, it's up to his father, I think, to look out for him. . . .

But his father had washed his hands of Louis-Joseph—indeed, it seems likely that he was among those proposing that the young man be declared incompetent.

With the passage of a year, the comte de Schomberg, friend and admirer of Mme d'Épinay though he was, could no longer tolerate her son's presence among his men.

Mme d'Épinay to Galiani, Paris, 13 September 1773. . . .
My son has left his regiment. The debts that he contracted and I have been unable to pay, and a personal quarrel with one of his fellow officers, have obliged him to resign. . . .

More precisely, Louis-Joseph's new debts had sent him to prison again—this time at Nancy. In October, by paying his creditors part of what they were owed, his mother obtained his release. It was the end of all thought of a military career. The "ex-lawyer," as Galiani had called him—who was now, at twenty-seven, an ex-musketeer into the bargain—was not "sent to the islands." That November, he was sent to less distant exile, to Berne; and there he disappears for a time from our story.

On 28 December 1771, Mme d'Épinay wrote to Galiani of the death of their good friend Helvétius from "*un accès de goutte remontée dans la tête.*" "All his friends are inconsolable, and have good reason to be so," she wrote. "Only he is happy."

Galiani's reply was philosophical, with classical echoes:

Naples, 25 January 1772.
Ma belle dame, if it served any purpose to weep for the

dead, I would mourn with you the death of our Helvétius; but death is only the grief felt by the living. If we do not grieve for him, he is not dead; just as, if we had never known and loved him, he would scarcely have existed. Everything that is, exists within ourselves—in relation to ourselves. For us, Helvétius's death is the gap he leaves in the ranks of the battalion. Let us love one another the more, we who remain, in compensation. As major of the unhappy regiment, I order you all: "Close ranks!—Forward, march!—Fire! Let us give no indication of our loss."

During the spring of 1772, Galiani, beset by a series of bureaucratic annoyances at work, discovered a source of consolation at home.

Naples, 21 March 1772. . . . As a distraction, I am rearing two cats and studying their habits—a completely new field of scientific observation, I find. Cats have been bred for centuries, and yet no one seems to have studied them thoroughly. Mine are a male and a female; I have isolated them from other cats in the neighborhood, and have been watching them closely. Would you believe it—during the months of their *amours* they haven't miaowed once: thus one learns that miaowing isn't their love language, but rather a signal to the absent. Another incontestable discovery: the language of the male is entirely different from that of the female. In birds, this difference is more marked; I don't know that it has ever been noted in quadrupeds. Furthermore, I am sure that there are more than twenty different inflections in cat language: it is indeed a true language—they always make the same sound to express the same thing. I would never end were I to tell you all my observations; but even these samples must certainly convince you that I'm up to scratch in matters of Neapolitan felinity. . . .[1]

Naples, 30 May 1772. . . . At present I am working on a history of cats. I have made several discoveries. Polygamy has of course been permitted in the cat kingdom from time immemorial; mating is excluded during pregnancy, but not during lactation—which to me confirms that there is nothing sinful in sleeping with a wet nurse, despite the opinions of Jamburin, Amorin, and Sanchez, all of them Jesuits, who assert the opposite. And lastly I discover that the gallantry of male cats and their homage to their ladies takes the form of giving them precedence—of saying, so to speak, "after you," and letting them pass ahead: in such a way that from time to time the gentleman's nose is given a soft brush by the lady's tail. Whence I conclude that we, instead of giving our arm to ladies, should . . . After which they, like their feline counterparts, should turn around and puff gently into our faces. From now on I intend to pay my court to ladies exclusively in this manner. Please be prepared for this when I return to Paris. . . .

The following summer there was another death disturbing to Mme d'Épinay—that of the friend who had been Galiani's model for the "marquis de Roquemaure" in the *Dialogues*.

Mme d'Épinay to Galiani, Paris, 10 August 1772.
You had no news from me last week, my dear abbé: I was too full of grief to write. We have lost the poor marquis de Croismare, suddenly, and through his own folly. He had the mad idea, despite our warnings, of having his new quarters painted, and of remaining in them while the work was being done. He fell down dead after spending a quarter of an hour with the painters. It is a terrible loss for me, and for all of us. The idea of "nevermore" repels me: I cannot accustom myself to it.

Galiani to Mme d'Épinay, Naples, 5 September 1772.
Your letter containing the news about our dear marquis was delayed in reaching me. Don't be surprised that it didn't touch me nearly as deeply as I'd have expected. That this should be the case astonished me—all but horrified me—and I determined to look more deeply

into the matter. Now I have come to see that my reaction is not due to our long absence from one another, nor to any hardening of my feelings. But one's attachment to the lives of others varies with the degree of one's attachment to one's own life; and to one's own life one is attached only in proportion to the pleasure it affords. I now understand why peasants die tranquilly and are unmoved by the deaths of others. Therefore, if you have shed more tears than I, it is unquestionably an indication that, despite your griefs and your other troubles, your life in Paris is less arid than mine in Naples, where I feel attached to nothing except my two cats. One of them disappeared yesterday, owing to the negligence of my servants. I was furious, and discharged them all. Happily, it turned up again this morning: otherwise I'd have hanged myself in despair.

And Galiani added still another doubtful consolation to his friend amid her troubles: "Such is my state of mind. In your opinion, which is preferable—anguish, or apathy?"

Mme d'Épinay sometimes apologized to the abbé for the melancholy tone of her letters, saying that they were "fit only to be used as hair curlers." Even so, throughout her troubles she continued to entertain him with stories of life in France. One of these concerned a *dindon*, a turkey, that escaped from the arms of a Harlequin performing in a farce at Besançon. The turkey, perched on the edge of a box occupied by members of the hated new Parlement, caused the delighted audience to break into a popular sentimental ditty—

> *Où peut-on être mieux*
> *Qu'au sein de sa famille?*

—*dindon*, in French slang, meaning "idiot," and the song itself suggesting that the turkey had now found his true home. A grim echo of this refrain is recorded in the memoirs of Galiani's friend the baron de Gleichen. On 17 July 1789, four days after the fall of the Bastille, Louis XVI, passing in his carriage through applauding crowds in the Place Louis

XV on his way to a meeting of the Estates General, heard a burst of music. A young man called excitedly through the window: "Sire, they're about to play '*Où peut-on être mieux qu'au sein de sa famille*'!" indicating the crowd's warm reception of the king as their paterfamilias. The king was heard to murmur, "God, what a family!" (Three and a half years later, the same square was the scene of his execution.)

Another story, of a kind Mme d'Épinay knew the abbé particularly enjoyed, dealt with a visit paid by one of his friends, a member of the Spanish embassy in Paris, to the renowned explorer and astronomer Claude-Marie de La Condamine, now a deaf septuagenarian:

Paris, 2 May 1772. . . . I'm going to tell you what happened to the chevalier de Magallon the other day. Paying a morning call on La Condamine, he found him in a dressing gown beside his fire. Nearby, on a stand, was what looked like a small chest. His servant announced the chevalier and closed the door after him. La Condamine started to rise, putting his weight on the little chest. It gave way; he fell with it; and there they were, he and the chest, he crying out "*ai, ai*, a mop, a mop!" The chevalier, not having seen what had happened, thought the old man was dying. Speech seemed to him of no avail: he was terrified and rang for aid. Then he saw that the chest was the poor old invalid's commode. It had opened as it fell, and its owner was floundering in all it had contained. The chevalier was convulsed by a mixture of helpless laughter and nausea. When the servant appeared, both men were shouting "A mop, a mop!" Then, after first aid had been administered, they wanted to talk, and looked for the old man's ear trumpet. It was found in the midst of the mêlée, no more presentable than its owner. It was wiped off, but the chevalier thought it advisable to give the persistently aromatic effluvia time to evaporate before it was put to use. He said farewell by signs, and is still running.

Mme d'Épinay was perhaps unaware that some years before, La Condamine had been the subject of a remark by Horace Walpole, whom she had met during one of his visits to Paris.

Horace Walpole to Horace Mann, 5 June 1763. . . . [La Condamine] lodged in Suffolk Street: his servant's bawling to him disturbed the other lodgers: the landlady sent two men as bailiffs to turn him out. On this, he printed in the public newspapers a letter to the people of England, telling them that he had travelled in the most barbarous countries, and never met with such savages as we are—pretty near the truth, and yet I would never have abused the Iroquois to their faces in one of their own gazettes.

Grimm returned in the spring of 1772 from his trip to England with the son of the landgrave—"more French in spirit, and more German in accent, than ever," as Mme d'Épinay put it. After a fortnight in Paris, during which he saw to it that the young heir took dancing lessons and was entertained by Diderot, the Holbachs, Mme Geoffrin, and Mme Necker, Grimm escorted him back to Germany. The empress Catherine, who had her own opinions of German princelings, dubbed Grimm "M. le Souffre-Douleur" ("the Willing Victim") or "Son Excellence Souffre-Douleurienne"—"never happier than when he is near, close to, beside, in front of, or just behind, some German Highness." Now Grimm received his reward for that assiduity. "Do you know," Mme d'Épinay wrote to Galiani on 11 April, "that the Emperor [Joseph II] has sent him a sheaf of diplomas that make him a baron of the Holy Empire? He is very shamefaced about it. I have never seen a baron more embarrassed about his barony—or, to put it better, his titles, since the baronies themselves are mere wishful thinking."[2]

Soon thereafter Grimm fell ill—so dangerously ill, of an *étranglement des intestins,* that even Dr. Tronchin was grave. Mme d'Épinay sent frightened letters; and Galiani himself, until reassuring news reached him, was "in torment." "That *chaise de paille*"—Grimm's rush-bottomed work chair—"is killing him," he wrote on 27 June, after the crisis had passed.

> When one keeps one's behind pressed to a hard surface day after day, how can one hope to evacuate sufficiently? For heaven's sake, have him cleared out well, and then do for him what one does for children—open his underpants at the back and tell him to run around the streets. He can say that it's the ceremonial custom of German barons who have no baronies, and whose feudal income from the lands of the Holy Empire doesn't cover the cost of proper underwear.

(Galiani frequently referred to Grimm himself as *"la chaise de paille,"* substituting, on occasion, a classical equivalent: παλαιοηαθέδρα.)

> *Mme d'Épinay to Galiani, Boulogne-sur-Seine, 18 July 1772.*
> Oh, most charming of abbés! Your letter of 27 June is divine. It touched me to tears, and poor Grimm as well, and made us laugh like mad—it was the only moment of levity I've had for two months. Grimm says that you guessed correctly, that all his trouble comes from not having open underpants. And he sends you a thousand affectionate greetings. We badly needed that divine letter, he and I.

Grimm's recovery was slow. He fell into such a depression, such a state of what seemed to be general indifference, that Mme d'Épinay feared for him and for their future together. Then, as he slowly recovered, she spoke to him "hesitantly, but from the heart." She was reassured by his response; but there remained something she could not fathom. Only later did she learn that he had been torn between his attachment to her, Diderot, and his duties for the Newsletter, and an offer that had come from Germany: a permanent post at one of the princely courts. Although he chose, ultimately, not to accept that offer, he would soon accept another of the same kind.

To Diderot, Galiani sent, about this time, a new lament about life in Naples:

> Here I no longer have the time or the desire to read anything. When you're alone, with no one to talk to or to argue with or show off to—nobody you can make listen to you—reading is impossible. For me, Europe is dead. I've been put into the Bastille. I now belong to the vegetable species.

Galiani and Diderot continued to correspond. On one occasion, the abbé, appealed to as a Latinist, discussed with the Philosopher the probable meaning of Horace's Ode on the destiny of Rome:

> *Delicte, majorum immeritus lues,*
> *Romane, donec, etc.* [Book 3.6]

—lines which, Galiani readily confessed, he too had never been sure he understood.

Meanwhile, Mme d'Épinay had been enjoying music of a kind she particularly loved, provided by a charming recent acquaintance, the marchese Alvise Mocenigo, the Venetian ambassador to Paris. Now he had been recalled.

> *Paris, 30 November 1772.* . . . The chevalier de Mocenigo told me on his departure that he will reach Venice only at the end of February. So be patient about the letter I have given him for you. It contains nothing of importance.
>
> I have never enjoyed music as much as during the six months I have known him. I don't know whether you've ever heard him sing, but, since Caffarelli, I had never heard anything so perfect. I've had much enjoyment from this, because not a week has gone by without my having two or three musical sessions with him, each of them lasting four hours. Before he left, he gave a supper

ds and me. It was a swan song: he sang like
᾽ miss him. From the time we first met he
tive to me, doing whatever I might ask.
᾽ Mora and the chevalier found this com-
..u made all kinds of feeble jokes about it—you
are certainly not ignorant of the tastes the ambassador
displayed here in France. My reply to all that was "*Tanto
meglio!*" Nothing equals the friendly companionship afforded to a woman by men of those persuasions. To the
rest of you, so full of yourselves, one can't say a word
that you don't take as provocation. If you think we're
being the least flirtatious we must take care in our responses: we must pretend not to believe a word you
say, or it's all up with us and we run the risk of finding
ourselves compromised without knowing how or why.
Whereas with those gentlemen one knows quite well
that they want no more of us than we of them—one
feels in no danger, and deliciously free. They find us
pleasing, they say so, we reply "I'm glad, because I find
you charming," they make us a bow, and things go no
further. Were I to be young again, they are the only
men I'd care to see—no question about it. Meanwhile,
I couldn't miss my ambassador more.

Galiani to Mme d'Épinay, Naples, 12 December 1772. . . .
You are right to love the chevalier de Mocenigo. I remember Mlle Clairon having similar feelings for the duc
de Villars, and I realized at the time that such men, with
their attentions and courtesy, make continual apology
to women for the wrong they do them in their imagination. Perhaps, too, they regret not being women
themselves to the degree they would like, and admire
you as texts of which they are mere annotators. Thus,
you have been a Tacitus, a Suetonius, of whom Mocenigo was the Casaubon.[3]

In January 1773, the renowned French actor and director
Jean Aufresne brought his company of players to Naples. In
Paris, Aufresne had broken with the Comédie-Française

some years before; he had taught French *déclamation* to the sixteen-year-old Marie Antoinette when he was with his troupe in Vienna; and now, to Galiani's delight, he opened a Neapolitan season with Diderot's comedy *Le Père de famille*.[4]

> *Galiani to Mme d'Épinay, Naples, 15 January 1773*. . . .
> Tell this to Diderot: tell him that my Neapolitans are convinced that his is the best of all French plays, and consequently the finest drama produced by the human mind. They do find the father a little too indulgent with his children. Italian fathers are far more severe than French fathers, and perhaps M. d'Orbesson is somewhat weak even for a French parent. You'll never guess the secret reason for the inexpressible pleasure Italians take in this play. It's the role of the Commander. He is a character uncommon in France, but frequently met in Italy, where there is even a term for him that is lacking in French. He precisely fits our designation *seccatore*. A *seccatore*, you see, isn't a bore, exactly, or a bad man, or a fool. He is a man who has a mentality that is "different," a certain kind of good sense that others find repellent, a man who is gruff, severe, tactless, who doesn't "fit in." So, in order to correct the poverty of the French language, when you meet up with a *seccatore* (and they do exist in France), just call him "Commander," and that will take care of him.

Galiani continued in his next few letters to report, as one drama critic to another, on Aufresne's Neapolitan repertory, which included plays by Molière, Marivaux, Goldoni, Beaumarchais, and Voltaire. When Voltaire's *Mahomet*, with its attack on religious intolerance, was forbidden by the Neapolitan censor (as it had been banned in Paris a generation before), the troupe presented several other Voltairean dramas, one of them *Zaïre*, a love story laid in ancient Peru. *Zaïre* was very successful, Galiani reported, "except that the Neapolitans found it rather pious": certainly a surprising complaint about a work by Voltaire. Before a private performance of *Le Père de famille* in the theatre of the royal palace, doubtless ordered by the queen, Ferdinando IV announced, so Galiani wrote, that he "expected not to enjoy watching those Frenchmen—quite the contrary: he liked to laugh, not to blubber. To protect him during the performance his courtiers made a show of yawning, looking bored, smoking, chattering—while their master wept copiously nonetheless." Ferdinand had seated the French ambassador beside him in the royal box, Galiani wrote, *"pour lui en marquer son avis"*—in order to observe this emissary's response: a response that, we may imagine, would have been adapted to the circumstances.

> *Naples, 29 January 1773.* . . . The Neapolitan visit of the French actors prompts a philosopher to reconsider many things. The scale of their success has been astonishing: never in my experience has there been so little hostility, such absence of derision. Joyful acceptance has been unanimous. You would laugh were you to see our theatre: one might think oneself in an enormous schoolroom. Everyone is concentrating on the libretto: heads are lowered, only occasionally raised toward the stage: the entire audience seems to be happily studying French. Politically speaking, this event has had a greater effect than any number of family pacts. Morally, it must be thought of as a mission: Father Superior Voltaire has dispatched members of his order to convert a nation— to plant the standard of his faith. Voltaire's poetry is teaching us how to write good prose.

XI

A Woman Alone

DURING GRIMM'S FREQUENT visits to Germany and during his illness, Meister had become de facto master of the Newsletter, aided not only by Diderot and Mme d'Épinay but also by a number of lesser assistants. In April 1773, Grimm left once more for Germany, this time en route to a further destination—Russia: he was again acting as escort to Prince Ludwig of Hesse-Darmstadt, one of whose sisters was to be married in October to the empress Catherine's son, Prince Paul. In early June, Diderot, too, left Paris, to spend some months in Holland, whence he would make the same journey across Europe to St. Petersburg, Catherine having invited him to be her guest. Both Grimm and Diderot were to remain abroad much longer than either had expected—until October 1774.

On 15 April, Mme d'Épinay's daughter, Mme de Belsunce, had written to Galiani that her mother was again ill—depressed, into the bargain, by Grimm's absence and the imminent departure of Diderot. Shortly afterward, Mme d'Épinay herself wrote to the abbé:

Paris, 24 April 1773. . . . I must write you . . . that I feel I'm dropping down a well. I cannot accustom myself to being abandoned by all those I love, at a moment when my health makes me doubt I shall ever see them again. . . . This makes me feel utterly wretched. *Adieu, aimez-moi.*

Galiani to Mme d'Épinay, Naples, 15 May 1773.
You are absolutely right. Between illness and abandonment, there is only one choice. The former is unhappy life; the latter is death, and death is the worse. But Grimm will soon return. As to the Philosopher—well, I wonder. If he were to imitate Descartes![1] Or if he were to be detained by the flattery of a royal *philosophe*! Besides, he is quite capable of *forgetting* that he should return. He confronts time and space like God, imagining himself to be everywhere and eternal. . . .

Mme d'Épinay to Galiani, Paris, 13 June 1773. . . . The Philosopher left Friday for The Hague and Russia. His farewell made me sad—all my friends cast so far from me. God knows when I'll see them again, and *if* I'll see them again. He's a strange child, that Philosopher! He was so astonished, the day of his departure, at having to set off, so frightened at having to go farther than Grandval, so miserable at having to pack his bags. As for his friends, I'm persuaded he thinks he'll run into all of us wherever he goes. And yet, that's a happy way to be. . . .

That spring, there had been discussions, in the letters, of the phenomenon of electricity, with Mme d'Épinay quoting Diderot's opinions. It was Galiani who had first broached the matter, his interest having been aroused by certain "electrical experiments" witnessed at an evening party in Naples given by the British envoy, Sir William Hamilton, and his cultivated first wife, Catherine. Mme de Belsunce, in one of her letters to the abbé, had asked him to write her the "story" of that evening—doubtless in an effort to cheer her mother.

Galiani to Mme de Belsunce, Naples, 15 May [sic] 1773.
. . . You ask to hear the story of the bolt of lightning—
but I don't know that there's much to tell. It happened
in the midst of a large evening party here in Naples,
clearly to demonstrate that Neapolitan boredom is proof
even against lightning. No one was hurt. The bolt passed
through the skirts of a lady sitting on a sofa—a lady
celebrated for her easy ways. It destroyed the gold in
the fabric, but spared what was under the skirt: thus
does Heaven protect wantonness at its most brazen.
Wantonness may thus be equated with justice—since
justice too, offers itself to all the world. . . .

It is particularly surprising to find Galiani extending his
strictures against "Neapolitan boredom" to the salons of
Palazzo Sessa, Hamilton's residence at Naples, where, as his
biographers Brian Fothergill and Carlo Knight attest, wit,
erudition, and intellectual curiosity were exemplified in the
host himself, and where visits of distinguished travelers continually enlivened local society. Justly famed for his antiquarian and vulcanological interests, Hamilton was, in
Fothergill's words, "at the height of his power, influence and
renown, and was perhaps the most prominent personality at
the Court of Ferdinand and Maria Carolina." Writing to his
London supervisors in 1775, Hamilton himself asserted, in
reference to his life at Naples, that "my situation in point of
self-comfort can never be more agreeable than it is at present"; and his own desire for transfer—which would dissolve
as his stay at Naples continued—arose from a wish to play,
on the diplomatic stage of Vienna or Madrid, a still more
central role in world affairs.

Meanwhile, Galiani persisted in his attempts to lighten
Mme d'Épinay's spirits:

Naples, 5 June 1773.
You must well know, *ma belle dame*, that after we're
both dead, our correspondence will be printed. What a
pleasure for us! How diverting! For this reason I'm
working as hard as possible to make my letters predom-

inate over yours, and begin to flatter myself that I'm succeeding. Readers will notice, in yours, a somewhat monotonous emphasis on friendship. Always tender, always affectionate, always caressing, ever applauding. Mine, on the contrary, will display a charming diversity: at times abusive, at times sarcastic; I can be in a wretched humor, and I may even begin in one tone and end in another, and I'm invariably in good health. That, especially, is my superior talent. For certainly, your four most recent letters—what a pitiful, lamentable impression they will make in the collection! So: admire my adroitness even in my occasional scoldings; and keep well, if only for the success of our future anthology. Do tell me, quickly, that you are disobstructed; otherwise I shall have a blockage in my head, and shan't know how to write you.

Adieu. Excuse my insults; accept them as expressions of a friendship that would go down in history, were history ever to speak of anything other than the follies and miseries of mankind.

Mme d'Épinay to Galiani, Paris, 26 June 1773.
You are unbearable, reminding me that our correspondence will be published after we've gone. I was aware of that, but had forgotten. At this moment I can only tell you that I have an immense dread of immortality. Besides, my dear abbé, you know that rests [in music] are one of the rules of beauty; and since my letters will be alternated with yours, the whole will make a sublime collection.

Allow me to announce that I am beginning to be somewhat less obstructed. . . .

I accept your affection, my dear abbé, your abuse, your excuses. Everything that comes from you is precious to me, you may be sure of that. History will doubtless speak of our friendship, since it speaks of men's misfortunes: is there any greater misfortune than being separated from those one loves?

Gradually, her health improved—though improvement would always be temporary—and she began to tell the abbé about various books she was reviewing, most of which she justifiably found lamentable. With her as sole remaining member of the old quartet in Paris, the Newsletter under Meister's direction was a shadow of itself. During that spring, there had been an occasional echo, merely, of its former tone. A paragraph in the issue for March concerned a dancer at the Opéra, Mlle Marie-Madeleine Guimard, who, according to *Larousse du XXème Siècle*, *"ne se piquait pas d'une vertu farouche"*:

Mlle Guimard's new house is almost finished: Amour has met the costs, Volupté designed the plan; and in Greece itself, that latter divinity never had a temple more worthy of her cult. The walls of the salon are completely covered with paintings: Mlle Guimard is portrayed as Terpsichore, with all possible seductive attributes. Before the work was finished, Mlle Guimard quarreled, for some reason, with M. Fragonard: the quarrel was so sharp that he was sent away, and an arrangement made with another painter. Later, curious to know what had become of his work at the hands of his successor, M. Fragonard found a way of getting into the house. He reached the salon without meeting anyone. Seeing in a corner a palette and paints, he immediately conceived a revenge. With a few strokes of the brush he effaced the smile from the lips of Terpsichore and gave them an expression of anger, of fury, without lessening in the least the likeness to the lady. The sacrilege committed, he quickly decamped. As chance would have it, Mlle Guimard herself arrived a few moments later with a group of friends, come to judge the talents of the new painter. One may imagine her indignation at seeing herself so disfigured. But the angrier she grew, the more closely she resembled the caricature! A painter's epigrams can, on occasion, match those of any poet. . . .[2]

And in the Newsletter for May:

Imminent death is seldom a stimulus to wit: therefore we shan't forget the remark made by the last Grand Master of Malta. He greatly enjoyed spending money, and this taste had led him to make a very considerable number of expenditures, financed from the funds of the Order. On one occasion he had taken 40,000 écus from a fund that was to have been spent on Masses for souls in Purgatory. His confessor, told of this sin, spoke to him of the need to make amends before dying. "Don't worry," the Grand Master replied. "Don't worry, Father: in a few hours I'll be with all those good souls, and we'll have time up there to settle everything."

Although the Newsletter continued to appear until the early 1790s, it would never regain its former lustre. Before leaving for Russia, Grimm had withdrawn from it yet further, increasingly occupied with his German connections. Both he and Diderot returned to Paris changed, from their winter in St. Petersburg. Diderot wrote from Hamburg to Sophie Volland that Catherine "had the soul of Caesar [from The Hague, he would write "of Brutus"] and the allure of Cleopatra," and he would long remain under her spell. Grimm would never emerge from it.

Catherine, in turn, was no less enchanted by Diderot. His admirer even before their meeting, she was amused in St. Petersburg by his informal ways; she listened to his libertarian views, never wavering from her convictions of the virtue of absolute rule. She was awed by the breadth of his knowledge and by his intellect. Every day, beginning at three o'clock in the afternoon, behind doors that, by her order, remained closed, he would discourse to her—"on society," as he put it in a letter to his wife; and letters he wrote later to Catherine suggest the range of what she called his "lessons." While he and Grimm were in Russia together, they were both made members of the Imperial Academy of Sciences. The friendship of Diderot and Grimm, those two figures of the Enlightenment, with Catherine, the absolute ruler of an oppressed populace, is an outstanding paradox even in that inconsistent age.

Of the paradox that was Catherine the Great, Byron would later observe, in *Don Juan*:

> *. . . for though she would widow all*
> *Nations, she liked man as an individual.*

From her "solitude," Mme d'Épinay continued to give the abbé private and public news.

> *Paris, 28 November 1773.* . . . My daughter arranged a delightful entertainment to celebrate my convalescence—a charming little comic opera in which she herself acted like an angel. Couplets, little children—all manner of things to lighten the heart.
>
> The festivities at court[3] had the opposite effect—on some of the actors. Yesterday they gave the old opera *Bellérophon* [by Lully]. One of its features, as everyone will tell you, is an enormous divine monster. What no one will tell you is that during the dress rehearsal a quarrel sprang up among the five or six little Savoyard chimneysweeps who had been put inside the monster to make it move; and they began to fight. Seeing the head of the beast going one way and its feet another, M. Rebel[4] climbed up onto the stage, lifted the monster's tail, and shouted "*Hé hé*, you little bastards, if I get hold of you . . . etc."—everything that can be said to such people through such a very peculiar megaphone. Whereupon the monster quickly resumed a respectful demeanor, to the relief of all present.

In other letters, she relays to the abbé news sent her from Russia by "the baronial *chaise de paille*" concerning himself and Diderot at Catherine's court; she relates some of her discussions and disagreements with Meister, particularly on the subject of political economy; she reports on Helvétius's posthumously published *De l'homme* (a discourse on the nature of man, of which Diderot was to write a refutation).

She admires Necker's *Éloge de Colbert*, which she calls "a masterpiece." On these and other themes, she is also writing articles in the Newsletter. Gluck's new opera, *Iphigénie en Aulide*, has taken Paris by storm, praised by all except those who refuse to listen to any music other than that written by Lully or Rameau. And she ridicules the new fashion of towering coiffures, each illustrating a "subject," a style launched by the hairdresser Beaulard:

> On one lady's head, we see the reopening of the Parlement; on another the Russian-Turkish peace treaty; on yet another, an English garden, or the battle of Ivry, with a portrait of Henri IV—in fact, all possible motifs from the ancient and the modern world. No longer do ladies' coiffures harmonize with their gowns. . . .

It was a fashion reminiscent—as we know from sculpture—of that favored by Roman ladies in the age of Trajan; and Galiani replied that Paris, in this respect, was well behind Naples, where for several years coiffures "twenty-two inches high and fifteen wide, not including feathers and other décor," had been the mode. The lady's face, he said, "in the midst of all that *atmosphère*, looks like a navel: a pretty navel *chez vous*, a hideous one *chez nous*."

Her improved health continuing, Mme d'Épinay attends the Holbachs' "synagogue"—their salon in the rue Royale —for the first time in two years; she visits Mme du Deffand. Still, it is for her a long and lonely winter. She tells the abbé one of her daydreams:

> *22 February 1774.* . . . Do you know, my abbé, what is my castle in Spain? I'll tell you, but it's for your ears alone: I have rented a charming house in the Place du Carrousel, a house with garden and terrace. Beneath this terrace there are innumerable little boutiques, the kind of place where you used to find "sublime things." Well, in this house I'm going to occupy the first floor, my daughter the ground floor, M. Grimm the second; and on this same second floor there is a charming little apart-

ment where I like to think you will come and stay for
a few days. Yes, yes, yes, yes, abbé—you *will* come
there. . . .

Writing in the Newsletter of the death of Louis XV in
May 1774, Meister did not forget that most subscribers were
themselves royal or princely:

It was on Thursday the 10th, at one o'clock in the
morning, that Louis XV drew his last breath. Throughout his illness, he had retained complete presence of
mind, and although in great pain displayed a patience
and a courage that were truly heroic. . . .History will
preserve the precious appellation unanimously bestowed upon him by the nation—*le Bien-Aimé.* . . .

Meister recorded a public letter the dauphin had written
to the comptroller general, asking him to distribute two
hundred thousand livres to the poor, to pray for the king:
" 'If you find that this would be too dear, in view of the
needs of the Nation, you will take the sum from my privy
purse and that of madame la dauphine.' Could a new reign
begin under more pious or felicitous auspices?"

Mme d'Épinay had reason to be cautious. Increased absolutism during the last years of the reign had, in any case,
created general apprehension. Since her husband's disgrace,
a portion of her income had been virtually a governmental
grant, which could be revoked; her son-in-law was a public
servant, in frequent summer attendance at Versailles. In her
letters to the abbé, she began at times to use a cipher when
referring to grandees: *"mon cousin"* and *"ma cousine"* for the
new king and Marie Antoinette; *"ma société"* for the court.
In other letters, open references to the young couple are
heavily complimentary.

Paris, 15 May 1774.
It's been a fortnight since I last wrote to you, my dear
abbé—we have been so shaken by unforeseen events.
We have lost one king, and now have another, whose

great concern is the welfare of the populace and of his subjects. His ambition is to restore order and decorum—a desire he expresses emphatically. The reign of *ces demoiselles* [Louis XV's mistresses] has come to an end: all women, lawful wives and mothers, will bless him. Come and see for yourself this change for the good. Things won't be as lively as in your earlier time here, but everything will be more interesting; and since it won't be forbidden to love one's friends out of pure affection, society will be all the better. We are inaugurating the reign of persons we can respect—of persons who are honorable.

Paris, 7 July 1774. . . . The queen is more gracious, more charming, more delightful than ever. At Marly, she has created a very free atmosphere. Gaiety reigns, and goodness and benevolence are the virtues held dear by our masters.

Even before receiving the first of those letters, Galiani, too, wrote cautiously: the Queen of France and the Queen of Naples were sisters:

Naples, 28 May 1774. . . . *Ma belle dame,* don't be callous or *overly* circumspect in these moments when one's curiosity is at its height. I don't ask you to be indiscreet. Don't bother to tell me what's happening in this or that ministry, or in the Parlement, or with the princes of the blood. Forget finances, war, politics. Tell me what is going to happen to writers. That's what concerns me. Of all reigns, that of Louis XV will be the most memorable. As to that of Louis XIV, all that will be remembered is that Voltaire wrote about it under Louis XV. Besides, it's the later reign that produced Montesquieu, Voltaire, Diderot, D'Alembert, Boulanger, Rouelle, La Chalotais and the eclipse of the Jesuits. When one compares the cruelty of the persecution of Port-Royal with the mild reproof meted out to the Encyclopaedists, one sees the difference between the reigns of the two kings. The earlier monarch sought renown, and mistook clamor for glory: the later was a gentleman, who practiced the most wretched of professions—kingship— with the utmost reluctance. Such a reign will not be met with again, anywhere, for a long time to come.

Tell me, at least: will the changes announced in the newspapers be confirmed? . . .

Mme d'Épinay knew well enough not to obey all the abbé's injunctions:

Paris, 23 July 1774.
I am profiting from an opportunity to write freely.[5]
. . . As you know, there was a wild blaze of enthusiasm here.[6] Well, it has gone out, like a blaze in straw. At present the mood is the exact opposite. There were grand promises of improvement, great denunciations of flatterers, loud assurances that luxury was improper; much attention was to be paid to the public good; there was a large desire to *learn*. But all that is going by the board, and huge new expenses have been incurred. The various cabals have all had their turn, and there is no prospect of stability. There have been great projects of reform, yet nothing will be done. The lady is young, and thinks of nothing but pleasure; every day she forfeits some of the credit she might have earned: to the garnering of that goodwill she seems quite indifferent. I enclose a list [apparently a code] that will enable me to keep you informed. Burn this letter and keep the list. . . .

She continued to send Galiani details of governmental changes, cautiously supplementing the official news he read in his French and Italian newspapers. Two events would particularly please them: the appointment, as minister of the navy, of their friend Sartine,[7] who, when head of the Paris police, had eased the publication of Galiani's *Dialogues*; and the instantaneous and utter oblivion that befell Morellet's

Réfutation of Galiani, now finally published, just as Galiani's recommendations concerning grain distribution were being officially adopted.

In Russia, "the travelers"—as Mme d'Épinay had come to call them—had lingered beyond all expectation. Catherine's urgings to stay were irresistible; departure was repeatedly postponed; Grimm was ill, and then busy in Holland, with Diderot, on Catherine's affairs. They returned to Paris in the autumn of 1774, Diderot by ordinary coach, Grimm in a private carriage with two young Russian brothers, the counts Nikolai and Sergei Rumiantzov.

Mme d'Épinay to Galiani, Paris, 24 October 1774.
He arrived at two o'clock. He is marvelously well, plump and rosy. Oh! *mon abbé*, what a moment! I wept like a child, and couldn't stop. But he doesn't seem as happy to be here as I had thought he would be. He seems distracted. Well, that's what happens when you go to warm yourself in the icy North: everything else seems insipid once you've rubbed your nose in the snow. However, we must give him time to reaccustom himself to things here before making up our minds: it won't do to hurry. He asked for news of you. You'd have enjoyed listening to the details he gave us. They don't sound exaggerated—just a little euphoric, perhaps. Natural enough, of course.

Don't ask me to think of anything unconnected with him! Next week, he'll settle in here. His well-being will be my only concern. How happy I'll be if he's aware of that!—and if he isn't, I'll be happy anyway. I'm certainly going to be well: I'll no longer have reason not to be.

The Philosopher arrived on Friday. They traveled together from The Hague to Brussels, and—there being no place in our friend's carriage—the Philosopher took the public stagecoach. I asked our friend on Saturday morning: "Did the Philosopher arrive yesterday?" "Certainly. He must have. I put him into the coach myself

the day before I left Brussels, and asked for a recei‚
An excellent idea, no?
    . . . Adieu, my dear abbé. Your news, please. Lo\
me, love *us*. Bonjour.

Then, two weeks later, at the end of an unusually long
letter, dated 7 November 1774, which again chronicles public
affairs in veiled language, come two paragraphs born of her
concerns.
Of the abbé's nostalgia for Paris:

Would you like to hear a remark made by Mme Du
Deffand, one that depicts her admirably? She was invited
to supper, two months or so ago, by Mme de Marchais:
there was to be music. She replied that she didn't think
she could come, because she wouldn't be able to leave
her friend M. de Pont-de-Vesle, who was very ill, but
that she would try to see Mme de Marchais for a moment
before going to her friend's sickbed. In fact, she arrived
at nine o'clock. "I've come to have supper with you all,"
she announced. Of course, everyone asked for news of
her friend. "Oh," she said, "he died. If he hadn't, I
wouldn't be here."

And then, at the end of that letter, a cry:

I'll not speak of the traveler. I'll wait until he's less
euphoric—when someone is drunk there's not much to
say about him. Would you believe it?—he plans to return to where he's just been—this time for three years!
I think he hasn't entirely made up his mind: at least, so
he says. If he persists in that plan, it will simply kill me,
that's all. And, were I to survive despite my grief, I'd
drag my life out like any other woman abandoned and
alone.

That was their reunion, after eighteen months' separation.

Galiani to Mme d'Épinay, Naples, 10 December 1774.
A plague on that German! So he's still drunk? And
doesn't see that with his stupid talk about traveling

again, going back there, he's keeping you from getting well according to my prescription? But—be patient, *ma belle dame*—wait until he's slept off his Northern dream. When he's had enough of it, I'm sure he'll rub his eyes and tell himself he was mad. . . .

In this Galiani was mistaken.

There was one noteworthy change, however: on his return from Russia, Grimm formally ceded the direction of the *Correspondance Littéraire*, the Newsletter, to Meister. But without Grimm, and later without Diderot and Mme d'Épinay, the Newsletter could not retain its verve. Meister succeeded in continuing publication through the first years of the French Revolution, chronicling for his royal and titled readers (with necessary discretion) the fall of the Bastille, the meetings of the Estates General, and succeeding public events. But inevitably his links with these subscribers made him unpopular with the new leaders in France. Despite his carefully inserted praise of aspects of American republicanism—of George Washington, of the French translation of John Adams's *A Defence of the Constitutions of Government of the United States of America*—the Newsletter was doomed by its incompatibility with the times, and publication ended with the number for May in the violent year 1793. Meister retired to his native Switzerland, where he died in 1826. His last years were embittered by the slipshod nature of the first publication of large portions of the Newsletter in book form: a feckless enterprise in which not only his own role but also Grimm's were inadequately chronicled.

XII

Les Conversations d'Émilie

MADAME D'ÉPINAY now enjoyed a triumph.
"Imagine!" she had written to Galiani on 23 August 1773,
after the first half year of Grimm's and Diderot's absence. "I
too am writing dialogues. But mine are between my granddaughter and myself."

During the summer months, when Mme de Belsunce and
her family were at suburban Boulogne-sur-Seine, Mme
d'Épinay, now forty-seven, showed herself an affectionate
grandmother, writing to Galiani of childish sayings that
"made her ponder" and of the role she characteristically assumed as tutor. She had grown particularly close to her
granddaughter, Émilie, sometimes taking her to stay in Paris.
That summer of 1773, with Grimm and Diderot away—"My
friends are at the four corners of the world"—the company
of the six-year-old girl was particularly precious. Mme d'Épinay's words to Galiani were her first mention of *Les Conversations d'Émilie*, the book which, during her lifetime and for
some generations beyond, would be by far the best known
of her works, preceding by several generations the discovery

and publication of her autobiographical *Histoire de Madame de Montbrillant*.

That autumn, the abbé asked Mme d'Épinay to send him cotton cloth of a quality he could not find in Naples, sufficient to make him a dozen shirts:

> *Naples, 11 September 1773.* . . . I shall never forget your motherly sweetness, and at the same time your laughter, when you caught sight of one of my shirts lying on my bed in your country house. To you it seemed impossible that there should be a creature so presumptuous as to call himself a man, with a shirt so short and ridiculous. So: estimate the amount of linen needed to clothe that child—that man, so-called. . . .

For various reasons, a long time passed before the cloth could be sent. On 15 March of the following year, Mme d'Épinay wrote that she had been expecting to send something else, "another masterpiece of my own making," but that this probably would not be ready for another six months. In the Newsletter for June the book was announced (with an incorrect title) as forthcoming. As usual, Mme d'Épinay's anonymity was respected:

> The principles of education have perhaps never been so deepened and developed* as in our own day: we lack only good elementary books that would facilitate the application of those principles. A very witty woman, whose intellect is superior even to her wit, has just written such a book, for the use of her daughter. It contains what we consider an excellent implementation of the moral catechism outlined by Jean-Jacques [Rousseau] in his *Émile*. Sharing his conviction that until the age of ten, children are absolutely incapable of grasping a long series of ideas and arguments, she has been very careful to avoid giving her lessons any systematic order.

*Here the present translator's prose is intended to reflect the deterioration in style, under Meister's editorship, of portions of the Newsletter not composed by Mme d'Épinay or Diderot.

The only method she thought she should follow, and from which she never departs, is always to enable the child to discover—independently, whether by instinct or reasoning—the answers to her questions: that is, always to tell the child the truth, never using arid definitions, which leave only false ideas in the mind. . . .

Although, thanks to the simplicity with which the book is written, one cannot but be aware of an intelligence full of grace and finesse, we greatly fear that its real merit will be appreciated only by readers who have reflected deeply on the guidance of the human mind and heart in their earliest development.

What might be added is that in the *Conversations d'Émilie* Mme d'Épinay speaks to her granddaughter with the same charm we have seen in her letters to the abbé, and with the same naturalness and lack of pretension—qualities seldom prominent, perhaps, in today's educators as they grapple with analogous or identical issues. Notable, too, is the subtle change as the grandmother, after addressing the theme of behavior in the child's earliest years, turns her attention to the passing of childhood and the young woman's entry into *le monde*.

The first edition of *Les Conversations d'Émilie*, a small volume with a charming engraved frontispiece depicting a mother and child of the period, was published anonymously in the autumn of 1774.

Mme d'Épinay to Galiani, Paris, 15 November 1774.
I have taken the liberty, my dear abbé, of giving your name to M. le baron de Bülow, chamberlain of the duke of Gotha, who was sent to me here by that court; and M. Grimm joins me in asking you to give him a good welcome. He has kindly consented to bring you a small parcel from me. He does not know what it contains, and there is no need to tell him. It is a book that I wrote when I was so deathly ill last year. I wanted to leave my daughter an idea of how she should raise her children. When you read it, you will become acquainted with my

granddaughter: in her part of the conversations, there is almost nothing that she didn't actually say to me, or that is not very close to her own words. . . .

Bülow's departure having been delayed, she again recommended him to the abbé in a letter of 3 December, this time qualifying her book as "a kind of testament I wanted to leave my daughter—an indication of the way I was bringing up her little girl."

And early in the new year, with an author's pleasure:

> *Paris, 9 January 1775.*
> *Bonjour, bon an, mon cher abbé.* . . . You haven't yet received my dialogues. They are public news here, despite the precautions I had taken to remain unknown. They are a wild success—it's quite funny, really, because they weren't written to impress anyone who doesn't have children or grandchildren. Even mother Geoffrin has felt obliged to say good things about them—and is very annoyed, I think. I learn all this from my sickbed,[1] and it makes me laugh. I keep wondering "Where is my abbé?" . . . Were you to find the dialogues unsatisfactory I'd be very upset, because your approval means more to me than all others put together. . . .

A few days after this letter was written, the book that was causing such pleasure in Paris arrived in Naples. Galiani was feverish, suffering from "a very painful carbuncle" on his nose: still, even to those who have come to know his fluctuations of mood, the begrudging and petulant tone of his first letter about the *Conversations* may come as a surprise:

> *Naples, 14 January 1775.* . . . Baron Bullo [*sic*] has arrived, and has given me your book. You would like to know my opinion of it—I see that from here; but I have had a fever, the pages weren't cut, and the paper is very displeasing. So I have read only bits and pieces. This evening I'll tell you only that it seems to me very original, a new kind of book. An infinite number of didactic

dialogues have been published, but they are all too high-toned for the children at whom they're directed. You begin with a baby's first babble—something never done before; but, in fact, starting as you do with *do, re, mi,* you touch the basis of all knowledge. I'll tell you also that you have been immensely helped by Émilie, who played her role perfectly: without that, you'd never have carried it off.

My nose is frightfully painful, so I'll leave you. All I want is a dozen cotton shirts. . . . We have agreed as to quality and price. My nose hurts. Good night.

Was the abbé jealous—he who had published dialogues himself, and nothing since? The reply he received was more polite than he deserved:

Mme de Belsunce to Galiani, [Paris,] 6 February 1775.
I am distressed to have to write to you, M. l'abbé. Everyone expects bad news when they see my handwriting, and they are right. If Maman were able to write herself, I'd hold back my pen. But for the past week or so she has been feverish, sweating profusely, and consequently very weak. This is almost unremitting, and her nights are not good. Still, she tells me that she pities your poor nose as much as she can. Out of gratitude, *you* must pity *her*: she needs sympathy at least as much as you do—which is to say, greatly.

Maman is very flattered by your opinion of her dialogues. If your view had been otherwise, you and I would have quarrelled. To my mind, this little book is a masterpiece of its kind, and Maman is playing down her own great merit when she says that all my daughter's answers are precisely the child's own words. That is certainly true in some instances, but if Maman hadn't had the talent to rephrase, arrange, and add, the effect would have been much diminished. A child's constant chatter and nonsense, charming though they may be, become wearing and monotonous. . . .

Her letter was crossed by one that the abbé had written
to her mother on 28 January 1775, intended as something of
a palliative:

Do you know, *ma belle dame*, that you have made me
choke with laughter? Had I died, your book would have
been to blame. The tenth conversation is something
incredible (the term "masterpiece" has been debased).[2]

... I have been trying for several days to decide what
your book is good for, and I think I have found the
answer: I will use it as a touchstone for judging people.
Here is a sample of the barometer:

Those saying that your book is good, and useful, but
that it could have been better done and made more
instructive: Narrow, limited minds.

Those utterly detesting it: Shits, heartless, soulless.

Those finding it "perfect": Flatterers.

Those appreciating the originality of its gaiety and
naiveté, being greatly amused by it and finding it utterly
useless, since education is entirely a matter of chance—
as much so as conception: Sublime Beings—Diderot,
Grimm, Gleichen, and your humble servant. . . .

To that, with scarcely a break, the abbé added:

I'd be glad if you'd send me some ladies' garters—
not the perfumed kind, but elegant nonetheless. The
rucked skirt has arrived here, and Neapolitans seem unaware that it calls for new garters. It's time I spread the
word. I'd like a few with silver clasps, and holes punched
for adjustment: here in Naples thighs tend to be dev-
ilishly massive.

Replying (again through her daughter, because she herself
was "swathed in poultices") to these supposed amends,
which the abbé apparently considered generous, Mme d'Épinay sent word that she "couldn't be happier" about the abbé's
opinion of her work. She "agreed with him absolutely"—
except that education, by "perpetually surrounding a child
with good examples and good advice, might increase that

child's chances of being virtuous." Fortified by her Paris success, she could let Galiani have his say.

The fancy garters he requested are unmentioned by mother or daughter. Perhaps they were sent—like so many other essentials of that time and of the present day—by diplomatic pouch.

XIII

The Imaginary Socrates

GALIANI'S brother, Berardo, died in the spring of 1774, leaving his affairs in disorder and three daughters for whom husbands must be found. Lapsing into his callous vein, the abbé wrote in this regard to Mme d'Épinay.

> *Naples, 13 August 1774.* . . . I am arranging marriages: that is *all* I am doing at present. I hope to have a pair of them out of the way by October, and when that's done I'll have only a hunchback to take care of. She's bright, however, even though ugly and deformed, so she'll help herself find a husband, and that will relieve me of some of the burden. If I once free myself from this terrible situation, ah! how many books, how much writing, what good things you'll see pour out of me!

As time went on, he wrote of being besieged at home by countless other relatives, of "floundering in a deluge of family affairs." At work, he spent his days "listening to platitudes." His laments about Naples were endless:

The duca di Bovino, master of the royal hunt, was the only courtier who read Horace, and he died the day before yesterday. . . . To add to my troubles, my French servant, Dutout, has just left me, after fifteen years. He was seized by a violent longing for his native Savoy, and nothing could hold him. This upsets all my domestic arrangements, and I'm more perplexed about whom to hire to prepare my morning chocolate than the king of France in deciding whom to appoint foreign minister. Dutout may come to Paris, and if so he'll give you my news. I recommend him to you and M. de Magallon, and to all my friends.

Mme d'Épinay's reply: "If your servant comes to Paris I'll welcome him as I would anyone coming from you. I only fear I shan't be able to restrain myself from kissing him."

Galiani had always been fascinated by the theatre, including the informal outdoor performances by groups of wandering players that were a feature of Neapolitan life. His own person—minuscule, vivacious, gesticulatory—was expressive of that theatrical consciousness which, in Naples, constantly veers close to performance. There was more than a touch of *commedia dell'arte* in this little abbé: we have seen Grimm compare him, in some of his aspects, to the sprightly Arlecchino—our Harlequin; and Marmontel, in his memoirs, would later do the same.

Galiani himself is sometimes credited with being the first to record, in his posthumously published lexicon of the Neapolitan dialect, the origin of that other great star of the commedia dell'arte, the exuberant Pulcinella—or Polecenella, as he was sometimes called in Naples. (In English, he, or his close relative, is known as Punch.)

During the last century, a troupe of strolling players came to Acerra, a small town in the fertile province of Campania. One day they ventured outside the town, into vineyards where peasants were harvesting the grapes. At such times, when men and women are at work together, and the wine is flowing, there is much merry-making and banter. The players found themselves greeted with a variety of rustic sallies; and, being practiced in buffoonery in their profession, they set about defending themselves by replying in kind. However, among the harvesters there was a fellow called Puccio d'Aniello, a comical-looking character with a long nose, his skin reddened by the sun. He was quick-witted and sharp-tongued; and when the players turned their particular attention to him, quite a battle of wits ensued. Soon it became apparent that he outshone them on all points; and the players, giving way, slunk back to town. They marveled at what had happened to them; and, true to their profession, soon realized that such a person would be a fine asset to their company. Returning to the vineyard, they hired him on the spot. He proved a great success, making everyone laugh with his sallies—always wearing a black half-mask, white shirt, white breeches, white stockings. Thus the name of Puccio d'Aniello became famous; and after his death, which occurred within a few years, his place was taken by another actor, who assumed the same name and costume. The name, somewhat varied by local pronunciations, became famous; and every city in Europe now has a Pulcinella—spelled in one way or another—of its own.[1]

The classicist Galiani went on to speak of Pulcinella's equally legendary predecessor, a masked, roistering character named Maccus, of Greek origin, who was featured in the ancient Oscan city of Atella, not far from Acerra. These plays—farces said by Horace to have been presented, in the classical Greek tradition, to cheer audiences following the performance of a tragedy—were produced well into Roman times, and eventually banned because of their obscenity. Other ancient sources have been proposed as the origins of the figure of Pulcinella; and we may bear in mind that the name itself resembles that of another very active species: the Vulgar Latin *pullicenus,* whence the Italian *pulce* (flea).

(Until recently there existed in Acerra a public square named Piazza Pulcinella, and on a nearby house a plaque recounted a different version of the legend, announcing itself as the birthplace of a tailor, one Andrea Calcese, known as "Ciuccio"—"Donkey"—who "created Pulcinella in the seventeenth century," or possibly devised the masked appearance, distinctive, to say the least, of Pulcinella. Acerra is now encompassed in the industrial zone extending from Naples toward Caserta. Piazza Pulcinella has been eliminated; and the sole remnant of the supposed house of Pulcinella can be glimpsed behind a barricade of planks. Surveying his legendary territory of Acerra today, Pulcinella would need all his sense of humor. And yet another town, Aversa, also near Naples but not mentioned by Galiani, identifies itself as "the birthplace of the original Pulcinella." It is emblematic that these Neapolitan claims, while analogous to those concerning the "Casa di Rigoletto" at Mantua, and the "Tomba di Giulietta" at Verona, should be associated not with tragedy, but with farce.)

In the summer and fall of 1775, Galiani sent Mme d'Épinay news of an event in which his interest in Pulcinella's various origins and the phenomenon of the theatre played its part. Linking Cervantes' Don Quixote to a well-known living Neapolitan academic figure, he had developed the central character of a comic opera—a fictitious personage who would assume the nickname "Socrates."

Naples, 19 August 1775.
I'm working seriously at directing a comic opera: if it's a success I'll tell you more.

9 September 1775. . . . After a surfeit of boring duties, I've been seeking relief in Horace and in supervising the production of my comic opera. It's to be called *Il Socrate immaginario* [*The Imaginary Socrates*], and it's the craziest thing you could imagine. I'll send it to you when it's printed.

16 September 1775. . . . Nothing special to report tonight, so let me tell you about my comedy. It's an imitation of *Don Quixote*, and deals with a worthy provincial gentleman who has taken it into his head to revive the philosophy of the ancients, together with their music, gymnastics, etc. He thinks he's Socrates; he's cast his barber as Plato (another Sancho Panza); his wife is shrewish and beats him, so she's Xantippe. He's constantly going out into his garden to consult the *genius loci*. Finally, they give him a sleeping potion, letting him think it's hemlock; and, thanks to that opiate, he wakes cured of his madness. The plot really deserves to be made into a merry little novel: it would be unique, I think— the *Don Quixote* of our century.

Because Mme d'Épinay would, in reading this work, need help with the Neapolitan dialect and parochial allusions, Galiani added: "When the piece is printed I'll send it to Caracciolo, and if he'll undertake to explain its language and humor, you'll find yourself laughing." He knew that she would recognize allusions he had enjoyed concealing in his text—references to Parisian matters of which his characters could know nothing, and which his Neapolitan audiences might laugh at without fully appreciating: allusions that, as she would realize, he had put there for her.

Galiani to Mme de Belsunce, 11 November 1775.
You'll have learned from my letters to Maman that I've been amusing myself by writing a comedy called *Socrates*. Now it has been performed, and has created a sensation—such a sensation that it has been suppressed by order of His Majesty. You cannot imagine how delighted I am to find myself detested by our local élite as cordially as I was by the Economists. . . .

Galiani to Mme d'Épinay, 9 December 1775.
Some time ago I wrote you that I was supervising the

production of a comic opera called *Socrates* and that I was greatly enjoying it all. Then you fell ill, and I said no more of it. Now I must tell you that the piece has enjoyed the most sublime of all possible successes: it has been banned by His Majesty's most explicit order, after six public performances and even a command performance at court. In France, only *Le Tartuffe* has been deemed worthy of that honor.[2] So: put *Socrates* on the same level as *Le Tartuffe* with respect to the scandal it has caused and the cabals, intrigues and spite it has engendered. Such is my situation here: such the dismay that my wit generates in the skulls of these imbeciles. Envy me, don't pity me: this business hasn't done me the slightest harm. You can't imagine what "explanations" the piece has set off here—all the local allusions that have been discovered in it. Only the Apocalypse has ever been so ludicrously interpreted. I'll be damned if I understand what it is that people manage to unearth in my lines.

Writing in this vein to Paris about *Il Socrate immaginario*, Galiani made no mention of his two Neapolitan collaborators. For the necessary position of professional librettist, familiar with theatrical and operatic requirements, he was able to enlist a friend, the noted Giambattista Lorenzi, a worldly abbé like himself. Lorenzi put Galiani's comic, often farcical lines into rhyme, and helped to invent and develop minor characters. For the music, Galiani found his composer in Lorenzi's friend, the thirty-five-year-old Giovanni Paisiello: an earlier collaboration between Paisiello and Lorenzi on a comic opera called *Don Chisciotte della Mancia* had doubtless been a source of Galiani's inspiration. Paisiello gladly entered Galiani's game, burlesquing, here and there, phrases by Lully and others involved in the Parisian musical wars. This triple collaboration of Galiani, Lorenzi, and Paisiello on *Socrates* has come to be considered an early signal of the onset of the greatest period of *opera buffa*, leading to the best work of Cimarosa and culminating in the genius of Mozart.

Nor did Galiani tell Mme d'Épinay that his Don Tamaro Promontorio, the provincial "Socrates the Second," and Tamaro's wife, Donna Rosa, whom in fits of delusion he called Xantippe, were caricatures of a well-known pair of Neapolitans: the baron Saverio Mattei, the self-important professor of Greek and Hebrew at the University of Naples and impassioned exponent of the Socratic philosophy; and Mattei's wife, Giulia, a notoriously jealous shrew.[3] The story ends "happily"—in a sardonic sense—for all, with a general resumption of provincial routine.

Like *Don Quixote*, *The Imaginary Socrates* has another dimension: farce though it is, Galiani infused it with a feeling of melancholy and defeat. "For two hours," a modern commentator has written, "Galiani's provincial Socrates and Plato have enjoyed a sense of freedom, an illusion of happiness; but it has all been a dream, a flight from reality in which the characters wear masks, so to speak, as a protection from daily life—that 'real' life which, as Galiani looked about him in Naples and the provinces, he perceived as a nullity."[4] And, as another modern Italian writer has put it: "The remark by one of Galiani's characters, the barber Antonio, his Plato—'*Viva, Socrate, viva!* I don't understand anything you say, but I know that whatever you say is right'—is a proper synthesis of what the general French reader, according to Galiani, thought of the *philosophes*."[5]

In the team of authors, Paisiello's inclusion has never been questioned: his name alone was printed on the published composition. No one doubts that it was Galiani himself who discovered a Don Quixote in Saverio. And in much of the language of the play, especially in the discussions among academics (which Galiani wrote in classical Italian, rare then in *opera buffa*), one hears the voice that, in past years, had enlivened even the weighty questions of the grain trade.

In Naples, however, those French *Dialogues* were little known. On the mid-October evening in 1775 when, from his seat in the third tier of the Teatro Nuovo, Galiani watched the first performance of his *Socrates*, the applause was enthusiastic; but it was for Paisiello's music and for Lorenzi, whose drollery the audience recognized, rather than for Galiani, whose long absence in France had left him, as yet, an unfamiliar figure to the Neapolitan public. After a short series of successful public performances, there was a command performance at court; and on the following day the royal edict closed the opera. Like the more drastic order regarding Galiani that had been sent from Naples to Paris some years earlier, this edict, too, was signed by Tanucci, who was now prime minister:

> *Portici, 24 October 1775.*
> *Bernardo Tanucci to the presiding officer of the executive committee of the Theatres of Naples.* The king, having heard the opera at the Teatro Nuovo entitled *Socrate immaginario*, is of the opinion that it is indiscreet and should not be publicly staged. And he has ordered me to inform you and the executive committee that he forbids further performances.

No more definite reason for the order has been recorded. Some have suggested that it was issued out of respect for Mattei, who, as a professor at the university, was a government official; others, that it expressed official displeasure at Galiani's broader and entirely recognizable satire of Neapolitan provincial pretensions.

How Paisiello and Lorenzi reacted to the closing of *Socrates* is not known. The general manager of the Teatro Nuovo, Gennaro Bianchi, sought compensation from the body of local magistrates officially concerned with theatrical performance (it had formally sanctioned the production): the royal order was "ruinous," Bianchi claimed, leaving him with debts that "might send him to prison"; and, by a subsequent royal order, he was partially recompensed from the pockets of the magistrates themselves—an explicit penalty, said the sardonic Tanucci, imposed on the poor judgment of those dignitaries.[6]

Some years later, Lorenzi would include the text of *Socrates*—with a preface by himself that omitted any mention of Galiani—in Volume 4 of his own *Opera teatrali*, and it would be republished several times during the next century bearing Lorenzi's name alone. Nevertheless, Galiani's name always remained professionally associated with the opera; and ultimately—for the first time, in a mid-nineteenth-century edition annotated by Michele Scherillo, the Neapolitan theatrical historian—he would be confirmed in print as co-author, coming eventually to eclipse Lorenzi.

Scherillo had possibly seen an exchange of letters between Galiani and Paisiello about the triumphant Neapolitan revival of the opera in 1780. (Thanks to recommendations by Galiani and Grimm, Paisiello was by then Master of the Royal Music in St. Petersburg.[7])

> *Galiani to Paisiello [Naples, n.d.]*
> *Carissimo amico*, I am doubtless not the first to tell you that at Naples we are ever eager to hear your divine music, and that several of your operas have been given here recently. His Majesty ordered new performances of the famous *Socrates*, without the slightest change in music or libretto, and this has enjoyed enormous success—especially with the role of Socrates being sung not by Gennaro Luzio as before, but by the great Casacciello, who entered perfectly into the part. The king and queen came several times, as well as His Highness the archduke governor of Milan, a prince of large mind and great quality, who enjoyed it immensely. May you always be my friend. I send my greetings to Donna Cecilia. Warmest regards from your *Devotiss. Obbligatiss. servo ed amico* Ferdinando Galiani.

And, in one of Paisiello's letters to Galiani from Russia, introducing a grand-ducal pair who were about to visit Naples:

> *Tsarskoye Selo, 18 September 1781.*
> *Signor Consigliere ossequiosissimo*: . . . They are great lovers of all the fine arts: I hope they may be pleased with that aspect of our country; and of course there is much else that I am sure they will enjoy. I don't know whether

they will reach Naples in time to find the theatres still open: I have been hoping it might be possible for them to hear our [*il nostro*] *Socrates* and see how such a work is given in Naples, because they are great lovers of opera buffa. . . .

Since then, *Socrates* has been sung in many Italian and foreign cities. Recorded both professionally and privately, it has become widely known.

A notable tribute to it, by a great poet, is found in a passage of Antonio Ranieri's memoirs of his friendship with Giacomo Leopardi, in which Leopardi is described attending a performance of the play at the Teatro del Fondo in Naples in the 1830s:

> I see him yet, seated there, leaning on his right elbow, shielding his eyes from a troublesome light, our friend Margaris standing behind him—both of them enjoying the famous *Socrate immaginario* by the abbé Galiani, set to music by Paisiello, sung by Lablache, with its famous chorus, truly Aristophanic: *Andron Apanton/Socrate Sofotatos* ["Of all men, oh Socrates, you are the wisest!"] —our description of the opera having made him eager to hear it.[8]

That was in the closing, Neapolitan phase of Leopardi's tragic life, when the enjoyment of theatrical performances, whether on stage or by itinerant actors, constituted one of his few amusements. It took place more than half a century after those first productions of *Socrates* in the Teatro Nuovo, which had relieved Galiani of his impulse to envy the success of *Les Conversations d'Émilie*.

XIV

The Last Letters

A STORY of two friends, both writers, who correspond for years; he grows briefly jealous of her unexpected public success; he repents, but is stimulated to counter it with new work of his own; he succeeds; the correspondence becomes sporadic, but the friendship continues until her death.

The later years of the friendship are revealed in fragments. Mme d'Épinay had written her last articles for the Newsletter in 1775. Now, as time went on, she wrote fewer letters even to Galiani, and of these a number have disappeared. (There is no trace, for example, of her undoubted response to Galiani's announcement of *Socrates*.) She wrote repeatedly of her wretched health, but it was only in mid-January 1775, when Grimm arrived in Naples and described her suffering, that Galiani fully understood the gravity of her condition.

Grimm, now constantly in the service of Catherine and of German princes, was again accompanying the Rumiantzov brothers, this time on a tour of Italian cities. As Grimm and

Galiani were enjoying this Neapolitan reunion after a separation of almost seven years, letters came from Mme d'Épinay reporting her suddenly improved health. The two men recognized and respected this gallant show.

Galiani to Mme d'Épinay, Naples, 20 January 1776. . . . What a blow it would have been had *bad* news of your health arrived just as the *chaise de paille* and I were in each other's arms, eager to enjoy this long-awaited happiness to the full and actually beginning to do so! What a horrible situation for the two of us, reunited only to weep! Instead—your letter arrives—I had just left him—I run back to where he is staying—we embrace madly—and quickly make our plans for Vesuvius—Cockayne—the Christmas crèches—and a thousand other *niaiseries napolitaines.*—Ah! what a blessed, happy letter! It revived us!

Now that I'm seeing him again, why not you as well?

After Grimm's departure, Galiani wrote to Mme d'Épinay that although he could tolerate some of the social reforms enacted or proposed by the new French ministers, and applauded by Diderot and other members of the Enlightenment, he was particularly opposed to one—the abolition of the *maîtrises* (guilds) and of the award of the official title *maître* (master) to properly qualified artisans, particularly in the arts and crafts, after years of study.

Naples, 18 May 1776. . . . It is a mortal blow to French manufacturers: the effect will be felt in thirty years, not before. . . . We are in a century when prescribed remedies are doing at least as much harm as the vices they are meant to supplant. . . . We are seeing the total collapse of Europe: the time for emigration to America has come. Everything is rotten here: religion, laws, arts, sciences; all will be rebuilt in America. This is not mere chatter, or a hasty conceit spewed up by our present quarrels with England! I said it all more than twenty years ago, and I have always seen my prophecies come true. So don't buy a house in the Chaussée-d'Antin: buy one in Philadelphia.

This is the first indictment by Galiani of the great world of European culture that he had enjoyed in Paris and held dear so long thereafter. In that spring of 1776, as they both apparently knew, the Second Continental Congress was drafting, in Philadelphia, the document that was to be the formal declaration of American independence.

Mme d'Épinay to Galiani, Paris, 10 June 1776. . . . I think you're right: it wouldn't be a bad idea to settle in Philadelphia. I'll suggest it to my grandchildren, as advice coming from you. But as for me, I could never bear to be so distant from the bit of earth that contains the precious remains of my dear dog Ragot. . . .

Galiani replied with news of the mysterious murder of his favorite cat, his "master in the study of cat language"; and then, for a time, the two commented sporadically on events pertaining to the American Revolution. In February 1778, thanks in part to the popularity and persuasions of Benjamin Franklin, the first American ambassador to Paris, France formally recognized American independence, and promised aid. Among the countless French expressions of solidarity with the new republic was an eloquent printed message by Diderot, "To the American Insurgents." Galiani wrote to Mme d'Épinay about refugees—"American Tories," as they would come to be called—arriving in Naples: "There are many English here, seeking shelter from the storms in America: most of our Neapolitans assume they have come for Carnival. Meanwhile, *les Washington et les Hanckocke* [*sic*] will be fatal to them."

Mme d'Épinay to Galiani, Paris, 3 May 1778. . . . Voltaire has bought a house quite near me that he'll be moving into next September. His niece is seriously ill —the reason for his not going to Ferney as planned. He speaks of traveling those 120 leagues as though it were a mere excursion to Chaillot.¹ He continues to share with Franklin the applause and acclamations of the public. The moment they appear in a theatre, or pass along a street, or attend a function at one of the academies, there's a great ovation. Princes come and go, unnoticed, but when Voltaire sneezes, and Franklin rejoins "God bless you," it begins all over again. Here's a line of Latin that is to be inscribed on the frame of Franklin's portrait:

ERIPUIT CAELO FULMEN, SCEPTRUMQUE TYRANNIS*

Would you like a translation of that into French verse, jotted down by D'Alembert when he woke up the other morning?

> *Tu vois le sage courageux*
> *dont l'heureux et mâle génie*
> *a ravi le tonnerre aux cieux*
> *et le sceptre à la tyrannie.*

On 25 July 1778, with French troops now in America, Galiani wrote to Mme d'Épinay: "At this very moment, you [France] will have determined the outcome of the greatest revolution in the world: whether America is to reign over Europe, or Europe is to continue its reign over America. I would place my bets on America. . . ." On 17 April 1779: "Those accursed Americans have involved you in a ruinous war. *Tantae molis erat Americanam condere gentem!*"† On 31 July 1779: "We are in a year that will be remembered for centuries. . . ."

23 September 1780. . . . Ever since the subject of grain legislation was first broached, it seems that God has been sending famine to the world, as though to confound politicians. This year we are very straitened here, and

---

*From heaven he seized its lightning, and from tyrants, their scepters.

†Galiani is paraphrasing the *Aeneid*, I, 33: "*Tantae molis erat Romanem condere gentem*"—"So great an effort was it to found the Roman people."

to make matters worse Spain is drawing grain away from us. Ah! What a wonderful thing is *l'économistification*! Let us have peace; for at least we could have herring to eat, and cod, and American wheat.

That was the last reference by either of them to the American war, which ended a year later with Cornwallis's surrender at Yorktown.

Other events, in Paris and Naples, affected the friends. In 1777, making what would be her last change of residence in Paris, Mme d'Épinay moved—despite Galiani's advice against settling in his once-beloved city—into a house newly built in the Chaussée-d'Antin. A floor was reserved for Grimm, but Grimm was seldom there. Mme d'Épinay, who deplored his incessant travel and was jealous of some of his Rhenish and Russian friendships, had several new names for him: *"le papillon germanique"*—"the Germanic butterfly"; *"le voyageur mi-russe mi-allemand mi-français mi-italien, le vrai cosmopolite."* "I have never known such a relentless traveler," she wrote. "Fate has turned him into a tennis ball that ricochets between Petersburg and Paris, Paris and Petersburg. *Pazienza!*"

Grimm, meanwhile, had been urging Galiani to come to Russia. Catherine had bought the library of Galiani's brother, Berardo, the archaeologist and translator of Vitruvius; and, through Grimm, she repeatedly invited the abbé to St. Petersburg.

Grimm to Galiani, St. Petersburg, 31 December 1776. . . . Do you know, you should have yourself sent to this court as minister from yours. Think about this: it is no idle suggestion. You'd send up the price of furs, you'd need so many in this climate; and the carriages would then have to be enlarged, though here they're all capacious, as in England; but, those details apart, you'd get along very well. Besides, how does Ferdinando Galiani dare live in the same century as Catherine without ever seeing her? How can he allow me to have this advantage over him—me, one of the lesser members of our family? It is now more than three months that I've been here—spending my life with her, every day, one day like another, seeing only her, often from morning to night, going only to the court, dining with her in public or privately, chatting, talking for hours on end —freely, with complete confidence: doesn't that sound like a dream? I don't know how long this dream will last, but one would think that keeping me entertained was one of the duties of the Empire. . . .

In Naples, at the same time, Maria Carolina, who had long been resentful of Tanucci, now seventy-eight, for "continuing to treat her husband like a child," had secured the old man's reduction to the grade of minister without portfolio and his replacement as prime minister by the marchese di Sambuca, former ambassador to Vienna. Galiani felt no regrets. He wrote to Mme d'Épinay that Tanucci had shown little regard for him since his recall from Paris, and had made small use of him. "Such a change of ministry would be nothing in Paris, but in this lethargic place it's a great event: it has helped to dispel the depression into which I've recently fallen because of the incurable sickness of my angora cat." Later, after Mme de Belsunce had permitted herself an observation to Galiani on that theme: "Your daughter has been scolding me because in my letters I've spoken only about my quadrupeds: but I assure you that had I written of our local bipeds, she'd have much greater cause to complain."

The administrative change brought him a minor bureaucratic promotion—appointment to a magistracy that determined legislation in privately held lands. "It gives me greater authority, a little more work, and no increase in salary, but it opens the way toward the last of those items. I've become greedy, and have been spending more money than ever before."

Official Naples continued unenlightened and ungenerous:

Galiani to Mme d'Épinay, Naples, 1 August 1778. . . .
We have had a very bad harvest. The usual decrees were issued, and of course prices immediately shot up. As you

may imagine, I have not been consulted or made use of or regarded as knowing anything about such matters. The reason for this is that nobody here has the slightest idea that I've written a book on the subject. They know I once wrote something—in French, wasn't it? A nice little fairy tale? Or a bit of poetry? Something along those lines? Don't think I'm joking. . . .

Little is known about the depression into which Galiani fell at this time and which lasted about a year. It followed the death, apparently sudden, perhaps self-inflicted, of a woman about whom he wrote to Mme d'Épinay: "If I could bring her back to life for but two hours, talk with her, learn the reason for her despair, her thoughts, her last wishes. . . ." In no extant letter does Mme d'Épinay refer to the matter, except perhaps by an exhortation at the end of a letter in February 1779: "*Addio, carissimo abate. Sanità e allegrezze, per quanto è possibile.*" Catherine, in Russia, wrote to Grimm, who had told her of his friend's low spirits: "What is it that is weighing so heavily on the abbé? I had thought that in Naples, in the most beautiful climate in Europe, one took things more lightly." She ordered that he be sent a Russian medal. After a bureaucratic interval of two years, it arrived in Paris, in Grimm's care.

> *Mme d'Épinay to Galiani, Paris, 3 December 1781.* . . .
> Good news. Your medal arrived last evening. It is very handsome. Our friend says that you were wrong not to have asked that it be gold, and I say that you were perfectly right, for quite apart from the fact that you would certainly have sold it, this one in bronze is incomparably more handsome than those in gold. Now we'll see how we can send it on to you. . . .

Though he did not go to Russia, Galiani was able to do the empress various services, including the formulation of a Latin inscription to be placed on the base of a statue of Peter the Great in St. Petersburg. She subsequently sent him other medals and gifts, and she saw to it that he was elected, as Diderot and Grimm had been, to the Russian Imperial Academy of Sciences.[2] "In the depths of southern Italy," he wrote to her in one of his replies, "there exists a small being . . . now known even in his own country as 'Galiani, friend of the Empress of the Russians.' " But even before that, he may have smiled at Mme d'Épinay's assurance that "bronze is incomparably more handsome." In his letter to her about "spending more money than ever before," he had not mentioned that for several years he had been buying ancient gold and silver coins and medals unearthed by peasants in lands near his monasteries, and was continuing to do so. Never acknowledged in letters to his friends, this became known only after his death.

In a letter to Galiani of 7 September 1777, asking him to welcome to Naples "M. de Witt, son of the burgomaster of Amsterdam," Mme d'Épinay had added: "He will tell you, my dear abbé, of my state of vegetation, from which I emerge only to suffer." Galiani may have learned the meaning of those words from the burgomaster; and he commented on them in answer to a worried letter, now lost, from Mme de Belsunce.

> *Naples, 22 November 1777.* . . . Why are you so worried about your mother's taking opium? What are you afraid of? Don't you know (but of course you do) that the entire Orient—that is, half the human race—lives with opium, or rather *in* opium, until decrepitude? The Occident drinks wine instead. Haven't you known old women who were unremittingly drunk? Well, your mother will be continuously drunk on opium. I knew the contessa Borromeo, who began to take opium and musk when she was fifty, because of frail health. You cannot imagine the havoc she made of her life. She died recently, aged one hundred and two.
>
> You must get it firmly into your head that, since life

is nothing but an accumulation of trouble, suffering and grief, *Dieu fit de s'enivrer la vertu des mortels.* [God created inebriation as a human virtue.] Asiatics, Europeans and Americans take opium, wine and tobacco as palliatives to the circumstances of their lives. The nepenthe of the ancient Greeks was nothing but opium. Ambrosia and nectar are simply hydromel, a drink made from honey, which can be intoxicating.[3] Wine was not yet known to the Greeks in the era of their most ancient mythology. The conquests of the Egyptian king whom we call Bacchus transplanted the grapevine, native to Armenia, into Asia Minor.

But an end to this tremendous—and certainly very novel—dissertation on the subject of Maman's opium! Let her take as much as she desires; and since Fréron and his *Année littéraire*[4] are no more, and the Economists are silent, you can see that it's the only soporific available to her. I hope that she won't be impatient in her search for relief, that she will have a long life, and eventually be cured of all maladies except old age.

Mme d'Épinay had a particular reason for taking opium: it enabled her to write, and she was eager to complete a new, enlarged edition of the *Conversations d'Émilie* in the little time she supposed remained to her. The year before, while desperately ill, she had written to Galiani:

> *Paris, 22 July 1776.* . . . What a curious thing is Destiny! I was so close to the other world, and so well prepared to go, that there are moments when I imagine I'm already there. I look at this magic lantern of a world with detachment, and say. . . . . You know how to read unwritten lines, my dear abbé: you can easily complete this little paragraph yourself.

During the next few years she was able to work at the new *Conversations* whenever intermittent improvement, or opium, made such writing possible. She and her husband had recently exiled their ever-troublesome son Louis-Joseph to Switzerland, providing him with a modest allowance and threatening him with disinheritance should he return to Paris. In Berne there was soon another threat of arrest for debt: his parents paid. In Fribourg, where he married into a bourgeois family of Swiss officials, he scandalized them by incurring debts yet again. This time it was the empress Catherine who came to the rescue. A portion of a letter from Grimm tells the story:

> *Grimm to Catherine II [1778 or 1779]*. . . . I want particularly to tell Your Majesty that nothing in my entire life has cost me more effort than proposing that you buy those diamonds. Why should the empress buy diamonds of which she has no need, solely because their owner finds herself in adverse circumstances? So an inner voice has constantly reproached me. But this unfortunate woman was Mme d'Épinay. One does not always wish to exhibit one's distress; and if she had dealt with jewelers she would probably have lost a third of their value. . . .

In May 1781, Mme d'Épinay could tell the abbé that her book was done, and that she was sending it to him. It would be brought to him by their friend Domenico Caracciolo, who would soon be passing through Naples on his reluctant way to take up his new post as Neapolitan viceroy in Sicily.[5]

> *Mme d'Épinay to Galiani, Paris, 12 May 1781*. . . . If he doesn't die of grief on the way, he will bring you my book.[6] This edition is in two volumes, and has been out two months. You'd have had it earlier if I hadn't wanted to send it to you post-free. You must read the prefaces, the *avertissements*, etc., and then you can skip the first four conversations, which are unchanged; but you must read all the rest, because that is completely new work.
>
> Don't forget to remind M. de Caracciolo that last summer I gave him a book concerning money that Grimm and I thought you should have. He has sent it on to Naples with his own books.

. . . As for me, I am like those little German toys that always bob up again after being overturned twenty times. . . . I wanted to profit from this occasion to give you a sign of life—the best I can do. *Aimez-moi*. . . .

Galiani to Mme d'Épinay, Naples, 9 June 1781.

Your ravishing letter reached me in Rome, just as I was stepping into a coach to return here. It greatly lightened my crossing of the Pontine Marshes. I reread it four or five times, and always with ecstasy.

Caracciolo arrived the day before yesterday, Thursday. . . . He talks continually of Paris, but he will be living far from Paris, and if France continues to mistrust those who are its best friends in the government, he will come to share my own feelings—no great longing to be in France, while missing Parisian friends. His baggage isn't unpacked, so I don't yet have your book. I'm wildly impatient to read it, and I send you a thousand thanks—also for the book about money. . . .

I have received two letters from Grimm, one in Rome along with yours, the other here this week. The news he gave me of M. Necker's resignation puts me into such bad humor that I have no desire to reply.[7] Is it possible that in France this century is unenlightened, the nation not at peace, the sovereign lacking all courage? That there is no era, never a time, when a great man can remain in his post? Is this possible? What does it all signify? Must we see in it an eternal law, existing ever since our dear father Adam's famous apple—the apple that delivered mankind over to the wicked and the foolish, and put an end to heroes? If that law exists, we can only bow our heads and obey; if it does not, I will curse parliamentarians, intriguers, cabalists, and all who lack understanding, as being responsible for this debacle.

Naples, 16 June 1781.

Only this morning Caracciolo gave me the two books

that you sent me as presents. I thank you for this generous gift. So far I have only turned the pages. . . . Your dialogues are utterly charming. Émilie's part is so real! Never have large truths been expressed more ingenuously. In a word, a great work. . . .

Now the spaces between the letters, both his and hers, begin to grow longer. Mme d'Épinay is remote in her weakness—*"la force me manque"*—and perhaps in the feeling that with her new book completed, her role is all but played out. Galiani laments the long gaps; but, though he must have been aware that he would soon lose her—or perhaps because of that very awareness—he wrote less frequently than he might have done. His last known letter is from the following autumn.

Galiani to Mme d'Épinay, Naples, 22 September 1781.
Do not imagine for a moment that because I haven't written for some time, I have been forgetting or neglecting you. I find myself talking to you constantly, infinitely enjoying what you say. And my favorite reading is the conversations with Émilie, whom I have never had the honor of knowing. But you I know, and I see you and hear you: I'm a party to all the conversations. Tell me a thing or two about this charming work. Who composed the very singular letter from *le sieur* Éloi Godard? Was it you? Are you so merry despite your suffering? Is it based on an actual letter? Or entirely imagined? I need to know everything about this unique piece. And the fairy tale! Had I written such a thing here in Naples, I'd have long since been shut up in the Castel Sant'Elmo. Hasn't it caused comment?

Her answer, delayed by illness, is the last but one of her letters to the abbé.

12 November 1781.
For more than three weeks, my dear abbé, I have wanted every day to write, and it has been impossible.

My hand is unsteady, and I cannot dictate at my ease when it's to you that I'm writing. I always feel that there's no room for a third party in our affairs.

Apropos of that, Mme de Belsunce would be very annoyed if she knew that you thought my last letter was in her hand. It was my chambermaid who wrote it. You don't know that my daughter thinks her writing resembles mine so closely as to be taken for it? She, by the way, has been in the Béarn for several months and won't be back until next spring.

This autumn my son and his wife and their children were with me here. The two children almost died of putrid [typhoid] fever, and the younger is still not completely over the effects. Their departure was postponed several times. I kept telling myself that soon I would be alone and less worried, writing to my charming abbé. Not at all. Because then, suddenly, my husband was at death's door from a disease I'll not name: you can easily guess. Finally my visitors were able to leave, and now I can answer your charming letter.

First, I am well: that is, as well as my condition allows. I'd be quite content to continue for thirty years as I am: manna and opium are my saviors.

To return to my book. It is your approval that truly counts with me. Yes, I wrote the letter from the bailiff; and I can tell you, without the slightest exaggeration, that it was written two years ago this summer, during a momentary relief from my nephritis, when I was so ill that I was being given four or five grains of opium every three hours. The result was that in twenty-four hours I had taken twenty-four grains of opium and dictated the bailiff's letter, following which my temperature soared and I became delirious. My secretary, seeing me rolling on the floor, one moment moaning with pain and the next dictating *folies*, confessed later that he, and my nurses, too, thought I'd gone mad. That wasn't the only time I've had occasion to notice that acute pain excites my natural gaiety: the conversation in which Émilie tries to tell a story—the bit you so liked in the first edition—was done while I thought I was choking to death. As for the fairy tale, it hasn't attracted enough notice here to cause me any trouble. Nobody has understood it: you could count on your fingers the number of people who have enjoyed it.

Adieu, cher abbé. I have written this letter in three installments, as my strength has permitted. There may be gaps in it, but you well know that there are none in my feeling for you.

In February 1782, M. d'Épinay died of the disease whose name Galiani could "easily guess" and was buried beside his parents in the church at Épinay-sur-Seine. "So ended," Diderot noted, "a man who had wasted many millions, and had never, during his entire life, said or done a good thing." The lady with whom he had been living—it is not clear whether this was still one of the "demoiselles de Verrières"—billed his estate for 64,000 livres she claimed to have lent him, and was quickly and quietly paid. Among his effects was "a harpsichord with gilt decoration"—perhaps the instrument at which, almost forty years before, he and his eighteen-year-old cousin, Louise d'Esclavelles, had exchanged confidences, interrupting her singing of "a recitative from *Thétis et Pelée.*"

About this time Catherine learned from Grimm that Mme d'Épinay's income had been slashed as a result of Necker's fiscal reforms, and she had vainly tried through the Russian ambassador in Paris to have the order revoked.

Catherine II to Grimm [St. Petersburg, n.d. (1782?)].
. . . Listen: rather than make further attempts with people who cannot or will not see to the righting of a wrong, bagatelle though it would be for the royal treasury to do so—you who help me with expenses that we both know may be fruitless: take a sum, say twice 8,000 livres, and give it to the author of *Les Conversations d'Émilie.*

If she should be reluctant to take it, lend it to her for fifty years. Above all, tell no one about it: simply let me know that I have lent that sum.

For Émilie, have a trinket made with her name in diamonds, and put it around her neck so that she'll remember me.

Six months later, Mme d'Épinay wrote once again to the abbé:

[Chaillot,] 22 July 1782.

I have not been able to write to you before this, my dear abbé, because only now am I able to put foot to ground after my eighth visit to the other world. I have taken an aversion to Paris, and have let myself be transported to Chaillot, where the *chaise de paille* and I have rented a charming house. I am delighted to be in the country. The pure, bracing air has been trying, but if I can accustom myself to it, as I hope to, I'll be the better for it.

I sent you some news about myself through my Émilie, but fear the letter went astray, to judge by your recent reproaches to M. de Grimm and the absolute silence between you and me. It is really impossible for me to write, my dear abbé. These few words that I'm risking today, to tell you that I love you and that you are as dear to me as ever, will cost me an hour's choking and coughing. But what won't one do for friends? I simply wanted you to know that I exist, and that my feelings remain the same, but that in every other way I am quite different. My speech suffers from my being toothless and breathless, and constant pain makes it difficult even to think. I never go to bed at night without marveling that I didn't die during the day. The sword ever suspended overhead doesn't exactly make for gaiety; and, resign oneself as one may, one finds that there is always something to do in this world. I assure you that I am one of the testiest old women imaginable [she was now fifty-six]; and I marvel at the care people are willing to give me and the patience they must possess to bear with me.

I have no wish to force you to display such tolerance, my dear abbé, and I embrace you with all my heart.

That embrace is the last message in the last letter in the twelve years of correspondence between Louise d'Épinay and the abbé Galiani.

Early in the next year, Mme d'Épinay's friend the marquis de Saint-Lambert, poet and member of the French Academy, longtime companion of her favorite cousin, Mme d'Houdetot (née Sophie de Bellegarde), was delegated by the secretary of the Academy, Jean d'Alembert, to tell the author of *Les Conversations d'Émilie* that she was the first winner of the recently established Prix Montyon,[8] a gold medal given for "the book published in the current year that might be of the greatest benefit to society." Frail though she was, she saw to it that her reply was prompt and properly formal. Characteristically, it was also personal.

> *Paris, 18 January 1783.*
>
> The French Academy has just given me, Monsieur, strong testimony of its indulgence, in awarding the *prix d'utilité* to *Les Conversations d'Émilie*. Greater weight was doubtless given to the intention, rather than to the execution, of the work; and perhaps to maternal zeal rather than to talent. The academy's vote would be a powerful incentive to continue one's work, in the hope of ultimately deserving such an award, were it not for the impediment of uncertain health. I might have hoped thus to further the ideals of the founder of the prize and, in some measure, to deserve the honor done me by the academy. I beg you, Monsieur, to be so kind as to convey my thanks to the academy. My pleasure in sending those thanks through you, Monsieur, and the academy's choice of the actual bearer of the news, are two circumstances that add immeasurably to my satisfaction.

D'Alembert to Mme d'Épinay, Paris, 19 January 1783. The academy accords me, Madame, the honor of responding that you owe it no thanks for its decision to award the *prix d'utilité* to your work. The academy has merely done justice to the excellent principles embodied in that work, and to the clear and simple manner in which they are presented.

Our assembly greatly hopes, Madame, that by further successful accomplishment you will give it an opportunity once again to do the same justice to your talents, and to your desire to put these to the service of mankind. Allow me to add that I share that sentiment with all my colleagues.

Louise d'Épinay lived only four months longer.

An account of the moments immediately following her death at the age of fifty-seven is included in a volume compiled by nineteenth-century editors of *L'Histoire de Madame de Montbrillant.* It claims to be a transcription of the coroner's report, and may be authentic.[9]

In the year seventeen hundred and eighty-three, Tuesday 15 April, at ten o'clock in the evening, we proceeded to the rue de la Chaussée-d'Antin, having been summoned to a house owned and inhabited by madame d'Épinay. In a room on the ground floor giving onto the garden and serving as a bedroom we were told that the *dame* Louise-Florence-Petronille-Tardieu d'Esclavelles, widow of Denis La Live d'Épinay, *seigneur* of Deuil, La Chevrette and other properties, had just died, about one hour before, in that place. . . . And after being shown a female corpse, which we were informed was that of the said *dame* d'Épinay, and those present having sworn that nothing had been disturbed or removed, we declared that official seals would be affixed, *etc.*

In her long, detailed will, Mme d'Épinay's bequests to Émilie included her gold medal—a proper legacy to the "onlie begetter" of the work for which it had been awarded.

To Grimm, expressing *"son estime et sa confiance,"* she confided her manuscripts, including *L'Histoire de Madame de Montbrillant*, asking him, if he thought them worthy of publication, to edit them himself.[10]

A lengthy obituary of Mme d'Épinay, written by Grimm, whose liaison with her had lasted twenty-seven years, appeared in the November 1785 issue of the Newsletter. It is eloquent and admiring, but Grimm prudently omitted any hint of intimacy or affection. There is an air of reserve in his remarks—a reserve absent from the closing paragraphs, fulsome in their praise of the empress Catherine.

It is not known when or from whom Galiani learned of Mme d'Épinay's death. For him it concluded the association of a quarter-century—a friendship that had encompassed affection, irritation, humor, gossip, philosophy, and comment on events involving all Europe. Rather than close the story of her life with that void, some writers have preferred to add another letter, one which passed as genuine until early in the present century, when Fausto Nicolini found it to be a forgery. It was apparently invented as a tribute to both Galiani and Mme d'Épinay, by, once again, early editors of *L'Histoire de Madame de Montbrillant*, and professes to be from Galiani to a certain Mme Du Bocage in Paris, a lady about whom little is known and who is not mentioned in the correspondence.

Naples, 19 June 1783.
Madame, Mme d'Épinay is no more! And thus I too have ceased to exist. In your last letter you suggested that I continue, with you, the correspondence I so long had the honor of exchanging with her. I appreciate the magnitude of the burden you offer to assume; but how could I reply? My heart is no longer among the living: it is completely entombed. Forgive me, madame, if I write you with such frankness, and display such ingratitude.

Mme la vicomtesse, who so often gave me news of her poor mother, lacked the courage to inform me of so great a loss; it was you whom she asked to assume that sad mission. She could not have chosen better: who, other than yourself, could have assuaged my sorrow, had that been possible? For me, however, there is no assuagement. I have lived, I have given sage advice, I have served the state and my master. I have acted as a father to a large family; I have written in the hope of benefiting my fellow beings; and, at an age when friendship becomes a necessity, I have lost all my friends. With them I have lost everything. We do not survive our friends!

XV

The End of the Affair

IN THE pages of *L'Histoire de Madame de Montbrillant*, Louise d'Épinay revealed herself to posterity. Galiani's nature was disclosed to the public, if less directly, through the impression he made on others, through his recorded conversation, and in the tone and perspicacity of his published writings and his dispatches to Tanucci. It is in the correspondence, however, that we see the two friends plain. Over fifteen years, each personality inspirited the other to a form of intellectual intimacy.

Now Galiani was alone; and what we know of the few years remaining to him we know from historians of Naples rather than from himself or his friends. Out of touch with Paris for the first time in a quarter-century, he gave, in later years, a less divided attention to his own city and, after a long denigration, began to commend it. A measure of this conciliatory sentiment toward Naples had been evident in the last phase of his letters to Mme d'Épinay, when he turned, from time to time, to Neapolitan matters. He of course had been familiar with the Neapolitan dialect all his life, and loved its abundant good humor. In Neapolitan, even the Bible and the *Iliad* become comic, Casanova had heard Galiani declare in Paris. With Lorenzi, Galiani had featured the dialect in *Socrates*, and shortly thereafter he began to study it. In this matter, too, a first confidante had been Mme d'Épinay, to whom he described the genesis of a work he hoped to produce on the theme.

> *Naples, 17 April 1779.* . . . I don't know whether I told you that I sprained my knee and had to stay home for a fortnight. Not knowing what to do to keep occupied, and being unable to continue my Horace due to a lack of books and people to turn to, I began something that Diderot once suggested to me. I have been working at it for a month, and it will soon go to the printer. I'm obliged to keep it secret, as otherwise it would be officially forbidden, like *Socrates*. I speak of it only to you. I've begun a dictionary of the Neapolitan dialect, with etymological and historical research into words peculiar to our jargon. It will be a curious book, useful to my country and enjoyable for those who understand our dialect.

Del Dialetto napoletano, the book Galiani published that September, is not the promised dictionary, but rather a 180-page preface to such a work, containing only a sampling of Neapolitan speech.[1] Even this caused difficulty with the printers: Neapolitans themselves, they were nevertheless unaccustomed to seeing their dialect in type. "You have no idea what Neapolitan printers are like," Galiani wrote to Mme d'Épinay. "Typography has certainly made more progress among the Hottentots."

The *Dialetto* is one of the most engaging of Galiani's works, abounding as it does in the humor of its subject. It found many readers, but was heavily received by local critics, one of whom, Luigi Serio, professor of *eloquenza* at the university, wrote in a "Risposta al *Dialetto napoletano*" that Galiani's familiarity with popular speech "seemed to be limited to what he overheard while passing through the streets in his carriage." There was apparently some justice in that stricture; but in the second edition, published a year later, Galiani laughed at those critics as pedantic buffoons. They came in two varieties, he said: professors like Serio, who called the work frivolous but in fact resented it as an intrusion into a field they considered their own; and professors of the opposite opinion, who deplored that serious attention should be paid to what was, after all, the mere jargon of the plebes, a linguistic *sterquilino*—a dungheap. In his letter to Mme d'Épinay, Galiani himself had called Neapolitan speech "our jargon": now he showed, or claimed to show, that it often resembled the Italian of Dante more closely than did other modern Italian speech; and he was certain, he said, that had Naples not fallen under foreign dominion so early and remained oppressed for so long, the regional language, full of Greco-Roman and other ancient overtones, would have continued to be recognized as a rich and splendid tongue. As Sainte-Beuve later wrote in one of his *Causeries de lundi*, "Galiani insisted on the pre-eminence and anteriority of Neapolitan over all the other dialects of Italy: he likened it to the Doric of the Greeks." Essentially untranslatable, *Del Dialetto napoletano* continues to give pleasure to Neapolitans of all nationalities.[2]

But there was still much about Naples that distressed Galiani. In 1780, in a new edition of his youthful *Della Moneta*—reflecting his greater freedom in expressing his opinion on such a matter—he called Neapolitan rural taxation monstrously unjust. "No other similar example [exists] in civilized Europe, but only in the African desert and in barbarous Tartary." And in that same year, when an eruption of Vesuvius caused panic and inspired an outpouring of religious and pseudo-scientific comment, he published a satirical pamphlet, its authorship facetiously attributed to a well-known local hack, and titled "Most Frightening Description of the Frightful Fright That Frightened Everyone on the Occasion of the Eruption of 8 August, Which Thank God Was of Short Duration: by Don Onofrio Galeota, Impromptu Poet and Philosopher." He likened the volcano's spewing of fire, lava, and pumice to other natural phenomena, such as perspiration or "the sneezing caused by opening a package of tobacco"; and, in a warning unheeded to this day, he was ironic about those who court danger by building on Vesuvian slopes. Quotations from Aristotle and Virgil abound in this thirty-page tract.

Perhaps it was the popularity of such works on local matters that brought permission for the revival of *Socrates* in 1780. And, shortly thereafter, Galiani received an official commission to prepare a treatise on relations between neutral nations and belligerents—a theme related to some of his previous work and now relevant to the neutrality of Naples and other powers in the current war between England and Bourbon France. "This work will be heavy going," Galiani wrote to Grimm; and, in one of his last letters to Mme d'Épinay: "Ah, if only I could be doing this in Paris, discussing certain passages beside your fireplace, or at the baron d'Holbach's dinners!" But he was pleased by the signs of official favor—and doubtless by the reward: a benefice from a rich Neapolitan abbey, Santa Maria della Vittoria. He was in royal favor as well: invitations to the palaces in Naples, Caserta, and Portici—"commands," they were called—came from Ferdinando and Maria Carolina following their enjoyment of the revival of *Socrates*, the opera they had previously heard once and promptly banned. He was asked for, and gave, his recommendations for public works: a canal should be cut to give certain Neapolitan suburbs access to the sea; a new map of the kingdom was needed; the kingdom's roads were a disgrace.

Galiani was quickly alert to the needs of Messina and cities at the tip of the peninsula when they were destroyed by earthquake in 1783. As a modern historian has written, "He courageously denounced the three great evils of lower Calabria: the arrogance of the barons, the waste of mortmain, the filth, wretchedness, backwardness, wildness of those southern cities and their inhabitants. . . . It should be forbidden to build churches, chapels and convents before re-

storing homes, and especially mills, oil presses, shops, cis-
terns and aqueducts: the Church and the Knights of Malta
should be obliged to forfeit illegally seized public lands."[3]
And, "by order of Her Majesty the queen," he composed "A
Brief Account of What, to My Knowledge, Took Place Concerning the Treaty of Navigation and Commerce with
France"—a history of the negotiations begun in 1765 and
endlessly prolonged. Tanucci had recently died, and Galiani
now felt free in this account to write bitterly of the man who
had sacrificed him and his life in France in the interest of
"statesmanship," and who had signed the order closing the
first run of *Socrates*.

There were clashes with Sir John Acton, the aloof, half-
British, half-French naval expert who had been borrowed, in
1779, from the entourage of Maria Carolina's brother the
Grand Duke of Tuscany to reorganize the Neapolitan fleet.
Increasingly favored by the queen, Acton had rapidly assumed wider Neapolitan authority, eventually becoming
prime minister. The veteran Galiani soon found himself
obliged to send a written apology to this touchy new superior, his junior by nine years, for some remarks he had made—
reasonable enough, but ill-chosen, and resented—about state
affairs: a forced apology the abbé was not to forget. Relations
between the two never prospered. In 1784, Acton had occasion
to write to Galiani—in French, his preferred language—concerning an honor to be done a royal visitor:

Saturday morning.

Here, M. l'abbé, we have a strange dispatch and the
demand for a still stranger *consulta*. The King of Sweden
has in mind to pay a compliment to our queen in the
form of a bear hunt, a simulation of the actual hunts
traditional in his country, where the animal is offered
in ceremonial homage to a lady. The queen immediately
said that we must rack our brains to think of a return
compliment to the King of Sweden, and that we will
only come up with boring ideas unless we consult Galiani. So, here is the dispatch ordering M. Galiani to

devise, and promptly, a masquerade that will be easy to present and not overelaborate, *since we do not wish to go to great expense*: something to honor the instigator of the Swedish revolution, a friend of arts and letters, protector of the so-called "liberal arts," of which he speaks continually: a masked ball in his honor, to be given on Sunday or Tuesday evening.[4]

Voilà donc ma commission faite, que je remplis en vous souhaitant le bonjour.

Easy to imagine the minister's saturnine pleasure in transmitting the queen's hasty order. The abbé's solution is not recorded: one feels for him, and relies on his inventiveness.

From court gossip of those years at Naples and Caserta, Fausto Nicolini has recorded the abbé's good-humored ripostes to sallies by the king and others — anecdotes that reflect his intimacy with the royal circle and the favor he enjoyed there but that make a pale contrast with his Parisian conversation. In general, he became steadily more conservative during his last years. In 1784 he showed himself suspicious when he learned that John Jay, one of the American negotiators, in Paris, of the peace treaty with Great Britain, had proposed to the Neapolitan ambassador, Don Luigi Pio, that Naples sign a commercial agreement with Philadelphia. For one thing, it was too early to admit the American republic—until recently a mere set of thirteen British colonies in constant disagreement, and now a newcomer in search of prestige—to terms of equality with the Kingdom of Naples: international disapproval would be certain. (Galiani saw France's support of the rebelling colonies as but another sign of French weakness.) Besides, what did the new nation have to offer Naples except tobacco? "Timber?" Galiani wrote. "We have enough of our own to last us for many years. And as for dried cod and salt pork—we get those cheaply from England and Holland." American vessels were welcome to come to ports in the Two Sicilies, especially to the free port of Messina, and to buy Neapolitan goods. Meanwhile, it might be well to investigate the rumored new

The Naples Diplomatic Corps in 1784, by Dominique Vivant Denon

commercial agreements between America and Holland, Portugal, Spain. . . .

Diderot had been in poor health since his return from Russia and Holland in 1774.

Newsletter, August 1784.

M. Diderot n'est plus: he died on 31 July, as peacefully and suddenly as he had always wished. For several years, his weakened condition had been evident. During the last six months, in particular, he had become dropsical, to a degree that carried him beyond medical aid. On the last day of his life, however, far from worsening, he seemed to have a little more appetite. That morning, he had a long, animated conversation with his friend the baron d'Holbach; and he had just said to his wife, "It's a long time since I last enjoyed eating," when she suddenly saw his eyes grow dull. She quickly asked if he was feeling worse: there was no answer: for him, the suffering was over.

The curé of Saint-Roch, the parish in which he died—in a house found for him by M. Grimm, acting for H. M. the Empress of Russia—felt it necessary, at first, to make a few difficulties, arising from the philosopher's all too well known reputation and from opinions expressed in his writings—opinions never publicly disavowed. However, those scruples were forgotten after a conversation with M. de Vandeul, M. Diderot's son-in-law, on the condition—and this is interesting, coming from a priest—that there be a funeral costing from fifteen to eighteen thousand francs.

"The loss of this famous man," the notice concludes, "is an affliction to letters, to philosophy, and to friendship."[5]

Galiani doubtless learned of Diderot's death, if only in the public news, after an interval; but no word from him about this loss survives. Diderot had had a falling-out with the ever more conservative Grimm at the time of Turgot's liberal reforms, but of this Grimm makes no mention in a letter he wrote to Galiani about the death of their friend:

> *Paris [probably 6 September 1785].* . . . Our incomparable Diderot had been living in a way made possible by the generosity of our incomparable Catherine. He died *chez elle*, so to speak: his old flat was on so high a floor that he could never reach the street without hiring someone to help him—a constant strain on his purse; the Empress ordered me to find him a suitable lodging, and I rented a splendid one on a ground floor. He had been living in it for a fortnight, happy as a child; he died while sitting at table, chatting after dinner. He is the only man of such eminence for whom his country did absolutely nothing; he never received an écu from the government; all was left to Catherine's generosity.

In May 1785, Galiani suffered a slight stroke. The effects gradually receded; during the next year, despite warnings, he traveled for a few weeks in Puglia, and, in 1787, to Venice, Padua, and Modena, visiting friends. After his return to Naples, the king and queen were struck by his altered look when he arrived at a palace reception, and insisted that he return to his home and rest. He was asthmatic and, like Diderot, dropsical; now he rapidly worsened. An exchange of letters with Maria Carolina provides a pair of self-portraits, though portions of the queen's homily suggest also the hand of a "spiritual adviser," perhaps the court chaplain. Even so flexible a wit as Galiani's may have been somewhat tried by this free discussion of his own imminent death.

> *Maria Carolina to Galiani, Naples, [October] 1787.*
> I am writing to tell you of my sorrow at the loss of a man so useful to the king and the country; and at the same time to assure you that I shall not forget your niece, of whom you have spoken to me several times. That will give me an occasion to show my gratitude for your faithful service. However, after reassuring you

about persons for whom you feel concern, I must say something about yourself: in doing so, I think I can perform the best possible service for you, and give you the greatest proof of my gratitude. You will soon be making the journey into eternal life, rendering an account of the use you have made of the uncommon talents granted you by Providence, and acknowledging to what extent you have erred. God is infinitely merciful, infinitely good; and your present illness is itself an evidence of His mercy. Beware of abusing this: I beg you not to display that obstinacy that derives from loose living; do not listen to the flattery of false friends, which may lead to eternal damnation. Believe me: throw yourself into the arms of a merciful God; renounce your errors; by setting a good example, impress those who have been scandalized by your past actions. My gratitude for your good services and my admiration of your talent and intelligence make me shudder when I think of the peril in which you stand.

I have been wanting to speak with you, but am told, to my regret, that you can no longer leave your house. I blame myself for not having spoken of these things the last time I saw you. Mark my words: throw yourself into the arms of God the infinitely merciful, the Father who forgives all: make your suffering and your untimely death an offering to Him; close your doors against those who would mock this letter, were they to read it. . . . I would visit you, did my position not preclude it. Thank the Supreme Being for having granted you your talents. . . . His arms are open, in forgiveness of your errors. . . . I trust that you do not doubt God's existence: you have too much talent [*sic*] for that. . . . Rely on His mercy. . . . With gratitude from one who grieves to lose you, Carolina.

Galiani to Maria Carolina, Naples, 18 October 1787.
Among the infinite mercies granted me by Heaven, I regard as one of its greatest favors that of having moved

Your Majesty's most gracious heart to wish to come to see me and urge me to think of duty, virtue, and eternal salvation. For that I shall always be grateful to the All Highest, always seeing it as the act of a Most Clement Sovereign, indeed, of an affectionate mother. Nevertheless, I cannot truthfully say that my soul has strayed so far from the proper path as Your Majesty, in your most magnanimous letter, seems to fear. I do not wish to deny, and cannot, that I have been and still remain a sinner; and I constantly pray Heaven to show me mercy. I can assure you, however, that the eternal maxims of morality and of the *true Christian religion* [the emphasis is Galiani's] are ever close to my heart, and I pray God that they may be there to the end. I feel strong enough to come and kiss Your Majesty's hands once again, and to serve you as God wills. However, should the doctors forbid it, and there be no appeal, it would be an infinite goodness on Your Majesty's part not to abandon my sister-in-law, the marchesa Galiani, and her husband, Don Tolomeo Rossi. And since your goodness is inexhaustible, I dare beg also that you retain, in his post as commercial magistrate, Don F. Azzarito the younger, my relative whom I helped to educate and whose merits are recognized by all his colleagues in the legal profession.

I must not try your kindness further, and far less must I be guilty of vainglory; but I cannot refrain from saying that, though I have often sinned as a man and as a Christian, I cannot recall having done so as a magistrate or as a servant of the state.

Sono ai piedi della Sua Maestà
Umilissimo vassale,
Ferd. Galiani.

A few days later, Galiani received the last rites: he insisted on wearing his wig and on being helped by servants to accompany the officiating priest to the door. One account of his final days has it that "he died as he had lived, laughing and making others laugh with him." Another, that he was "a harlequin to the end." Still another, that "he declared himself greatly worried about one detail of his will: in what category to include his aged, infirm horse. 'Mobile property?'—the horse was undeniably alive, but could scarcely stand. 'Immobile?' Whatever his decision, he said, his heirs would undoubtedly wrangle about it." When Acton called, Galiani refused to see him: "Tell him that my carriage is waiting, and that his will soon arrive." From the empress Catherine, on one of his last days, came a jeweled snuffbox bearing her portrait and a letter of thanks for the part he had played during the past several years in the long drafting and negotiating of a trade agreement between Russia and the Kingdom of Naples. He died on 30 October 1787 at the age of fifty-nine, and the following day joined his uncle the archbishop in the church of the Ascensione at Chiaia. No trace of either tomb remains in that church today.

In the convulsions of society that followed the outbreak of the French Revolution, the later story of Mme d'Épinay's friends and descendants constitutes a detailed chronicle. Of the four principal characters in the present story, only Grimm lived to see the fall of the Bastille and to suffer through the ensuing violence.

After Mme d'Épinay's death, Grimm became Émilie's legal guardian, having apparently convinced her parents that, because of his royal and imperial connections, he could do more for her than could they in their remote province. He placed her in a convent school in Paris; and his letter to Galiani recounting the death of Diderot concluded: "As soon as I find a suitable husband for Émilie, I'll invite you to lunch at Baia, dinner at the port of Misenum, and supper in the grotto of the Sybil." In 1785, when Émilie was eighteen, he did find her a husband, a comte de Bueil, whose château was at Varennes, twenty-five leagues from Paris. Her parents gave her a dowry of 100,000 livres; Catherine, a present of 12,000 rubles. Grimm himself was appointed by Catherine as Russian minister at Hamburg, but he seems seldom to have traveled there. He often stayed at Varennes; and during the turbulent years that followed, when Émilie's husband was for a time an officer with the émigré army of the prince de Condé, he shepherded her and her children over the border to Gotha. He himself lived in Gotha, in retirement, until his death, at eighty-four, in 1807—in the new, Napoleonic age, which, in its turn, would soon close. The empress Catherine was appalled by the revolution in France; she lived until 1796, and left Grimm well provided for. And one of Émilie's daughters—a great-granddaughter of Mme d'Épinay—married and living nearby, composed the inscription for his gravestone in a rural cemetery: "Here lies a learned man, and devoted friend. Though he attained an advanced age, his death came too soon for us, and for the world."

Mme d'Épinay's daughter and son—Mme de Belsunce and the ever debt-ridden Louis-Joseph—met briefly in Paris for the settlement of their mother's estate. He returned to Switzerland and she to Méharin, only to leave it again, in haste, as a threatened aristocrat, early in the Revolution. For a time she was an all but penniless refugee in Spain. When the convulsions subsided, she was rescued by Émilie and Bueil, with whom she spent the rest of her days in the château at Varennes, to which they had returned.

The fate of Émilie's father is obscured in the chaos of those times. Not so, however, that of one of her brothers, Henri de Belsunce. In August 1789, a few weeks after the fall of the Bastille, this grandson of Mme d'Épinay, a major in the élite Régiment de Bourbon, was shot and stoned to death at Caen. It was a time of famine in Normandy; the day before, Belsunce's regiment had protected a convoy of grain from the assaults of a hungry crowd. Now a mob gathered again. Belsunce appeared: he was tall and handsome, an easy target. He fell, and women in the crowd tore out his heart and ate it.

There had not as yet been many examples of such savagery,

and there was horror at court. Émilie was summoned to Versailles, where Marie Antoinette kissed her and wept. The Newsletter for April 1790 opened with a memorial ode:

SUR LE JEUNE COMTE DE BELSUNCE
Massacré par le peuple dans une émeute à Caen.
Romance, Par Mme Laugier de Grandchamp

The final quatrain suggests the author's relation to the young victim:

Cher compagnon de mon heureuse enfance,
Toi qui péris pour conserver mes jours,
Fidèle ami dont l'ombre me devance,
Je vais te joindre: adieu donc, mes amours!

And in 1794, at Naples, one of Galiani's great-nephews, Vincenzo Galiani, a medical student, was a member of a group of young people who displayed sympathy with French republican ideals. Thirty were imprisoned; three were sentenced to death, of whom young Galiani was one. His distraught family appealed to the queen—that sovereign whose benevolence the abbé Galiani had entreated for members of his family and who had repeatedly assured him of her esteem and gratitude. But the times were transfigured, and Maria Carolina was a sister of Marie Antoinette—who, on 16 October 1793, had been led to the guillotine. A year later, on 3 October 1794, young Galiani was hanged, sharing the fate of innumerable others caught up in the tragic cycle of retaliation that was played out in Naples, as in Paris, with irreparable loss.[6]

Giovanni Paisiello, who had composed the score of *Socrates* and corresponded with Galiani from Russia, returned to Naples; in 1799 he declared himself for the Parthenopean Republic. Jeopardized by the return of the Bourbons, he was allowed to go to Paris at the request of his admirer, Napoleon Bonaparte. While there, he composed the music for the emperor's coronation mass. Returning again to Naples, he was spurned by the vengeful Bourbons, and died in comparative poverty in 1816.

. . .

Louise d'Épinay and Ferdinando Galiani were spared awareness of these griefs. Their lives, fraught with infirmities and sorrows, gladdened by benign pleasures, had been passed in a more hopeful era, and in the active belief that knowledge and self-knowledge might ultimately prevail over the destructive passions of mankind. That sense of rational and cultivated being, in whose diffusion these two had played their part, was overtaken, but not extinguished, by the familiar violence of history. And we may now see it as—like civilization itself—a sustained if interrupted theme.

NOTES

CHAPTER 1 Madame d'Épinay; or, Poor Relations

1. For the various editions of *L'Histoire de Madame de Montbrillant*, see Chapter 14, notes 9 and 10.

2. The *fermiers-généraux*, or tax-farmers, had for centuries been entrusted with the collection—actually performed by their assistants —of indirect taxes. Their main interest lay in profits derived from the difference between the fixed sums which they paid the Treasury for their posts and the amounts their assistants managed to squeeze from taxpayers. Tax-farmers constituted one of the wealthiest sections of any French community. Their inevitable unpopularity was to lead in 1794 to the rounding up and execution of all surviving tax-farmers (including the scientist Antoine-Laurent Lavoisier).

Charles Dickens's "Monseigneur" in *A Tale of Two Cities* is a tax-farmer: "A sumptuous man was the Farmer-General. Thirty horses stood in his stables, twenty-four male domestics sat in his halls, six body-women waited on his wife" (Book I, Chapter 7). And further on: "Two score and twelve were told off at the daily roll-call for execution. From the Farmer-General of seventy, whose riches could not buy his life, to the seamstress of twenty . . ." (Book III, Chapter 13).

3. Mme d'Épinay's description of this episode in the pages of *Madame de Montbrillant* is not unlike the picture painted by Choderlos de Laclos in his 1782 epistolary novel *Les Liaisons dangereuses*, the action of which takes place in 1768.

4. Denis-Joseph was the principal heir because the eldest son, Louis-François, was mentally defective, living in a monastery with a lay attendant and a personal servant. Little more is known about him: he is not mentioned by Mme d'Épinay. She refers to the fourth and youngest son, Alexis-Janvier, only as an infant. Of the siblings, only Alexis-Janvier and Sophie (later Mme d'Houdetot) seem to have been endowed with full mental balance. (Ange-Laurent died insane at the age of fifty-four, and we shall see the end of Denis-Joseph.)

5. Hippolyte Taine, in *L'Ancien Régime*, speaks disparagingly of "*les parvenus, les financiers qui achètent ou se donnent un nom de terre.*"

6. Opera by Pascal Collasse (1689).

7. Much later, in the early years of the nineteenth century, George Sand's paternal grandmother, who had been Francueil's second wife, told her little granddaughter about his charm (she had been the comtesse de Horn, a widow of thirty, when they married in 1777, Francueil being then over sixty): "Your grandfather was handsome, elegant, always faultlessly turned out, graceful, jovial, courteous, affectionate, even-tempered, until the day he died. . . . His mind was for me an endless encyclopaedia of ideas, knowledge and talents. . . . He played

duets every day; he was an excellent violinist and made his violin himself (he constructed other musical instruments, and clocks as well); he was an architect, an expert with the lathe, a painter, locksmith, decorator, cook, poet, composer, carpenter, and a marvelous embroiderer. In the evening, when we didn't entertain or go out, he would sit beside me and draw. . . . Among our friends were young women who had made more splendid marriages, but who never tired of telling me that they envied me my elderly husband." (George Sand, *Histoire de ma vie*, Chapter 1.)

8. In 1770, Rousseau began to read sections of his unpublished *Confessions* in Paris salons. Learning that they contained inaccurate references to herself, Mme d'Épinay complained to her friend Gabriel de Sartine, lieutenant general of the Paris police, and the readings were stopped. However, those passages, and equally inaccurate passages concerning Diderot and others, remain in the printed *Confessions*.

On the other hand, at the request of Diderot, then engaged in a controversy with Rousseau, and with Diderot's participation, Mme d'Épinay sharpened certain passages concerning Rousseau in her autobiographical *Madame de Montbrillant*. But this would remain unpublished until after Rousseau's death: he never saw it.

9. "Not an excessive number for those days. . . . Another *fermier-général* had twenty-four servants in livery, not counting scullions, kitchen help, and Madame's six maids . . . thirty horses. . . . The duc de Choiseul, in disgrace at Chanteloup, maintained four hundred people, including fifty-four in livery. . . . One *président* in the Parlement had about thirty-six servants and fourteen carriage horses, not counting his wife's own staff. Thus 'M. de Montbrillant' was living on a scale that was almost modest." (Editor's note in *Madame de Montbrillant* [1951], II, 292.)

Mme d'Épinay herself writes that her husband had at least eight horses, including "two superb saddle horses from Denmark," and that at the time of his father's death he was writing to Denmark for more, in order to have "a team of eight carriage horses." Elsewhere she speaks of his having twenty-four saddle horses.

10. Unlike her daughter by Francueil, this son was not "recognized" by M. d'Épinay. Nor, one imagines, did Mme d'Épinay expect that he would be: he was not wanted by the family as a possible heir. He was baptized with a name unconnected with the names of his parents—Jean-Claude Le Blanc de Beaulieu. Of him, George Sand wrote what she says she had been told by her grandmother: "Born in the village of Le Blanc and raised in a place, or on a farm, called Beaulieu, he was given those two names and sent to a seminary at an early age. . . . He was the image of his mother." Jean-Claude Le Blanc de Beaulieu became bishop of Soissons in 1802, resigned his see in 1820, and died five years later.

CHAPTER II *Melchior Grimm and Denis Diderot*

1. Mme Geoffrin, whose Paris salon Grimm frequented, wrote, via the Polish embassy, to her friend King Stanislas-August, whom she had enrolled among the subscribers to the Newsletter: "Here is your first number, together with Grimm's accompanying letter. Your Majesty will see that it is important that no copies be made. The German courts are very loyal to Grimm in this particular. I may even say to Your Majesty that negligence on this point could have serious consequences for me, the matter having passed through my hands." Another subscriber was Empress Catherine II of Russia.

2. Élisabeth Badinter, *Émilie, Émilie, ou L'Ambition féminine au XVIIIe siècle* (1983).

3. "Mlle Durand" in the Memoirs. Perhaps that was the real name of this apparently admirable woman.

4. Some months before, on 15 November 1755, Grimm had paid homage to Mme d'Épinay in the Newsletter by printing an unsigned poem addressed to her on her name day (Saint Louis, 25 August).

> *Vers à Mme d'Épinay*
> *le 25 août, jour de sa fête*
> *Les plus brillantes fleurs qu'un instant vont éclore,*
> *Un autre instant les voit flétrir;*
> *Je parcourais en vain tous les jardins de Flore*
> *Ne sachant laquelle choisir;*
> *Lorsqu'au bord d'un ruisseau j'aperçus l'immortelle*
> *Qui me dit: "Cueille-moi, tu dois me préférer;*
> *Je présente a Chloé une image fidèle*
> *Des tendres sentiments qu'elle sait inspirer."*

5. An appointment that ended after only eighteen months. An indiscretion—Grimm's slighting reference to a member of the French government in one of his dispatches to Frankfurt—discovered and reported by the censor, brought an official French demand for the termination of Grimm's employment. In addition to his income from the Newsletter, Grimm enjoyed a sinecure that paid him two thousand livres a year, as "*secrétaire des commandements*" to Louis, duc d'Orléans (1725–85), who was a lover of the theatre.

6. In 1747, as editor of the *Encyclopaedia* (then in its early stages of preparation), Diderot had been imprisoned at Vincennes for several months. His eventual triumph—publication of the entire *Encyclopaedia*—was achieved only in 1772, and even then he would discover that the printer had indulged in some surreptitious purging. Volume VII, the first to appear after the long hiatus, in 1759, opens with an excellent preface by Diderot.

Grimm's article for the *Encyclopaedia*, "Poème lyrique," offers interesting opinions about French and Italian music at this time. It begins: "The Italians have baptized the *poème lyrique*, or musical drama, 'Opera'; and this term has been adopted in France." The article deals chiefly with Italian opera and with dance as a component of opera ("Dance has become, in all countries, the companion of musical drama").

7. Marcel Proust, *À la recherche du temps perdu*, vol. 2, *Le Temps retrouvé*.

CHAPTER III *The Young Abbé from Naples*

1. In 1754, Intieri, a man of means, founded and endowed, at the University of Naples, the world's first professorship of economics (then called *commercio e meccanica*). Antonio Genovesi was the first occupant of the new chair.

2. A recent tribute to *Della Moneta* is contained in Giuseppe Nardi's introduction to the edition published by the Banco di Napoli in 1988: "In my opinion Ferdinando Galiani's *Della Moneta*, in the subtlety of its doctrine, the precision of its method, and the keenness of its thought, stands out markedly above all other writing of the period. . . . It anticipates by a century the school of the marginalists and economic determinists, commonly thought to constitute the beginning of the modern science of economics."

And John A. Marino, in *Pastoral Economics in the Kingdom of Naples*, also 1988, calls Galiani "the master of monetary theory," and writes: "Galiani's precocious, anonymous publication of *Della Moneta* at the age of twenty-one catapulted him into the front rank of European economic thinkers, and this work became one of the cornerstones of the new academic discipline of political economy. Naples further distinguished itself with the foundation of the first European chair of political economics, in 1754. . . . The establishment of the science of political economics in the university curriculum marked a new birth for the practical affairs of economics and government. Antonio Genovesi, the dynamic holder of the chair from 1754 to 1769, became the teacher of a generation of enlightened economic thinkers and reformers."

3. The volume also involved Tanucci and the editors in disputes with the German scholar Johann Winckelmann, the first archaeologist to distinguish between Greek art and Roman copies. The fullest account is found in Winckelmann's *Lettera sulle Antichità d'Ercolano* (1762).

Eleven years later, Galiani tried to persuade Tanucci to order the printing of a less luxurious edition of the Herculaneum volumes for general sale. In France alone, he wrote, pointing to the great success of the *Encyclopaedia*, there was a far wider reading public than Tanucci, in Naples, seemed to realize: "All the goldsmiths and jewelers, all the painters of coaches and overdoors, all the designers and decorators, need this book. Does Your Excellency know that the great fashion here today is '*à la grecque*'—that is, in the style of Herculaneum? At this very moment the Venetian ambassador is having a gold box made for himself, with reliefs taken from the Herculanean pictures. All bronzes, inlays, and pictures are copied from the Herculanean. The picture of a woman selling little winged cupids, I have seen copied in more than ten houses." (22 June 1767) But Tanucci refused. "The *Encyclopaedia* is not a book, but an entire library, and so it finds an infinite number of buyers. Besides, people are beginning to be sick of Herculaneum: the pictures are seen everywhere." (11 July 1767)

It is true that other volumes on the antiquities had already been published, and would, to our own day, continue to appear; but none has been of the quality of the Neapolitan edition. Tanucci's view that a taste for the antique was passé was of course mistaken. "*Le goût grec*," which had burgeoned so rapidly, spread and became diffused throughout the Western world in every aspect of art and architecture.

4. The congenial, cultivated pope, who had enjoyed the Iannacone farce and rewarded the donor of volcanic stones, had died in May 1758. Some of the geniality that had characterized Celestino Galiani, the pontiff's friend, pervades the eulogy by Celestino's nephew; in form, it is a brief biography. Among Benedict XIV's good works, Ferdinando praises particularly the care he directed to the neglected monuments of pagan Rome: he had concerned himself with the restoration of the Pantheon and the preservation of the remains, as we see them today, of the Colosseum.

CHAPTER IV   *Paris (I)*

1. The Parisian Jean-Claude Richard, abbé de Saint-Non (1730–1804), antiquarian and engraver, traveled in Italy with Hubert Robert and Fragonard; on his return he published, between 1781 and 1784, the famed illustrated volumes of *Voyage pittoresque, ou Description des royaumes de Naples et de Sicile*.

2. King Carlo and Queen Maria Amalia took with them their second son, also named Carlo, who was to succeed his father on the Spanish throne. Remaining in Naples with Ferdinando was their first-born, the ten-year-old Filippo, mentally defective and officially declared unfit to rule. He lived for another eight years.

Carlo scrupulously took with him nothing that could be considered the property of the Kingdom of Naples, even an antique cameo ring that he himself had found among the ruins of Herculaneum and had sometimes worn.

3. According to *Larousse du XXème siècle*: "*Morellet avait l'intelligence vive et étendue, un style facile et élégant, une grande aptitude à faire valoir les idées d'autrui*."

4. Humphrey Carpenter, *W. H. Auden, a Biography* (Boston: Houghton Mifflin Co., 1981), p. 363.

5. The *Encyclopaedia* ultimately consisted of thirty-five volumes: seventeen of text, twelve of plates, four of supplementary text, and a two-volume index.

6. Tanucci was mistaken: only a few months later, D'Alembert published his essay "Sur la destruction des jésuites en France, par un auteur désintéressé." The suppression of the Jesuits in France had begun. Permitted for a decade to remain only as secular priests, all members of the order were expelled from France in 1774.

7. "As a model for his horse, Bouchardon had chosen a Spanish horse belonging to the baron de Thiers. He preferred to have the free use of a horse belonging to a friend rather than borrow one from the royal stables and have to deal with His Majesty's grooms. Connoisseurs agree that M. Thiers' horse is very beautiful, the only disadvantage being that it is not in its first youth. It is gentle, and came to display a remarkable affection and friendship for the sculptor; it was almost as though it were aware of the special circumstances, and knew that it was to share the honors of immortality with the genius of the artist. Bouchardon often spent hours lying prone beneath the horse, which would remain motionless in whatever position it had been made to take. Thus we may now boast of having, at last, a bronze horse that is not one of those fantastic, rearing beasts we see baring its teeth, its nostrils flaring and mane flying, its muscles contracted—but a noble, graceful, gentle animal, ravishing in its rare and exquisite beauty."

Bouchardon died before the work was finished, and the last touches on the sculpture, together with the making of the pedestal, were entrusted to the sculptor Pigalle.

8. "Truly, the day before yesterday, when the statue was transported from the sculptor's studio to the new square, one had an opportunity of seeing how greatly the king is loved by his people. It brought tears to one's eyes to watch the celebration—the joy, the acclamations of the populace as they greeted this new sculpture. They festooned it with olive wreaths—they did all but burn incense: the cries of '*Vive le Roi!*' were endless. I never saw anything like it."

In 1792, when the square was rebaptized Place de la Révolution, Bouchardon's equestrian statue of Louis XV was toppled from its base and destroyed. It was replaced by a colossal sculpture symbolizing Liberty. Nearby, the guillotine was installed—the machine used to decapitate Louis XVI (the equestrian's grandson), Marie Antoinette, and many other unfortunates. Mme Roland, standing beside the guillotine in June 1793, is said to have apostrophized the new sculpture in her much-quoted words: "*O Liberté, que de crimes on commet en ton nom!*"

9. Among the Bourbons, Louis XV was "*Le Roi Très Chrétien*" in the diplomatic language of the day; Carlos III of Spain, "*El Rey Católico*"; Ferdinando IV of Naples, "*Il Re.*"

10. *Letters of Mozart and His Family*, ed. and trans. Emily Anderson, 3rd ed. (New York: W. W. Norton and Co., 1989), pp. 43–44.

11. *Ibid.*, p. 40.

12. A popular annual Neapolitan festival, now in decline, taking place around the church of Santa Maria di Piedigrotta, which stands at the foot of a slope below a tunneled Roman road and adjacent to the long-venerated "Tomb of Virgil."

13. It is unclear whether this anatomical disquisition was printed in the Newsletter as supposed fact or as a joke to test the credulousness of readers.

The present writer, cautious and no scientist, having asked an obliging friend to submit the passage to an authority on the rhinoceros, can gratefully report the reply of William Conway, general director of the New York Zoological Society: "Pure bunk. I have had several opportunities to peer down a rhinoceros's throat· it is definitely a single-tongued beast."

14. From the context, this would seem to be the mediaeval church named for the patroness of Paris. In 1764 that ancient building was still standing, during preparations for the construction of its grandiose successor on the site. The new church, designed by the architect Souf flot, would also be called Sainte-Geneviève; during the Revolution it received its present name of Le Panthéon.

15. "France, less favored on the whole as to matters spiritual than her sister of the shield and trident, rolled with exceeding smoothness downhill, making paper money and spending it. Under the guidance of her Christian pastors, she entertained herself, besides, with such humane achievements as sentencing a youth to have his hands cut off, his tongue torn out with pincers, and his body burned alive, because he had not kneeled down in the rain to do honor to a dirty procession of monks which passed within his view, at a distance of some fifty or sixty yards." (Charles Dickens, *A Tale of Two Cities*, Book I, Chapter 1.)

"Some of the prescribed horrors might be omitted: the tearing-out of La Barre's tongue was only simulated. . . . The crowd might wait for hours around the scaffold uncertain of what the eventual outcome might be. . . . As the rain poured down throughout a long summer's day, would the young chevalier de la Barre receive a last-minute reprieve from the Parlement of Paris?" (M. Chassaigne, *Le Procès du Chevalier de La Barre* [1920], quoted in John McManners, *Death and the Enlightenment* [N.Y.: Oxford University Press, 1981], p. 389.)

CHAPTER V   *"The Hot Baths on Ischia"*

1. Apropos of the composition of this document, the Italian scholar Raffaele Guariglia has written of Galiani: "He was a perfect represen-

tative of the glorious Neapolitan eighteenth century, not only because in all fields—in philosophy, law, politics and art—does he express the very thought of that era; but he had, too, that century's *esprit*, its delightful irony—in a word, the spirit that tempers the seriousness of a proposition with the pungent skepticism of criticism. In the pages of official reports, in which he speaks frankly and fearlessly, and even in arid documents recounting fruitless disputes and diplomatic negotiations, the figure of Galiani always carries with it a singular fascination—of which he himself was well aware, and which he knew how to exploit." ("Un mancato tratto di commercio tra le Due Sicilie e la Francia," in *Rivista di Diritto Internazionale*, 2nd ser., vol. 3 [1914].)

CHAPTER VI *Paris (II)*

1. Edward Gibbon, *Decline and Fall of the Roman Empire*, conclusion of Chapter 25. He is speaking of the emperor Gratian.
2. Like his father, Ferdinando was addicted to shooting deer, bear, and other game. To quote Harold Acton, in *The Bourbons of Naples*: "Ferdinando manifested . . . neither ardour nor indifference for the Queen. On the morning after his nuptials, when the weather was very warm, he rose at an early hour and went out as usual to the chase, leaving his young wife in bed. Those courtiers who accompanied him having inquired of His Majesty how he liked her: '*Dorme come un' ammazzata*,' replied he, '*e suda come un porco.*' ('She sleeps as if she had been killed, and sweats like a pig.')"
3. Caracciolo had written to Galiani early in his London stay that he found the British very strange. "They want a republic and a king, monarchy and liberty. An impossibility. As I remarked to one serious Englishman: 'You want ladies to be beautiful, charming, elegant—and at the same time faithful? Too much to ask!' "

In his invitation, sent in mid-November, he had promised Galiani "plays, operas, balls, Parliament, universities, casinos, literary men, politicians, and whores."
4. Apparently a reference to England's intellectual and scientific flowering as it emerged from the Seven Years' War.
5. Anthony Powell, *Books Do Furnish a Room* (Boston: Little, Brown, 1971).

CHAPTER VII *Recalled*

1. Two details of the story are not clear: when it was that Galiani learned about the spy, and whether, on being recalled, he immediately understood that his indiscretion must be the reason. Certainly Choiseul's "angry letter . . . couched in very general terms" to Castromonte

made Galiani realize that something serious had occurred. Nowhere in the Galiani-Tanucci correspondence is there any reference to the nature of the offense.

Tanucci had written to Madrid on 9 May, reporting compliance with the king's order that Galiani be recalled. His letter is unusually craven in tone, assuring Carlos that neither he nor Ferdinando had played a role in Galiani's indiscretion, and humbly begging pardon for having given cause for suspicion. (The last line of Galiani's letter of 29 May raises doubts as to Tanucci's veracity on this matter.) Then, at the end of his letter, he writes: "To replace Galiani in Paris I have sent Perez, who has been on my staff here. He is slow, ponderous, capable at best of writing a routine letter—qualities in contrast to the *vivacité* that caused Galiani to go astray." (Tommaso Perez had been director of the royal porcelain works at Portici.)

Galiani's recall from Paris marked the end of his diplomatic service abroad. But even Choiseul let it be known to Carlos that in his opinion Galiani's undoubted abilities merited his being given a post outside diplomacy.

2. The château de Chanteloup was Choiseul's country house, near Amboise. Gatti, who in addition to being Galiani's friend was the friend and physician of both Choiseul and his wife, was attending the duchess at this moment.

3. Choiseul's blatant hypocrisy here and in the following letter is, one may suppose, merely an aspect of his métier, just as the persistently respectful tone of Galiani's references to him reflects his hope of reinstatement in Paris. It is clear from what follows that Galiani was well aware of Choiseul's underlying responsibility for his recall.

4. Galiani would never forgive Tanucci for having instantly obeyed Choiseul's demand for his recall. He believed, or pretended to believe, that, had Tanucci used in this instance a little of the talent for delay he had displayed in other matters, Choiseul's order, once he was out of office, would have been rescinded. But Tanucci clearly considered Galiani expendable, his recall another step in the long avoidance of signing the Family Pact.

CHAPTER VIII   *The Publication of the* Dialogues

1. During Grimm's stay in Germany in 1769, the duke of Saxe-Gotha had appointed him *conseiller de légation*, with an annual salary of sixteen hundred livres. Grimm, becoming what can only be called a courtier, was growing bored with the Newsletter.

2. Once again, see *A Tale of Two Cities*: Dickens's disgraced Marquis St. Evrémonde is thought to be an echo of the exiled Choiseul.

3. In the palace of the Tuileries, in space previously occupied by the Opéra. The Comédie later moved to what is today the Odéon and then, in 1802, to its present quarters attached to the Palais-Royal.

4. It is interesting to find Mme d'Épinay, so concerned with education and human conduct, thus speaking easily of "the people," meaning the general populace. It was the parlance of those times: as Jacques Barzun has said, "Her ideas did not change her vocabulary." That revenge of "the people" so soon to boil over in France might have destroyed Mme d'Épinay herself had she lived to meet it. Even today, can we be sure that the phrase has not retained some of its old meaning? Perhaps "people" are simply more careful about using it.

In view of what was to happen in the former Place Louis XV twenty years later, an item in the Newsletter for 1 July 1770 is of sober interest: "Madame la Dauphine, who was arriving from Versailles with Mesdames de France [her husband's aunts] to see the illuminations in the Place, was informed of the disaster that had just occurred, and turned back. Two days later she and M. le Dauphin sent their entire privy purse for a month to M. de Sartine for the relief of those who had suffered that fatal night."

CHAPTER IX   *Madame de La Daubinière*

1. Galiani nowhere expresses any objection to Gatti's relations with Mme de La Daubinière, nor does Gatti's account sound as though he expected any. Perhaps both knew her to be what was called *"une occasionelle"*; and Galiani, despite his affection, so regarded her.

2. *Le Tableau parlant*, which had opened on 20 September 1769 and had been praised (probably by Mme d'Épinay) in the Newsletter for October of that year. The song is sung by a *barbon*—a graybeard —who is wooing his beautiful young pupil.

3. It was perhaps a recent promotion that enabled Galiani to make this generous offer. In a letter of 24 November 1770 to D'Alembert he had written: "I have just been appointed secretary of the Commercial Court, and retain my post as councillor as well. Would you like to know what this new post entails? It entails a salary of two thousand livres."

4. The comte de Schomberg, mentioned earlier as a contributor to the Calas engraving, is not further identified in the letters. There were several branches of the Schomberg family among the nobility.

5. Giovanni Macchia, "Galiani Arlecchino e la *'nécessité de plaire,'* " in *La Caduta della Luna* (Milan: Mondadori, 1973).

CHAPTER X   *The Prodigal's Return, and Stories Exchanged*

1. A footnote to the printed French text of Galiani's letters about his cats suggests that he may have been acquainted with an episode in

the life of Paradis de Moncrif (1687–1770), the royal historiographer during the reign of Louis XV. Moncrif had published a parody of pedantic scholarship entitled *Histoire des chats*: "This work, and the protection of the house of Orléans, had brought Moncrif membership in the French Academy. Maurepas writes in his memoirs that the day of Moncrif's induction into the Academy, while he was in the midst of his oration about his own work, a jokester present let loose a cat he had been hiding in his pocket. The poor frightened thing miaowed loudly, several members of the audience responded in kind, and this unexpected accompaniment to the discourse put an end to the academic gravity of the occasion."

The Newsletter for November 1770 also speaks of Moncrif and cats: "The poet Roy having written an excessively biting epigram concerning him, Moncrif waited for Roy outside the Palais-Royal and took a stick to him. Roy was accustomed to such treatment. Protecting himself as best he could, he turned his back, and said: 'Velvet paws, now, pussy, velvet paws!' " Moncrif's very name, evocative of the French *griffe* (claw)—*nomen et omen*, as the saying goes—invited many a witticism.

Pierre-Charles Roy (1683–1764) died at eighty-one, following another beating, this one said to have been administered by a ruffian hired by the comte de Clermont, Roy's successful rival for election to the French Academy, against whom he had directed another of his salvos. Voltaire's beating by hirelings of the chevalier de Rohan in 1725 was only the most celebrated of bodily assaults on controversial French literary men during the eighteenth century.

2. Mme d'Épinay probably knew that it was Grimm himself who had asked to be given a title of nobility. His first request—to be awarded the Swedish Cross of the Order of the Polar Star—had been refused. Negotiations for both applications had been conducted by an international chain of titled officials—friends of friends of friends; and the price of the barony, four thousand florins, was met by the landgrave of Hesse-Darmstadt. For the use of a fuller version of the title, "Baron Grimm of Grimmhof," there would have been a further charge. But Grimm owned no property. There was no Grimmhof: he was *Grimmhofslos*. Diderot mockingly promoted him, calling him "marquis."

3. The sixteenth-and-seventeenth-century Swiss-born classical scholar Isaac Casaubon, whose name George Eliot would give, in the 1870s, to the moldy pedant of *Middlemarch*.

Regarding Alvise Mocenigo, whose singing and company Mme d'Épinay so enjoyed, Fausto Nicolini writes in *Gli ultimi anni della signora d'Épinay*: "Named, in 1773, Venetian ambassador to Vienna, he was refused by Maria Theresa. For this reason the Venetian state inquisitor was obliged to put him on trial, and he was sentenced to prison in the castle of Brescia. He was released in 1775. In 1779 he sought the dogeship, failing to win only because of the satires and pasquinades of which he became the target" (p. 253). In a letter to

Galiani of 17 January 1774, Mme d'Épinay writes: "I have almost taken a dislike to music since learning of the misfortunes of our Venetian Orpheus"; and on 9 July 1775: "Poor chevalier Mocenigo. Nothing will make me forget him." Several members of the Mocenigo family bore the same name: another Alvise Mocenigo (1701–78) was doge from 1763 until his death.

4. Diderot had written *Le Père de famille* in 1758. It played successfully in several French cities and in Baden and Hamburg, but when it at last reached the Parisian stage, in February 1761, it ran for only six performances. Hence the somewhat consolatory tone of Galiani's letter.

CHAPTER XI   *A Woman Alone*

1. The seventeenth-century philosopher René Descartes had, as Mme d'Épinay well knew, accepted Queen Christina's invitation to visit Stockholm in 1649 and had died there the following year.

2. Mr. Everett Fahy, of the Metropolitan Museum of Art, kindly supplies the following information: that a portrait of Mlle Guimet by Fragonard in the Louvre is reproduced in the catalogue of the loan exhibition of his work held at the Metropolitan in 1988; that several Fragonard drawings of her may be found in the Musée des Beaux-Arts in Besançon and a bust by Gaetano Muchi (1779) in the Musée des Arts Decoratifs; and that the lady's house in Paris was in rue d'Antin.

3. Celebrating the marriage of the comte d'Artois (the future King of France, Charles X) and Maria Teresa of Savoy.

4. The violinist and composer François Rebel was general manager of the Opéra.

5. It becomes clear from subsequent letters that the "opportunity" was the presence in Paris of the twenty-one-year-old Charles Stanhope (future third earl of Harrington), who was on his grand tour and would soon be leaving for Italy. This letter of 23 July from Mme d'Épinay was delivered to Galiani, apparently by a certain Lastrucci, Stanhope's *"premier valet,"* late in December.

6. The enthusiasm was that of the *philosophes* and liberals in general for the appointment of Turgot as comptroller general. Carlyle praises him in a famous passage in his *French Revolution*: "There is a young, still docile, well-intentioned King; a young, beautiful and bountiful, well-intentioned Queen; and with them all France, as it were, becomes young. . . . Instead of a profligate bankrupt Abbé Terray, we have now, for Comptroller-General, a virtuous philosophic Turgot, with a whole Reformed France in his head. By whom whatsoever is wrong, in Finance or otherwise, will be righted—as far as possible. Is it not as if Wisdom itself were henceforth to have a seat and voice in the Council of Kings?"

Notes

7. "*Je vois que M. de Sartine va devenir le pilote de l'état*" (Galiani to Mme d'Épinay, 1 June 1775). As naval minister, Sartine would, in 1778, take measures to reduce the prevalence of scurvy on shipboard. Doctors appointed by him supervised the sailors' diet, insisting on the provision of lemons, limes, vinegar, etc. (In 1794 the British navy formally prescribed similar measures—hence the American term "limey" for a British sailor, and, by extension, any Briton.)

CHAPTER XII   Les Conversations d'Émilie

1. From now on, the respites between Mme d'Épinay's periods of suffering would grow shorter. She speaks constantly of her "colic."

Among the tributes that came to her in her sickbed was one from the empress Catherine, who said that she was having the book translated into Russian; and there was a message from Voltaire, dated 28 January 1775, which begins with words quoted from his houseguest of the moment: "The daughter of the great-granddaughter of the great Corneille, Madame, is reading *Les Conversations d'Émilie*. She keeps exclaiming, '*Ah, la bonne maman! La digne maman!*' As for me, I'm constantly murmuring, 'Why am I not at the author's feet? Why do my eighty-one years deprive me of the joy of seeing and hearing her? Why must I live out my life so far from her?' Ah! Madame de Belsunce, how fortunate you are!"

2. The tenth conversation emphasizes attentiveness, memory, and precision of speech. The formal *vous* is used throughout. "*Vous avez l'esprit paresseux*," the mother tells the child.

The conversations are indeed charming, and an innovation for their time; but they are a charming and innovative primer: it is difficult to picture Galiani, with all possible good will, giving them sustained attention.

The first edition was published in Leipzig—so, at least, says the title page. There seems to be no clear reason why it should have been: the book was unlikely prey for the French censor. If Leipzig was its true place of publication, Grimm was probably responsible for the choice, as a consequence of his academic and other connections.

CHAPTER XIII   The Imaginary Socrates

1. *Vocabolario delle parole del dialetto napoletano*, article *Polecenella*, vol. 2, pp. 38–41.

There is a vast literature concerning the supposed origins of both characters, Arlecchino and Pulcinella.

2. In 1664, after its premiere at Versailles, further performance of Molière's *Tartuffe* was forbidden by the archbishop of Paris.

3. Mattei was also a lawyer, and one of the founders of the important musical library of the Naples Conservatory.

4. Franco di Tizio, *Ferdinando Galiani* (Chieti, 1988).

5. Piero di Nepi, in *Il Veltro*, January–April 1973.

6. Benedetto Croce, *I Teatri di Napoli*, 4th ed. (Bari, 1947), pp. 244–45.

Tanucci, master of the double meaning, is recorded on only one occasion as having entered a theatre. The anecdote is told in the *Souvenirs* of the baron de Gleichen, Galiani's former diplomatic colleague in Paris: "In the ceremonies of Holy Week, the Pope is borne from one part of the Vatican to another in a kind of litter, under a canopy, shaded on each side by a peacock-feather fan. The whole thing has a very Chinese look. It was copied to the last detail in the production of a comic opera called *L'Idolo cinese*, at Naples, precisely at the time of marchese Tanucci's greatest hostility to the Vatican. The Papal Nuncio, informed of this indecent farce, complained bitterly to the minister. Tanucci was much diverted by the news, and at once determined to see the play. To the Nuncio he wrote: 'Ah, Monseigneur, such a thing is impossible! Although I never attend the theatre, I shall certainly go myself, to confirm with my own eyes that the rumor is false.' Tanucci attended the performance, and wrote to the Nuncio the next day: 'I have seen the play. Put your mind at ease, Monseigneur. There is not a word of truth in what you were told. I assure you someone has been very malicious.' "

7. See Domenico De' Paoli, *Ferdinando Galiani: Socrate Immaginario* (Urbino: Istituto d'arte per la decorazione del libro, 1959).

8. Antonio Ranieri, *Sette anni di sodalizio con G. Leopardi* (Naples, 1880). See also the catalogue of the exhibition "Giacomo Leopardi" (Biblioteca Nazionale, Naples, 1987).

CHAPTER XIV *The Last Letters*

1. Voltaire died in Paris four weeks later, on 30 May. His body was transported hastily and secretly to a churchyard in Champagne, just in time to escape an episcopal order forbidding Christian burial.

2. The academy to which Galiani longed to be elected was the French Academy. "Speaking of academies," he had written to D'Alembert on 25 September 1773, "why doesn't it occur to someone that I'm ideally suited to be a foreign member? Not that this is important to me, but it would be delightful were it to happen." It never did: it seems not to have occurred to Galiani that official expulsion from France was scarcely a recommendation for membership.

3. Mme d'Épinay doubtless enjoyed Galiani's display of learning —and invention. Hydromel is the English mead.

4. The literary critic E. C. de Fréron (1719–76) had been hostile to the Philosophes.

5. After having been ambassador in London and Paris, Caracciolo was dismayed by the Sicilian appointment despite its superior rank, and he continually postponed his departure for Palermo. Galiani wrote to Mme d'Épinay: "Urge Caracciolo to pack up and leave. Since he has to go eventually, he should make up his mind and do it. '*Guai e maccheroni si mangiano caldi*,' as we say in Naples. The Sicilians are offended and humiliated to see a man backing away from taking his place as their sovereign."

Caracciolo had become as Parisian as Galiani. Congratulated by Louis XVI on his Sicilian appointment, he is said to have replied, "*Hélas, Sire, la plus belle place de l'Europe, c'est celle que je quitte.*" He had been living in Place Vendôme.

6. For this new, two-volume edition, published in Paris, Mme d'Épinay both refined and amplified the ten original conversations, and added ten more. The last takes place on Émilie's "attainment of the age of reason"—the eve of her tenth birthday. In the last conversation, perhaps inspired by Diderot and by what she had seen in Switzerland, Mme d'Épinay praises the republican form of government, particularly because of the greater attention paid in republics to public education.

7. Necker had asked Galiani his opinion of his *Essai sur la législation et le commerce des grains* (1775), and Galiani had replied: "Our minds are so in unison that it has always seemed to me that I ought to have said everything that you have said concerning political economy—that I might well have done so, and could have. You asked for my opinion of your incomparable book on grain, and there you have it. '*A buon intenditor poche parole.*' "

8. The "*prix d'utilité*" was named for its donor, the baron de Montyon (1733–1820), philanthropist and economist.

9. This coroner's report is reproduced from *Les Dernières années de Madame d'Épinay*, edited by Lucien Perey (Mlle Lucie Herpin) and Gaston Maugras (Paris, 1883). This, with its earlier companion volume, *La Jeunesse de Madame d'Épinay* (1882), is one of several early-nineteenth-century editions or adaptations of *L'Histoire de Madame de Montbrillant*.

10. The manuscript of the *Histoire*, bequeathed by Mme d'Épinay to Grimm, was impounded by the Revolutionary government when it was found in Grimm's Paris apartment following his flight from the Terror. (He had expected to return.) While in government hands, the manuscript was carelessly divided in two and stored in different libraries. The two parts were rediscovered and published during the nineteenth century in several deformed editions.

A dependable, accurate printed text of the *Histoire* was not forthcoming until the twentieth century: in three volumes, admirably edited by Georges Roth, published by Gallimard in 1951.

CHAPTER XV *The End of the Affair*

1. The dictionary itself, the *Vocabolario delle parole del dialetto napoletano*, proved to be a far greater labor than Galiani had expected, and he left it unfinished. After his death in 1787, it was completed, and it was published in 1789 by a group of scholars who in their preface paid tribute to Galiani: "merely to name him is to praise him." The title page repeats what Galiani had written in his manuscript, that the *Vocabolario* was the work of several *academici filopatridi*—patriotic academicians, or academic patriots. This was a satirical allusion to a recently formed group of pretentious Neapolitan scholars calling themselves l'Accademia delle Scienze—of which Galiani had not been invited to be a member. He had offended many Neapolitans, including scholars, by openly preferring the society of non-Neapolitans, and by his low opinion, expressed in *Socrates*, and no doubt in many conversations, of contemporary Neapolitan scholarship.

2. The most recent edition of Galiani's *Dialetto* is that edited by E. Malata, published by Bulzoni in 1970.

3. Furio Diaz, *Per una storia illuministica*, p. 334.

4. There is dramatic irony here. This Swedish king is the celebrated Gustavus III, the cultivated, enlightened, and charming monarch who was fatally stabbed by an assassin at a masked ball in the Stockholm opera house on 16 March 1792, and died two weeks later. He is the hero of several operas, of which the most famous is Verdi's *Un ballo in maschera* (1859), libretto by Antonio Somma.

5. Two years later, in November 1786, there appeared in the Newsletter a long eulogy of Diderot written by Meister in a particularly effusive style: "O Diderot! How many days have gone by since your genius was extinguished, since over your inanimate ashes fell the darkness of the tomb!" etc. This six-page panegyric was much admired and often reprinted.

6. Ferdinando II and Maria Carolina had gone to Caserta for the day, to be distant from the peculiar unpleasantness: executions of members of the respectable classes were not yet as usual as they would become a few years later, following the brief existence, in 1799, of the revolutionary Parthenopean Republic, inaugurated by the Neapolitan intelligentsia.

The Neapolitan historian Pietro Colletta, writing in 1848, has described the scene of the three young men, Vincenzo Galiani, Emanuele de Deo, and Vincenzo Vitaliano, "walking stoically to their deaths":

"The gallows was surrounded by soldiers and by cannon pointed toward the streets giving on the square. Troops had been stationed throughout the city; the artillery in the forts had been alerted; police and spies were everywhere. These precautions had alarmed the populace, but blood-lust was stronger than fear, and crowds flocked to the scene of the executions.

"Vitaliano's turn came after his two companions had been pronounced dead. As he climbed the steps to the scaffold there was a slight movement in the square. This alarmed the artillerymen, who sprang toward their cannon; and this, in turn, caused a panic in the already tense crowd, resulting in a general *sauve qui peut*. In the confusion, the hangman found himself standing alone with his last victim. Terrified, he thought only of ridding himself of the encumbrance and fleeing the scene: he drew his knife and plunged it into Vitaliano's heart." (*Storia del Reame di Napoli.*)

SELECTED BIBLIOGRAPHY

BY MADAME D'ÉPINAY

Lettres à mon fils. Reprint of the Geneva edition of 1759. Paris: Sauton, 1869.

Lettres à mon fils . . . et morceaux choisis. With an introduction and notes by Ruth Plaut Weinreb. Concord, Mass.: Wayside Publications, 1989.

Mes moments heureux. Reprint of the Geneva edition of 1759. Paris: Sauton, 1869.

L'Amitié de deux jolies femmes/suivie de/Un Rêve de Mademoiselle Clairon. Published by Maurice Tourneux. Paris: Librairie des Bibliophiles, 1885.

Les Conversations d'Émilie. Leipzig, 1774. Second ed. 2 vols. Paris, 1781.

Letters from Mme d'Épinay to Tronchin. Bibliothèque Publique et Universitaire de Genève, Tronchin Archives M78 F° 4.

La signora d'Épinay e l'abate Galiani: Lettere inedite. With an introduction and notes by Fausto Nicolini. Vol. 1, *1769–1772.* Vol. 2, *Gli ultimi anni della signora d'Épinay, 1773–1782.* Bari: Laterza e figli, 1929, 1933.

Les Pseudo-mémoires de Madame d'Épinay: Histoire de Madame de Montbrillant. With an introduction, notes, and other materials by Georges Roth. 3 vols. Paris: NRF Gallimard, 1951. (The first publication of the complete text.)

Les Contre-confessions: Histoire de Madame de Montbrillant, par Madame d'Épinay. Preface by Élisabeth Badinter. Notes by Georges Roth, revised by Élisabeth Badinter. Paris: Mercure de France, 1989. (A later, one-volume edition of the *Pseudo-mémoires.)*

BY FERDINANDO GALIANI

Opere di Ferdinando Galiani. Edited by Furio Diaz and Luciano Guerci. Milan and Naples: Riccardo Ricciardi, 1975. (Series *Illuministi Italiani,* vol. 6.)

Il Pensiero dell'abate Galiani. Anthology edited by Fausto Nicolini. Bari: Laterza, 1909.

Del Dialetto Napoletano. Naples, 1775. Reprint edited by Fausto Nicolini. Naples: Riccardo Ricciardi, 1923.

Vocabolario delle parole del dialetto napoletano, . . . degli Accademici Filopatridi. By Galiani and others. 2 vols. Naples, 1789.

Dialogo sulle donne e altri scritti. Edited by Cesare Cases. Milan: Feltrinelli Economica, 1979.

Selected Bibliography

Della Moneta. Naples: Banco di Napoli, 1988. (The most recent of many editions.)

Spaventosissima descrizione dello spaventoso spavento, etc. Self-published, Naples, 1779.

Discorso sull'Amore: Sopra la morte di Socrate. Opusculi: Capo d'Anno, Cicisbei, etc. Naples, 1825. And various modern editions.

Della Moneta e scritti inediti. With an introduction by Alberto Caracciolo and edited by Alberto Merola. Milan: Feltrinelli editore, 1963.

Dialogues sur le commerce des blés. With appendices by Fausto Nicolini. Milan: Riccardo Ricciardi, 1958. (There are many other editions.)

Dialogues entre M. le marquis de Roquemaure, et le chevalier Zanobi: The Monograph Manuscript of the Dialogues sur le commerce des blés. Diplomatically edited with an introduction, notes, and appendix by Philip Koch. Analecta Romanica, Heft 21. Frankfurt am Main: Vittorio Klostermann, 1968.

Lettere di F. Galiani al marchese Bernardo T. Tanucci. Edited by Augusto Bazzoni . . . from the Archivio Storico Italiano, Serie III e IV. Florence, 1880. And: Bernardo Tanucci. *Lettere a F. Galiani.* With an introduction and notes by Fausto Nicolini. 2 vols. Bari: Laterza, 1914.

Correspondance avec Madame d'Épinay—Madame Necker—Madame Geoffrin, etc. Diderot—Grimm—D'Alembert—De Sartine—d'Holbach. Revised edition . . . by Lucien Perey and Gaston Maugras. 2 vols. Paris: Calmann Lévy, 1881.

Amici e corrispondenti francesi dell'abate Galiani. Edited by Fausto Nicolini. Naples: Banco di Napoli, 1954.

(See under "General" for biographies of Galiani by Diodati, Mattei, and Carlo Pascal.)

GENERAL

Acton, Harold. *The Bourbons of Naples (1734–1825).* London: Methuen, 1956.

———. *The Last Bourbons of Naples (1825–1861).* London: Methuen, 1962.

Badinter, Élisabeth. *Émilie, Émilie, ou L'Ambition féminine au XVIIIᵉᵐᵉ siècle.* Paris: Flammarion, 1983.

Bailey, Colin B. *Ange-Laurent de La Live de Jully: A Facsimile Reprint of the Catalogue Historique (1764) and the Catalogue Raisonné de Tableaux (March 5, 1770), with an Introductory Essay and a Concordance to the French Paintings.* Acanthus Reprint Series of Historical Auction Catalogues, edited by Edgar Munhall. New York: Acanthus Books, 1988.

Billy, André. *Vie de Diderot.* Paris: Flammarion, 1943.

Bjoernstaehl, Giacomo Giona. *Lettere dei suoi viaggi stranieri, etc.* 4 vols. Poschiavo, 1784.

Bouvier, René, and André Laffargue. *La Vie napolitaine au XVIIIᵉᵐᵉ siècle.* Paris: Hachette, 1956.

Selected Bibliography

Campardon, Émile. *Les Prodigalités d'un fermier général. Complément aux Mémoires de Madame d'Épinay.* Paris: Charavay Frères, 1882.

Caporali, Gaetano. *Memorie storico-diplomatiche della città di Acerra.* Naples: Arturo Berisio, 1975.

Carcopino, Jérôme. *Daily Life in Ancient Rome.* Translated by E. O. Lorimer. Edited and with bibliography and notes by Henry T. Rowell. London: Penguin Books, 1941.

Castaldi, Giuseppe. *Della Regale Accademia Ercolanese, etc.* Naples: Dalla Tipografia di Porcelli, 1840.

Catucci, Marco. *Galianea: Ferdinando Galiani tra letteratura ed economia.* Rome: Bulzoni, 1986.

Cobb, Richard, and Colin Jones. *Voices of the French Revolution.* Topsfield, Mass.: Salem House Publishers, 1988.

Coletti, Alessandro. *La regina di Napoli: La vita appassionata di Maria Carolina, etc.* Novara: Istituto Geografico de Agostini, 1986.

Colletta, Pietro. *Storia del reame di Napoli dal 1734 al 1825.* 2 vols. Milan: Rizzoli, 1967.

Colonna di Stigliano, Fabio. *Napoli d'altri tempi.* Naples: Riccardo Ricciardi, 1911.

Cranston, Maurice. *The Early Life and Work of Jean-Jacques Rousseau, 1712–1754.* New York: W. W. Norton & Co., 1982.

———. *The Nobel Savage. Jean-Jacques Rousseau. 1734–1762.* Chicago: University of Chicago Press, 1991.

Craveri, Benedetta. *Madame Du Deffand e il suo mondo.* Milan: Adelphi, 1982.

Cuoco, Vincenzo. *Saggio storico sulla rivoluzione napoletana del 1799.* 1801. Reprint. Bari: Laterza, 1980.

Darnton, Robert. *The Literary Underground of the Old Regime.* Cambridge, Mass.: Harvard University Press, 1982.

Delamonce, Ferdinand. *Le "Voyage de Naples" (1719).* Edited by Laura Mascoli. Naples: Centre Jean Berard, 1984.

Del Puglia, Raffaella. *La regina di Napoli: il Regno di Maria Carolina dal Vesuvio alla Sicilia.* Pavia: Viscontea, 1989.

Diaz, Furio. "L'abate Galiani consigliere di commercio estero del regno di Napoli," in *Per una storia illuministica.* Naples: Guida, 1973.

Diderot, Denis. *Lettres à Sophie Volland,* in *Oeuvres complètes. Correspondance.* Edited by André Babelon. Paris: Gallimard, 1930. Reprint. Paris: Éditions d'Aujourd'hui, 1978.

Diodati, Luigi. *Vita dell'abate Ferdinando Galiani, regio consigliere, etc.* Naples: Presso Vincenzo Orsino, 1788.

Duchâtre, Pierre Louis. *The Italian Comedy.* Translated from the French by Randolph T. Weaver. New York: John Day, 1929.

Duclos, Charles. *Les Confessions du Comte de . . .* Paris: Éditions de la Grille, 1928.

Dupaty, Charles. *Lettres sur l'Italie.* 2 vols. Genoa: Chez Yves Gravier, 1818.

Fothergill, Brian. *Sir William Hamilton: Envoy Extraordinary.* New York: Harcourt, Brace & World, 1969.

Selected Bibliography

Gaborit, Jean-René. *Jean-Baptiste Pigalle, 1714–1785: Sculptures du Musée du Louvre*. Paris: Ministère de la Culture, 1985.

Gay, Peter. *The Enlightenment: An Interpretation*, 2 vols. New York: Alfred A. Knopf, 1966 and 1969; W. W. Norton, 1977.

Giannone, P. *Dell'istorico civile del regno di Napoli*. Naples: Niccolo Naso, 1723.

Gleichen, Charles-Henri, baron de. *Souvenirs, précédés d'une notice par M. Paul Grimmblot*. Paris: Léon Techener Fils, 1868.

Goncourt, Edmond et Jules de. *La femme au 18 ᵐᵉ siècle*. Paris, 1862. With a preface by Élisabeth Badinter. Paris: Flammarion (Collection Champs), 1982.

———. *La Guimard*. Geneva: Minkoff, 1979.

Gorani, Joseph. *Mémoires secrets et critiques des cours, des gouvernements, et des moeurs des principaux états de l'Italie*. 2 vols. Paris, 1793.

Grimm, Melchior. "Lettre à une dame occupée sérieusement de l'éducation de ses enfants." *Mercure de France*, June 1756.

———. *Correspondance Littéraire, Philosophique et Critique, par Grimm, Diderot, Raynal, Meister, etc. . . . notices, notes, table générale par Maurice Tourneux*. 16 vols. Paris: Garnier Frères, 1877–1882. Kraus reprint. Nendeln/Liechtenstein, 1968.

———. *Correspondance inédite*. Collected and annotated by Jochen Schlobach. Munich: Wilhelm Fink, 1972.

Hamilton, William. *Campi Phlegraei: Observations on the Volcanos of the Two Sicilies as They Have Been Communicated to the Royal Society of London*. 2 vols. Naples, 1776. *Supplement*, 1779.

Inthiery, Barthélémy. *L'Art de conserver les grains: Ouvrage traduit de l'Italien, etc.* Paris: Saugrain le Jeune, 1770.

Jahn, Otto. *Life of Mozart*. Translated from the German by Pauline D. Townsend. London, 1882.

Knight, Carlo. *Il giardino inglese di Caserta: Un'avventura settecentesca*. Introduction by Harold Acton. Naples: Sergio Civita, 1986.

———. *Hamilton a Napoli: Cultura, svaghi, civittà di una grande capitale europea*. Naples: Electa, 1990.

La Capria, Raffaele. "Lingua tosta e lingua molle" (review of a modern edition of Luigi Serio, "Risposta al Dialetto Napoletano," Naples: Colonnese, 1982). In Raffaele La Capria, *L'armonia perduta*. Milan: Mondadori, 1986.

Marino, John A. *Pastoral Economics in the Kingdom of Naples*. Baltimore: Johns Hopkins University Press, 1988.

Mason, John Hope. *The Irresistible Diderot*. London: Quartet Books, 1982.

Mattei, baron Saverio. *Il cuore tira la mente: Commedia in due atti*. Naples, 1856.

———. *Galiani ed i suoi tempi*. Naples, 1879.

Ménétra, Jacques-Louis. *Journal of My Life*. New York: Columbia University Press, 1986.

Il mestiere di Regina: Lettere, 1770–1780. (Letters of Maria Theresa of Austria and Marie Antoinette of France.) Edited by Marina Premoli. Milan: Rosellina Archinto, 1989.

Selected Bibliography

Monaco, Vanda. *Giambattista Lorenzi e la commedia per musica*. Naples: Arturo Berisio Editore, 1968.

Morellet, André. *Réfutation de l'ouvrage qui a pour titre Dialogues sur le commerce des blés*. London, 1770.

Nicolini, Fausto. *Monsignor Celestino Galiani: Saggio biografico*. Naples: Società Napoletana di Storia Patria, 1931.

———. *Croce Studioso della Maschera di Pulcinella*. Naples: Grimaldi & Cicerano, 1983.

Nietzsche, Friedrich. *Epistolario, 1865–1900*. Turin: Einaudi, 1962.

Pane, Roberto. *Il canto dei Tamburi di Pietra*. Naples: Guida, 1980.

Pascal, Carlo. *Sulla vita e sulle opere di Ferdinando Galiani*. Naples: Morano, 1885.

Proust, Jacques. *L'Encyclopédie*. Paris: Armand Colin, 1965.

Rey, Auguste. *Le Château de La Chevrette*. Paris: Plon-Nourrit, 1904.

Robinson, Michael F. *Naples and Neapolitan Opera*. Oxford: Clarendon Press, 1972.

Romani, George T. *The Neapolitan Revolution of 1820–1821*. Evanston, Ill.: Northwestern University Press, 1950. Reprint. Westport, Conn.: Greenwood Press, 1978.

Rossi, Joseph. *The Abbé Galiani in France*. New York: Publications of the Institute of French Studies, 1930.

Scherer, Edmond. *Melchior Grimm: L'Homme de lettres, le factotum, le diplomate*. Paris, 1887. Reprint. Geneva: Slatkin Reprints, 1968.

Serio, Luigi. *Risposta al Dialetto napoletano dell'abate Galiani*. Naples, 1776. Naples: Colonnese, 1982.

Smiley, Joseph Royall. *Diderot's Relations with Grimm*. Urbana: University of Illinois Press, 1950.

Strazzullo, Franco. *Le manifatture d'arte di Carlo di Borbone*. Introduction by Raffaele Ajello. Naples: Liguori, 1979.

Tyl, Pierre-Marie. *Madame d'Épinay (1726–1783): Une Femme au siècle des lumières*. Exposition catalogue. Hôtel de Ville, Épinay-sur-Seine, 19 Novembre–4 Décembre 1983.

Venturi, Franco. *Utopia e riforma nell' "Illuminismo."* Turin: Einaudi, 1970. (See also other pertinent books and articles by this prolific authority on the Enlightenment in Italy and elsewhere.)

Villari, Lucio. *Settecento adieu: Dall'Illuminismo alla Rivoluzione*. Milan: Bompiani, 1985.

Weinreb, Ruth Plaut. "Madame d'Épinay's Contribution to the *Correspondance littéraire*." *Studies in Eighteenth-century Culture*, Vol. 18 (November 1988). Published by the American Society for Eighteenth-century Studies.

Wilson, Arthur M. *Diderot*. New York: Oxford University Press, 1972.

Winckelmann, J. J. *Le scoperte di Ercolano*. (Includes Winckelmann's original *Lettera sulle antichità d'Ercolano* [1762].) With an introduction, appendix, and notes by Franco Strazzullo. Naples: Liguori, 1981.

———. *Reflections on the Imitation of Greek Works in Painting and Sculpture*. La Salle, Ill.: Open Court Classics, 1987.

ALSO

Civiltà del '700 a Napoli, 1734–1799. 2 vols. Florence: Centro Di, 1979. American edition: *The Golden Age of Naples: Art and Civilization under the Bourbons, 1734–1805.* 2 vols. Detroit: Detroit Institute of Arts, with the Art Institute of Chicago, 1981.

Raffaele Ajello, Ferdinando Bologna, Marcello Gigante, Fausto Zevi. *Le antichità di Ercolano.* Naples: Banco di Napoli, 1988.

Bernardo Tanucci: statista, letterato, giurista. Atti del Convegno Internazionale di Studi per il Secondo Centenario, 1783–1983. Edited by Raffaele Ajello and Mario d'Addio. 2 vols. Naples, 1988.

Pulcinella Maschera del Mondo: Pulcinella e le arti dal cinquecento al novecento. A Cura di Franco Carmelo Greco. Naples: Electa, 1990.

Certain of the most notable of the many relevant articles seen in American, British, French, and Italian newspapers and scholarly journals are mentioned in the text and in the notes.

INDEX

italicized page numbers refer to illustrations

271

Index

Index

280

A NOTE ABOUT THE AUTHOR

FRANCIS STEEGMULLER was born in New Haven, Connecticut, and educated in the public schools of Greenwich, and at Columbia University. He is the author of many works about French culture and society, and translator of Gustave Flaubert's letters and the Modern Library edition of Madame Bovary. A Chevalier of the Legion of Honor, Mr. Steegmuller has received many literary honors, including, in 1971, the National Book Award for his biography of Jean Cocteau. He divides his time between New York City and Naples. He is married to the novelist Shirley Hazzard.

A NOTE ON THE TYPE

This book is set in a typeface called GALLIARD, drawn
by Matthew Carter for the Mergenthaler Linotype
Company in 1978. Carter studied and worked with historic hand-cut punches before designing typefaces. His
Galliard design is based on sixteenth-century types of
Robert Granjon, of Paris and Lyon, a distinguished
publisher, printer, type-cutter and founder.

Composition by Crane Typesetting Service, Inc.,
West Barnstable, Massachusetts

Printed and bound by Fairfield Graphics,
Fairfield, Pennsylvania

Designed by Harry Ford